ALSO BY MICHAEL RAY TAYLOR

Cave Passages:
Roaming the Underground Wilderness

DARK LIFE

MARTIAN NANOBACTERIA, ROCK-EATING CAVE BUGS,
AND OTHER EXTREME ORGANISMS OF INNER EARTH
AND OUTER SPACE

MICHAEL RAY TAYLOR

SCRIBNER

SCRIBNER
1230 Avenue of the Americas
New York, NY 10020

SCRIBNER and design are trademarks of Jossey-Bass, Inc.,
used under license by Simon & Schuster, the publisher of this work.

DESIGNED BY ERICH HOBBING

Text set in Electra

Manufactured in the United States of America

1   3   5   7   9   10   8   6   4   2

Library of Congress Cataloging-in-Publication Data
Taylor, Michael Ray, 1959–
Dark life: Martian nanobacteria, rock-eating cave bugs, and other
extreme organisms of inner Earth and outer space/by Michael Ray Taylor.
p.   cm.
Includes bibliographical references and index.
1. Extreme environments—microbiology. I. Title.
QR100.9.T38   1999
579—dc21   98–43310
CIP

ISBN 0-684-84191-6

For Kathy, Alex, Ken, and Chris

CONTENTS

Dark *adj.* 1. Lacking light or brightness. 2. Somber in color. 3. Gloomy; threatening. 4. Obscure; cryptic. 5. Ignorant; uncivilized: *a dark era.* 6. Evil; sinister.

Life *n.* 1. The quality manifested in functions such as metabolism, growth, response to stimulation, and reproduction by which living organisms are distinguished from dead organisms or inanimate matter. 2. Living organisms collectively: *plant life.* 3. A living being. 4. The interval between the birth or inception of an organism and its death. 5. A biography. 6. Human activities and relationships: *everyday life.* 7. A manner of living: *country life.* 8. Animation; liveliness.

ONE

THE SAMPLES

Plimpton (as a word, not the man) has a meaning beyond being a man's name, because George Plimpton became a Walter Mitty for the second half of the 20th Century, dabbling in American sports and entertainment. Writers now speak of "doing a Plimpton." It means not only becoming part of the story . . . it means that your experience becomes the story.

—WILLIAM MCKEEN
in *Good Stories, Well Told*

AUGUST 8, 1997

After several wrong turns, I pull into what I take to be the proper drive. The sprawling Johnson Space Center near Clear Lake, Texas, just south of Houston off Interstate 45, resembles nothing so much as the campus of a midwestern state college magically transported from 1966. Ugly, nondescript buildings of painted block and textured aluminum squat over a confusing grid of roads, parking lots, and well-tended lawns. Professorial-looking men and women bustle about, frowning at their watches in white J. C. Penney shirts. Here and there, longhaired young people sit cross-legged in the grass, conversing on weighty subjects.

Building 13 is a cavernous affair, indistinguishable from the center's other beige crypts save for its large black identifying numerals affixed to one wall. A white tower topped with a tank labeled "Liquid N" stands beside the parking lot. As night falls, floodlights give it a vaguely ominous look, like the guard tower in a prison movie. Over half of Building 13 is devoted to an open hangar, crowded with cranes and hoists. Gleaming devices slated for future Space Shuttle missions, according to public relations posters propped in front of them, sit half assembled and draped in plastic. Signs attached to gigantic machines warn: "Hard Hats Must Be Worn!" and "Caution: Poison Gas."

At nine o'clock on a Friday evening, the footsteps of a young chemist—a paid intern not yet graduated from college—echo hollowly through the deserted space. When Anne Taunton arrived for work at six this morning, Building 13 was a hive of activity. Engineers pored over diagrams at their desks, shirt-sleeves rolled. Workers in pale blue coveralls eased hand trucks beneath gas canisters, ferrying them to points unknown. But now she and I seem to be the only people here. The long shadow of an articulated manipulator arm lies still upon the floor. I follow her toward the heart of the building, to a tool with which we hope to glimpse a new form of life.

Taunton is dressed in jeans, sandals, and an embroidered cotton blouse the same beige color as the walls. Twenty-two years old, she is blond, her face not unlike that of the actress Jenna Elfman except for her wire granny glasses that seem to impart a perpetual squint. She is a well-adjusted, straight-A student from the small town of El Dorado, Arkansas. In mild protest against this fact (and also to pay off a bet made during a charity fund-raiser), last year she had her navel pierced. In it she wears a small ring depicting an Arkansas razorback, the emblem of the university to which she will return in the fall to complete an honors thesis in chemistry.

We pass through the assembly area into a long corridor of offices and small laboratories. Taunton turns left, leading me into a darkened room about the size of a classroom at the state university where I teach journalism. The only light comes from two computer monitors connected to a piece of equipment dominating one wall: a $500,000 Philips field emission scanning electron microscope (FESEM). It can magnify images to over 100,000 times their actual size with unprecedented clarity. It captures objects that would be invisible to the most powerful light microscopes. NASA obtained the state-of-the-art machine in 1994 for materials science. Its primary purpose in Building 13 is to analyze structural stress on rocket valves, space shuttle door hinges, and other hardware on which human life in space depends. But by signing up for time during off-hours, any JSC scientist can use the FESEM to look for other things, including extraterrestrial life. Taunton has spent many late nights and early mornings at JSC doing exactly that.

She removes four stubs of coated metal from a Tupperware sandwich box. Each holds a tiny pebble. At the center of the electron microscope, a chamber the size of a small microwave oven rests on a table cushioned against movement by a square air bag. Taunton turns a handle and the door slides silently open, supported at each corner by gleaming pistons. A tray holding a stainless-steel disc emerges. She carefully places the stubs into drilled holes on the disc, which already hold three other pebbles. She pushes the assembly closed, seals an air lock, and switches on a noisy vacuum pump. We sit before the two lit monitors.

The three pebbles already on the disc come from Mars. They are newly sliced chunks of ALH 84001, the Martian meteorite that captured world headlines exactly one year earlier, when a JSC team led by David S. McKay—Taunton's boss—announced the discovery of what appeared to be fossilized bacteria trapped within carbonates in the rock. The other four pebbles are travertine, a carbonate mineral deposited by thermal hot springs. I have collected these over the past month in a series of trips into a mile-long, hundred-year-old drainage tunnel that winds beneath Hot Springs National Park in Arkansas, thirty miles north of my home. Although park literature describes the slightly radioactive water as emerging from great depths "naturally sterile," I have learned enough about hot springs to believe it might be otherwise.

With the help of a few dedicated scientists, I have spent much of the previous year looking inside our world, and I have found it to be alive. A vastly diverse class of previously unknown microbes inhabits the deep subsurface of our Earth. These organisms, which I choose to call "dark life," have been found in caves, mid-ocean volcanic vents, salt domes, Antarctic ice cores, mines, and the deepest holes ever drilled. They form complex ecosystems and food chains wholly independent of sunlight, photosynthesis, oxygen, and other standard requirements for life "as we know it." They draw energy from chemicals (sulfur, iron, manganese, elemental hydrogen), or from the natural radioactivity that abounds within the planet's crust, or from the scant light produced by deep-sea volcanoes. Much of what is known about them has been learned since 1990. New discoveries occur almost daily.

Because the few species studied can endure extremes of heat, pressure, cold, salinity, acidity, and other conditions hazardous to humans, microbiologists have lumped them together under the category "extremophiles"—but this name is misleading, in that it implies such life is a rare curiosity. In fact, nearly every researcher who goes looking for it finds it, often in great abundance. A few theorists have gone so far as to speculate that these dark ecosystems represent the greatest mass of life on Earth. Placed on one side of a scale, they argue, the deep organisms would weigh more than all five billion humans, all animals, all plants and trees, all fish and plankton and algae, all the far more familiar microbes of our bodies and bathrooms—more than all of these put together, more than the sum of everything we used to call biology.

Dark life is by far Earth's oldest, both in terms of when certain genes evolved and in the life span of particular individuals. Some organisms appear to be, for want of a better word, immortal, remaining dormant for long periods of time, yet continually capable of resurrection. When all available water freezes or evaporates, they hunker in stasis until it returns. How long is a matter of vigorous debate, but at the low, most conservative end, the number is tens of thousands of years. Some research suggests that the high end is hundreds of millions of years. Shrunken, dried microbes have been revived from ancient salt domes, from sub-Antarctic ice cores, and from NASA gear exposed to the cold vacuum of space.

So much living stuff is underground, and so little is known about it, that I was able to enter the Hot Springs tunnel feeling quite optimistic about the chances of an amateur scientist actually finding undiscovered life.

JULY 4, 1997

The summer heat shimmered in waves above the soft, sweltering asphalt. Three friends and I stood in a municipal parking lot a few blocks off the main drag of Hot Springs. We sorted through cardboard boxes in the trunks of our cars, gathering helmets, lamps, thermometers, and pH meters for the expedition ahead. I checked my watch: At that moment, the main chute of the Pathfinder mission to Mars should have been deployed; the spacecraft's air bags should have been inflated. It seemed a good omen in my own search for alien life.

My friends adjusted their borrowed helmets. While not exactly renaissance naturalists, we were nonetheless an overeducated bunch, college professors in the fields of communication, theater, computer art, and journalism. Not a biologist among us. But I *had* recently taken an undergraduate course in microbial collection technique at my university, after assisting in several underground microbial studies. In addition, I possessed the proper gear, twenty years of caving experience, and a biological collection permit from the U.S. National Park Service. And I knew the path to several sites where we were likely to find unknown extremophilic microbes, not quite a mile into the darkness. We descended a steep grassy bank bordering the parking lot, watching for the copperheads that often lounged there, and stepped into a knee-deep rocky stream, its bottom slick and mossy. As Pathfinder bounced over the frozen surface of Mars, we walked upstream to a yawning concrete arch and switched on our headlamps.

On September 16, 1541, Hernando de Soto and his dwindling band, ragged from months of wandering through the American wilderness, rode into the village of the Tunicas in what would later be called Arkansas. Tribes from distant lands had gathered there to bathe in the village's sacred springs: Quapaw, Pawnee, Natchez, Choctaw, Osage, and even a few Cherokee who had come from far mountains to partake of the healing waters and to trade. De Soto hoped to barter for corn and other supplies, and, as always, to question the native travelers as to where he might find the gold that had always eluded him.

When news of the approaching strangers reached the village, several visiting chiefs had already gathered to prepare a celebration in honor of a recently returned trading party. According to the report of Garcilaso de la Vega, "the young men were for war, but the medicine men claimed that the Great Spirit had revealed to them that the strangers would come in peace." Thus de Soto was allowed to spend a restful month at the springs before marching south.

A century later, French trappers stumbled upon the narrow canyon by following a cool mountain stream into which dozens of steaming springs flowed. Natural dams of the mineral tufa, or travertine, circled pools of differing temperatures. These allowed bathers to move gradually from cooler to warmer baths, according to their personal tastes. Unlike the hot springs of Europe, those in the "valley of vapors" did not produce a sulfurous smell, and the water was quite tasty. News of the site spread. By the early nineteenth century, the town of Hot Springs had become a fashionable resort, the "curative" powers of its water touted by the world's leading physicians. Yet both the central stream—which often flooded as torrents of rainwater poured down the steep canyon—and the massive tufa dams perched above it stood in the way of the town they had spawned. The nineteenth century had a method for dealing with such inconveniences: paving them over.

"The main street was once the bed of a mountain stream. . . . The dispossessed river now flows through a tunnel," Stephen Crane observed when visiting Hot Springs on March 1, 1895. "Electric cars with whirring and clanging noises bowl along with modern indifference upon this grave of a torrent of the hills." The springs had been capped and piped into a central collection reservoir. Hot water was distributed through pipes to a dozen public buildings Crane compared to the mansions of "peculiarly subdued and home-loving millionaires." These glamorous bathhouses stood in a tight row atop the ruins of the ancient pools and dams.

Although many of the bathhouses have now fallen into disrepair, they remain, historically preserved as part of Hot Springs National Park. The wild stream still flows, covered by its masonry roof. Few of the tourists who amble down Central Avenue realize what's beneath their feet. Below Bathhouse Row, several natural springs still pour into the stream without benefit of municipal plumbing, coating the walls with yellow and red mounds of travertine.

The word "travertine" comes from the Italian *travertino,* a corruption of *tiburtino,* meaning "the stone from the city of Tibur." Tibur was the ancient name for Tivoli, a city located west of the Sabine Mountains on the banks of the river Teverone, near Rome. As it ages and hardens, Italian travertine forms a multihued, easily quarried stone that has been used to decorate the Coliseum, St. Peter's Basilica, and bank lobbies around the world. Although the most famous architectural travertines come from Italy, the mineral is quite common elsewhere as well. It is found in many sedimentary, granitic, and volcanic terrains; in and near fault zones; and close to every known natural hot spring, whether active or extinct.

Travertine is composed primarily of precipitated calcite and aragonite. The whitish (or occasionally yellowish or reddish) ingredient of most cave formations, such as stalactites and stalagmites, is calcite. Both calcite and aragonite are crystallized forms of calcium carbonate, or $CaCO_3$, the main component of blackboard chalk and antacid tablets. The difference between calcite and aragonite is that the latter is characterized by an orthorhombic crystalline structure, meaning aragonite crystals grow in three dimensions along three mutually perpendicular axes. If you look into a child's bag of jacks, you will see a variety of orthorhombic shapes thrown together like aragonite crystals in travertine.

I was looking for travertine in Hot Springs because of a chance conversation I had had with NASA's Carlton Allen, a planetary geologist and lunar expert on David McKay's team. The original NASA paper on the Martian meteorite had put forth four separate lines of reasoning to suggest that microbial remains were trapped inside the rock. To me, and I suspect to most other laypeople, the most striking of the four was the visual one: tiny, rodlike structures that might be the fossils of ancient Martian bacteria. This claim was controversial not only because the structures came from Mars but also because they were so small, of an order of magnitude smaller than any known bacteria. Virtually all biologists felt that nothing so tiny could hold the necessary molecules for the existence of "life as we know it."

But Robert Folk, a prominent sedimentary geologist based at the University of Texas and one of the world's leading experts on travertine, insisted that he had photographed many such organisms in sedimentary rocks right here on Earth. He was convinced that these "nanobacteria," as he named them, were, among other things, agents of the chemical reaction that deposits travertine at natural hot springs. (Folk preferred the spelling "nannobacteria," after "nannocrystal" and similar geological terms. McKay had ultimately decided that the prefix nano-, with a single "n," was more widespread in scientific literature. Two other researchers had independently discovered the cryptic spheres and rods at about the same time as Folk; they had independently hit upon the same term, spelling it "nanobacteria." Both prefixes came from the Greek *nannos*, meaning a small, mischievous old man. By any spelling, many who knew him would consider this an apt description of Bob Folk.)

Allen, Taunton, and other members of the McKay team had begun studying travertine from Yellowstone National Park and other locations in an effort to identify *living* nanobacteria. If they succeeded in extracting DNA, cell walls, or other evidence of life's chemistry in nano-sized objects, such proof would go a long way toward supporting the theory that similar organisms had lived in the meteorite ALH 84001. Not incidentally, this would also prove that a new class of life existed on Earth, one that might have important implications for biology and medicine.

I've spent much of my adult life poking into caves and tunnels. Caves provide not only an opportunity for geographic discovery but also an intensely physical awareness of the vastness of geologic time. In much the same way, tunnels—old aqueducts, sewers, railroad tunnels, mines—allow explorers to make tactile connection to the geologic eye blink that humanity calls "history." Not long after moving to Arkansas, I began roaming the Hot Springs tunnels, and I'd seen some fine travertine in them. Allen and Taunton had told me they'd be delighted to have a sample of actively depositing travertine from an unsampled area, especially one removed from sunlight. If I collected it, they'd let me drive it down to Houston to watch them prepare and photograph it on the same scanning electron microscope that had given the world the tantalizing images of ALH 84001.

So here I was, slogging over slippery rocks where the Osage and the Choctaw once gathered in peace. Above our group hung a two-foot-thick layer of fog. It gradually descended as we moved forward. The air temperature shot up several degrees, and I could hear splashing somewhere ahead.

Water, heated geothermally during its 3,000-year course through radioactive rock a mile below, shot from a massive iron pipe with about half the strength of an open city hydrant. Hot trickles and spurts issued in from a dozen cracks, where small springs had jumped the channels laid for them by the tunnel's builders. I stuck a long thermometer into the main flow. The water was well below the boiling point, but, at 146° Fahrenheit, still hot enough to scald. I checked the pH and considered which of the assortment of sampling tools and containers my friends and I had carried would work best for removing tiny chunks of fresh travertine.

I noticed an outlet of water high in the ceiling splashing onto a pitch-covered wooden distribution pipe along the wall, its volume that of a shower nozzle turned wide open. The flow had deposited a few centimeters of travertine skin, coating the thick pipe as well as a number of iron bolts and straps that held it in place. I pulled a cold chisel from my pack, dipped the blade in ethanol, and flamed it with a butane lighter.

I climbed up onto shaky pipe, holding the sterilized tool out with one arm, taking care not to touch it against anything en route to the closest bolt. Trying to ignore the hot spray that quickly soaked my clothes, I laid the chisel against the tip of a travertine-coated bolt about as big as the end of my thumb. I pulled a short sledge from my pack and gave the chisel a sharp rap. The piece cracked off cleanly. I balanced it on the blade as I eased my way back down to place the sample inside a sterile collection bag held open by one of my colleagues. With a permanent marker I labeled the bag "Iron Nub, Tunnel Spring #1." In the center of the nub, closest to the rusted metal, were alternating bands of color that I hoped might correspond to iron-eating microbes.

My friends and I worked our way north, collecting additional stone chips and selecting springs to which I would return later to place glass slides in order to grow fresh accumulations of travertine. We were soon heated to the point where we had to lie down in the cool mountain water just to catch our breath. I dipped my head back into the flow, thinking of de Soto. By now Pathfinder's dish antenna had locked on to a tiny blue speck in the Martian sky.

Advances in science, like those of human exploration, rely on ever-shifting combinations of curiosity, technology, and chance. As I lay in the stygian wash, I recalled another subterranean pool I had entered a thousand miles away, nearly a decade earlier, reaching what was then a raw frontier of cave exploration and technology. If caves and tunnels offered me visions of geologic and historic time, they also provided a gateway to my personal past. As with many human explorers who had come before me, my present quest had begun when I entered a new world without recognizing it for what it was.

TWO

1988

The truth of nature lieth in certain deep mines and caves.

—DEMOCRITUS

INTRUDERS

None of us knew whether it was night or day. We lay 1,200 feet, more or less, beneath the desert, down countless rope pitches and miles of tortuous passage from the single entrance to Lechuguilla Cave in New Mexico's Carlsbad Caverns National Park. *And the earth was without form, and void; and darkness was upon the face of the deep.* With this exhilarating knowledge we had slept, or tried to, for five or six hours, wrapped in oversized garbage bags that wept condensation.

We shifted positions, shuffling strips of foam padding that cushioned and insulated us from the cold hard earth. The cave's constant humidity, which had kept us sweating for hours as we made our difficult way down, now leached away warmth. We stank of the day's work, our funk blending with Lech's peculiar soil-and-metal odor. If I had thought about it then, I would have attributed the cave's unique smell to traces of sulfur.

At ten the previous morning, we had somehow coaxed a rented Oldsmobile down the rugged "four-wheel drive only" road to an unmarked parking area, where we geared up beneath a cloudless June sky. From there we had made the two-mile desert hike to the entrance in shorts, T-shirts, and boots. Our crossing spooked a small herd of deer. I paused to watch them scatter over a rise, leaping through a cluster of the prickly lechuguilla bushes for which the cave was named. Low rocky hills dominated the landscape. These sun-blasted ridges and the rock below them had been alive 250 million years ago. A magnificent barrier reef geologists call El Capitán had stretched for over a hundred miles along the coast of a shallow inland sea that once covered the American Southwest. The living reef had died as the basin it enclosed grew too salty. Then, long buried under later deposits, the dead reef became limestone, the ideal stone for caves.

Lechuguilla's entrance was a rectangular hole 70 feet deep and wide enough to swallow a truck. We donned helmets, kneepads, and climbing harnesses, then took one last look at daylight before clipping into the rope. It felt odd to begin a long descent without nylon coveralls. Made of the same ballistic fabric as police vests, they had always been my preferred garb for caving in cooler climes. But coveralls would have been unbearable in this warm cave. My bare arms and legs, now tucked into synthetic underwear for sleeping, were caked with soil, sweat, blood from inevitable encounters with sharp rocks, and gritty bits of white aragonite that we had acquired while squeezing through a tight formation-lined tube.

I thought it was probably morning, or almost morning, in the desert far above me. I knew I was tired of trying to sleep. Had the desert floor been the roof of the World Trade Center, I would have been lying in the lower lobby. I could sense the subterranean equivalent of the streets of Manhattan stretching in all directions around me, calling me to explore.

The hope of finding virgin passage is perhaps the greatest lure of caving. It can entice otherwise sane and normal people (well, almost normal) to writhe through undulating tubes of hugging rock for hours, or to step backward off a cliff into hundreds of feet of empty darkness, tethered to life by braided nylon only a few millimeters thick. Three months earlier, as a member of the first American caving expedition to China, I had heard that many miles of virgin passage had been found at Lechuguilla. Dave Jagnow, a well-known caver from New Mexico, had shown the Chinese geologists who were our hosts some of the first slides taken of the Chandelier Ballroom, a newfound "Lech" chamber. Americans and Chinese alike had gasped at the room's pure white stalactites of branching, faceted selenite crystals up to twenty feet long. I had been caving for a decade and had begun the year before to cover expeditions for national magazines, but I had never seen any formation even remotely resembling the diamondlike sprays that Dave projected onto the wall of a damp field house in rural Guangdong. He casually mentioned that similar finds were occurring almost monthly in the cave. I vowed that, one way or another, I would see the place for myself. And I had done it now. I lay on a chilling bed of dry cave soil, surrounded by miles of the unknown, staring up at the darkness and smiling.

In such an utter absence of light, one's hearing sharpens exquisitely.

Ten feet away and slightly below me, a twenty-four-year-old caver rattled an aluminum space blanket. I had bought it explicitly for this trip at an outdoor-gear superstore in New Jersey. But last night I had insisted that my fellow Lech novice take it, along with a three-foot square of polyurethane foam, when I discovered that he had packed neither a sleeping pad nor the requisite polypropylene pj's. Cold as I was without the pad and blanket, I knew he was colder. His Army surplus thermals may have been fine for the shorter caves in which he had trained, but they were virtually useless when damp. Every few minutes he sat up, rearranged the crinkly blanket, muttered the word "sucks," and settled down again.

I heard the plastic squeal of a pack zipper, a sound at once familiar and comforting to anyone who has spent time camping out. The expedition's photographer, who was also its leader, rummaged quietly in a side pocket of his narrow mountaineering backpack. He unscrewed a Nalgene bottle (the only sort we carried), took two long swallows of water or, more likely in Lechuguilla, Gatorade.

Some of the small pools from which we drew drinking water imparted an unpleasant mineral taste. Most of us masked this with powdered drink mix. I had premeasured canteen-sized portions of powder before the trip. During an awkward crawl on the way in, a zippered sandwich bag had burst and sugared the inside of my pack. I now raised a finger to my tongue and tasted orange Gatorade. The sticky stuff seemed to coat every part of my skin and gear.

The photographer was the most experienced member of our group, not only as a general caver but also as that special beast (special even then, just two years after the great cave had first been entered): a *Lech* caver. In no other cave in the United States, not even the 350-mile-long Mammoth–Flint Ridge system in Kentucky, were multi-day underground camps so integral to exploration. New methods and gear for "speleo-backpacking" continually evolved among the Lechuguilla regulars. His thirst satisfied, the veteran replaced everything in his pack without resorting to the small Maglite hung on a nylon cord about his neck. He then settled back into his home-sewn polypro sleep sack, comfortable even though his thin frame should have made him the coldest of us all.

On a ledge across the room, the team's photo assistant shifted her breathing slightly. Although she made no other sound, I could tell she was awake. Even in total darkness, she commanded attention. I wondered whether the photographer listened, like me, to her wakefulness. Strong, young, and skilled in caving and climbing technique, she was from southern California: black hair, big eyes—the full Malibu.

We three men knew she was romantically linked to another well-known caver and that even as we lay in the darkness, he was pushing new passages with another team in some distant part of the cave. And of course we had attachments of our own, as well as a strong sense of professionalism about our mission. None of us, not even the handsome young novice, would seriously try to flirt with her. But in quiet moments in such intimate surroundings, supine in the abode of our most primitive human ancestors, I found it hard not to at least think about sex.

With this realization I must have fallen asleep, for I was startled by the pistol crack of someone firing a carbide lamp.

Although later banned from Lechuguilla because of the slight but not impossible risk that they might set the caves sulfur deposits ablaze, in 1988 antique carbide lamps—most of them manufactured for the coal-mining industry in the 1940s and 1950s—were still the favored light source of many cavers. The lamp's warm yellow glow brought our room into view. I lay in a steeply canted chamber about the size of a three-car garage. The floor and walls were of the disintegrated limestone that Lech cavers call "rock flour." If you kicked it, it floated out like a cloud of Pillsbury's best. Wonderfully soft stuff to sleep in. A few relatively flat heaps of it scattered about the irregular floor served as our beds.

"Damn bag sucks," said a male voice, and the light flickered out.

From the entrance, we had descended a series of climbs, stoop walks, and free-hanging rappels—the longest of them from an undercut cliff 145 feet above the dark floor—until we had reached a stadium-sized chamber called Glacier Bay. A natural avenue wound through the tilted space, ending in an area of tricky crawls and rope traverses at the Rift, a multilevel fissure 200 feet deep. We snaked through the Rift to the Overpass, which had opened up most of the known passage just the year before. Our guide said the cave didn't really begin until you had climbed, hiked, slithered, and rappelled from this point to the shore of Lake Lebarge, over 700 feet down.

Lebarge, a shallow, clear pond perhaps 75 feet in diameter, straddled the first of a series of huge passages that glistened with surrounding white gypsum in a myriad of forms: crystals, flakes, flowers, spikes, cones, and powder. Other lakes followed in the Lebarge Borehole, some of them lined with bulbous, milky mounds of calcite unlike any cave formation I had ever seen. In some places, rows of ghostly human-sized forms called "hoodoos" stood like sentries along the path. These were built of countless thin mineral flakes that had floated on the surface film of long-vanished pools, each accumulating mass over months or years or decades until it became heavy enough to sink in the still water and another began growing in its place. When the water retreated, the hoodoos remained.

The massive gypsum deposits lining Lechuguilla's limestone walls had suggested to some geologists that its tunnels were carved not by runoff flowing from the surface—as was long considered the case with all limestone caves—but by strong chemical reactions between ancient groundwater and hydrogen sulfide rising from a deep subterranean source. Hydrogen sulfide associated with petroleum deposits in the rich Delaware Basin field was believed to have been chemically converted to sulfuric acid, which could eat into limestone like gasoline poured into a Styrofoam cup. In the early 1980s few in the geological establishment had accepted this theory, originally applied to Carlsbad Cavern. But then the discovery and early exploration of Lechuguilla had confirmed it.

Evidence of rising, acid-rich springs clung to every chamber. This cave had clearly built itself from the bottom up, rather than the top down. The ancient chemical soup had deposited not only deep beds of gypsum but also sulfur, manganese, iron, and other ingredients to create bizarre mineral formations identified nowhere else on Earth. The exact chemical mechanisms by which the various strange formations had grown were the stuff of growing debate among geologists. Clues were just beginning to emerge from the world's active hot springs that biology might play a role in hot spring mineralogy, but few of those studying Lechuguilla considered this news particularly relevant to the study of cave formations. After all, the hot springs that had formed Lechuguilla had vanished long ago, leaving behind nothing but rocks and chemistry—so far as anyone knew.

Eventually, we reached the small pool called Last Water. The name had been an accurate description until a few months earlier. Explorers had since found deeper lakes in each of the three main branches of the cave. All the standing water in Lech was perched well above the region's natural water table. Although we were bound for the cave's largest known lake, discovered two months before and seen so far by only six people, we stopped to eat and fill our canteens at Last Water.

We'd been in the cave for five hours at that point, with three more to go before reaching our destination.

A natural collapse just inside the entrance pit had blocked Lechuguilla for thousands of years, until cavers dug through it on Memorial Day 1986. The miles of passage beyond had revealed no trace of humanity or, for that matter, bats or other traditional cave life. A few cave crickets inhabited the upper passages, but even they became scarce below the rappel into Glacier Bay. Lech was a truly virgin place, rare in the annals of human exploration.

From the beginning, Lech's cavers—working in concert with National Park Service managers—had agreed to lay narrow trails carefully through each room to preserve the untrodden floors. They had also agreed to haul out all solid wastes in an effort to conserve Lechuguilla's pristine chemistry. Thus the bottoms of our packs held "burrito bags": doubled locking freezer Baggies (the one-gallon size worked best) rolled inside a sheet of aluminum foil, along with a bathroom kit that contained kitty litter (to be dropped into the bag) and disposable baby wipes. Once a bag had been used, it would be wrapped in foil and would become a "burrito." Cavers heading out after a long trip took care not to bang their packs around, lest they later discover "burst burritos" among their gear.

In a warm cave in which one had to consume several liters of water per day, often for days at a stretch, the disposal of liquids was another matter. Few could carry it all out. Bits of yellow flagging signaled urinals throughout Lech. You could smell these long before you scrambled over the rocks to reach them. Cavers resorted to wide-mouthed bottles when exploring new areas, dumping them later at yellow flags along the trade routes. On the last day of any given expedition, however, all bottles were to be carried out full. I had heard sad tales, not all of them apocryphal, of tired cavers stopping for a drink as they climbed toward the surface and pulling out the wrong bottle from their packs.

Another problem arose when cavers failed to drink enough water. Moving through Lechuguilla involved sweaty work, especially the many rope climbs required to exit the cave. Dehydration was a continual threat. One of the first signs was a sudden onset of nausea. Atop well-traveled slopes throughout the cave, fuzzy fungal growths thus sprouted from small circles of dried vomit. As I continued to explore Lechuguilla over the next few years, I would become the source of such pollution in three or four places. But during this first outing into the warm depths, I had paused frequently to drink. I felt great.

As we had at last neared Lake Castrovalva, our guide became increasingly less certain of his route. The directions we had received were not as specific as they might have been. We spent several hours lost in the vicinity of the Easter Bunny, a sparkling gypsum totem which looked, if you squinted at the right angle, something like a three-foot rabbit sitting on its haunches.

The Bunny Maze proved a fine place in which to be turned around. Every visible surface in each tunnel we tried glowed a blinding white. Sparkling drifts of gypsum snow seemed ready for skiing; faceted gypsum barrels poked up like gigantic peppermint sticks. Eventually, we found ourselves at what blue bits of flagging identified as the FN Survey. The survey markers led us to the Prickly Ice Cube Room Overlook and down through the Mouse Hole, a major landmark, according to our directions. We were almost there.

In a 200-foot-diameter chamber at the base of the Mouse Hole, we were amazed to run into two separate teams surveying in that part of the cave. An hour later, as we crossed an area thick with rock flour, we ran into a third. Luckily for us, the third team was led by the caver who had first discovered Castrovalva and the chamber beyond it. He explained that they had named the lake after a serene but ultimately illusionary world in a *Dr. Who* episode. More to the point, he informed us that we were headed the wrong way. The route was far more complicated than the map we carried indicated, he said. He offered to leave his team and guide us there.

The generosity of this offer became apparent when the caver took us across a short rock-flour bridge, perhaps forty feet up and no more than three feet thick, which lost a part of itself with every crossing. It was not the sort of path one could cross too many times. From there, a series of labyrinthine crawls led to the dry-looking, innocuous antechamber to the lake. Even our guide missed some turns and had to double back. If not for him, we couldn't possibly have found the place.

Just before leaving us to return to his surveyors, who had already waited more than the thirty minutes he had told them he'd be gone, the caver pulled me aside. "Listen, you're going to write about this, aren't you?"

I admitted that sooner or later I probably would.

"Well, we needed to cross the lake to the formation areas to map, but none of the stuff on the far side goes anywhere. It's important to have some photo documentation in there. That's fine. But I don't see any reason anyone should ever go back after this trip. *Ever.* You'll see how delicate it is. If you play it up in an article, it'll get all kinds of traffic. That would not be good. You can find other stuff to write about, can't you?"

I said I wasn't sure, but I'd think about his request. Fortunately, I never had to wrestle with that particular moral dilemma. Unknown to our guide, another of his initial mappers had already written up Lake Castrovalva for a national caving newsletter. The article included, among other superlative descriptions, the line "They stood in awe at some of the most beautifully decorated cave they had ever seen." In coming years, this sort of cliché would become de rigueur for nearly all Lechuguilla trip reports.

The caver led us to a small arch, which we confirmed opened to a tunnel that resembled three coffins laid end to end. The far end of the rectangular passage sloped into water so clear that we didn't know we'd reached it until the first person made a splash. We could see that a few feet ahead, a ten-inch airspace opened to blackness.

Tucked into a rock shelf above the waterline were two one-man inflatable rafts. They had been hauled in—with great difficulty—by the original mapping team, after their discovery trip had revealed the extent of the water beyond. We decided to wait until "morning" to cross beneath the arch into a series of three small, wet rooms that would lead us to Castrovalva proper. We returned to the dry antechamber and made camp.

• • •

I awoke to footsteps.

A carbide lamp bobbed up the slope and away, heading toward the closest flagged rock, located several chambers back. Across the room the photographer fired a portable backpacking stove that whined like a jet engine. He bled the flame and set about boiling water for our breakfasts.

"Up and at 'em," he said, much too cheerfully.

One by one we took turns visiting the "designated rock." Warmed by instant oatmeal, we began packing gear for a full day of photography. Our target lake lay just beyond the small tunnel at the bottom of our slanted room. Gradually, we drifted toward this low exit, dragging our packs by their shoulder straps. We wrapped nylon duffels of photo gear inside doubled garbage bags, sealed them, and wedged the green bundles onto the rafts. Then we did the same for our own gear, our boots, and then finally our clothing.

Except for helmets and attached lamps, we would enter the water exactly as we had entered the world. The rafts would keep our clothes dry as we swam them to the other side. But we were skinny-dipping for a higher purpose: to keep the water clean. The dirt on our clothes and boots would have muddied the lake; the dirt on our bodies, we presumed, would at worst merely cloud it.

Water from Lechuguilla's deeper pools, and the water in this pool was the deepest yet found, had tested as absolutely pure, purer than the testing laboratory's "pure" standard. Of course, the laboratory had tested the water only for pollutants and known organisms, but it really looked clean. It contained no filterable agents that could be cultured on standard growth media. Nor did it contain the trace radiation common to groundwater in New Mexico. This meant it had reached this reservoir sometime before July 16, 1945, the day the Manhattan Project left tiny, measurable bits of Trinity in all the surface waters of the American Southwest.

Because we had two boats, we elected to cross in teams of two, swimming the gear across the 100-foot-long lake, which had an estimated depth of 50 feet. Stoop-walking past me in the coffin-shaped room, the photo assistant grabbed the towline and splashed forward. She was as blithely unself-conscious of her body as only an outdoorsy Californian can be. The two of us began to guide the first boat toward the arch while the photographer continued packing lenses and film in the second. We immersed ourselves in the cool 67° Fahrenheit water.

I whooped and hollered at the chill.

She had to duck to fit her helmet through the arch before turning to pull the raft. It completely filled the hole, stuck fast.

I pressed down on the inflated sides, wriggling and shoving until it noisily slid through. I ducked and followed. We repeated the process through two larger archways in the watery tunnel beyond, before the ceiling vanished far overhead. We were suddenly swimming in deep water, bound on all sides by immense bulbous calcite formations similar to those I had seen in Lake Lebarge, but larger and more profuse. Some crowded the walls; others seemed to float on the surface, as though their sides had lightly docked against the walls moments before.

Cave geologists had named these rose-colored mounds "mammillaries," for obvious reasons. I noticed that some of those projecting into the water were topped by dark, rigid mineral nipples. The mammillaries had grown by slow accumulation of calcite on all surfaces then underwater. Now ripened like massive fruit, each must have weighed tons.

I pushed the boat into deeper water. The photo assistant pulled, swimming backward. Overhead, wet stalactites dripped and glistened.

I hollered again, not from cold but to hear my voice bounce back from the black distance. Here I was, in a vast lake beneath the desert, the seventh human creature in this place, following a muscular Venus as she pulled an inflated shell across one of the most beautiful chambers I had seen in a decade of caving.

Moist mammillaries on the shore gave way to massive broken pillars and columns beyond. The ceiling's canted arches and vaults seemed exquisitely planned, like the broken ruins in Botticelli's "Adoration of the Magi." Layers of sweat and grime and

Gatorade powder rose from my flesh like original sin, and I was seized by an overwhelming urge.

Treading water, I removed my helmet and wedged it between gear bundles on the raft so that it pointed back at me. I pulled off my glasses and fixed the neoprene sports strap to the boat's nylon line. Then I held my breath and plunged. Shadowy rocks poked from below. I swam down, down, as though following a plumb bob's quiver toward the vibrating heart of the world. The lake's coldness on my open eyes felt strange; my vision turned suddenly tactile.

At last I rolled, and water rushed into my ear. Above I could see the bottom of the boat, our two small lights flickering over the disturbed surface, the photo assistant's legs scissoring as she guided the raft toward a small outcrop in the center of the lake. My heart pounded in my chest. The water felt purer than anything I had known. I blew out a few bubbles. Then I deliberately swallowed a great gulp of the stuff. No taste, just a quenching coolness. This is, I thought, as far from life at the surface as it gets.

Fully baptized in Lake Castrovalva, I kicked back toward the light.

"Tastes great," I said as I surfaced. "And less filling."

We tied the rafts on the island and rested for a few minutes. The second boat soon popped through the arch. The photographer requested that we unpack a flashgun, a converted flashlight that fired old-fashioned blue bulbs. He took a few quick shots from his raft, shouting "Fire!" as we bathed the room in brilliance. Then we repacked the gun and spent bulbs and swam on. The four of us climbed naked onto the stone shore of the formation-draped chamber beyond the lake. We unloaded the rafts, dressed, and spent hours photographing geologic wonders. I stood in awe at some of the most beautifully decorated cave I had ever seen. Massive stalactites in pink and orange pastels flowed into mounds of white rippled flowstone. Calcite cave pearls sparkled amid multilevel rimstone pools.

Much later, as we began the long journey back to daylight, heading out from what remains one of the most enjoyable caving trips I can recall, I once again drank deeply of Castrovalva. I never imagined that with every drop, I was swallowing life.

A decade later, after a half dozen additional expeditions to Lech, I would slowly come to realize that it was all alive. All of it: the water itself, the mammillaries, the gypsum bushes and crystals, the rock flour, the stalactites. Every surface I could see and many more that I couldn't thrived with unknown, invisible ecosystems, far more diverse in their species and their many strategies for survival than the population of any tropical rain forest. These creatures had played a role in shaping the strange beauty of the cave, just as their ancestors had governed the courses of the ancient sulfur springs that had carved its passages.

I had no way of knowing it in the summer of 1988, but clues to dark life and the colorful sculptures it could carve were at that moment being deciphered from the sulfurous springs in Yellowstone National Park and from other steaming pools near one of the ancient fonts of Western civilization.

✦

IL PROFESSORE

In the 14th Canto of *The Inferno*, the blind poet Virgil leads Dante Alighieri into the ninth and final circle of hell. The two men approach a small stream:

> Silently on we passed
> To where there gushes from the forest's bound
> A little brook, whose crimsoned wave yet lifts
> My hair with horror. As the rill, that runs
> From Bullicame, to be portioned out
> Among the sinful women; so ran this
> Down through the sand; its bottom and each bank
> Stone built, and either margin at its side,
> Whereon I perceived our passage lay.

"To understand this passage," said Benvenuto Cellini in a sixteenth-century commentary on Dante, "you must know that in the environs of Viterbo there is an extraordinary hot spring, which is reddish, sulfurous, and deep. From its bed rushes a brook, which the prostitutes of that area divide among them. Indeed, even in the most modest prostitute's dwelling, there is a bath that uses the water from that brook. It is therefore a good comparison, apt as to the reddish color, the heat, and the bad smell."

Although the dwellings of the prostitutes are long gone, the brook and spring and the ancient city of Viterbo remain. Since Roman times, the spring has gone by the name Bullicame, meaning literally "Boiling Ditch." The 149° Fahrenheit water flows into a large stone viaduct, part of the ancient distribution system. The sides of the viaduct, like the stone-built spring itself, are coated with thick layers of travertine that grow thicker daily. Long white tendrils of calcite and aragonite drip from the trough; small hillocks of white mineral deposits encircle the spring itself.

There are actually three major springs in the vicinity, all heated by the volcanic rumblings of nearby Monte Vico. Combined, they form the main tourist attraction of Viterbo, a city of 60,000 an hour's drive north of Rome along the mountainous spine of central Italy. Not all of the springs' famous bathers were of such ill repute as those mentioned in *The Inferno*. In 1235, Pope Gregory IX entered a steaming pool in the town center to be cured of "*mal della pietra*," an aching of the bones. The cure took; "*Terme dei Papi*" became a papal resort for centuries. Popes Boniface IX and Pius II swore by the restorative power of the hot, sulfurous water. Remains of a palace built near the spring in 1450 by Pope Nicholas V still stand.

The youngest spring of Viterbo is Bagnaccio, having erupted at its present site during the reign of Mussolini. Yet here, too, a ruined Roman bath testifies to a more ancient flow that once bubbled out a hundred yards away. A native might explain that the god Vulcan, who controlled the heat of the depths, shut off the flow as if it were a spigot, waited a few centuries, and then turned it on again. In the short span of four decades, thick deposits of travertine had accumulated at the new Bagnaccio flow, just as they had at Bullicame.

On June 20, 1988, Robert Louis Folk—"Luigi" when in Italy—stepped from a taxi parked along a highway six kilometers northwest of Viterbo. He was a small wiry man with a wispy beard and thick black-rimmed glasses. His hair, dark with flecks of gray, was cut short but still managed to blow in the breeze in a way that made it look wholly unkempt. He wore old clothes. His face seemed perpetually fixed in a mischievous smile.

An attractive young woman, a graduate student of geology named Paula Noble, stepped out of the cab after him. The driver pulled their nylon backpacks from the trunk and pointed up toward a small ridge above the highway.

"*Si*, Bagnaccio," Folk said. "*Grazie.*" The cab sped off.

Folk spoke to his student with animated hand gestures as the two walked over the ridge. They were surprised to find themselves in the elaborate ruins of a Roman bath. He spotted the dried remains of aragonite dams and ran to them, tracing the ancient watercourse through the ruin. He looked every bit the college professor that he was. With his small size, his energy, and the excited attention he paid to every rock in the path, he could also have passed for an experienced caver. He was somewhat claustrophobic, however, and had managed to avoid all but tourist caves throughout a distinguished career as the world's leading limestone petrologist.

A month earlier, Folk had retired from the University of Texas at Austin, where he had taught since 1952. Several years earlier, he had been appointed to the university's endowed Carlton Centennial Professorship in Geology. Despite his flowery title and the continued teaching it guaranteed, he fought the feeling he was being put out to pasture. He had published more than 120 papers in leading geological journals. His manual for basic sedimentary petrology—the study of the origin, composition, and structure of rocks laid down by water—was affectionately known as "the orange book" in geology labs from Harvard to Stanford. He had always kept busy, and he resented any implication whatsoever that he might slow down anytime soon.

Folk was born in Shaker Heights, Ohio, a middle-class suburb of Cleveland, on September 30, 1925. His father was a self-made lawyer from a farm family in the West Virginia panhandle, and his mother was a pianist and artist. Bob was a sickly, runty, bookish sort of boy who, as he would later put it, "never learned to do physical things very well, like ride a bike or swim or date chicks." From the age of five, he roamed the glacial moraines around Shaker Heights, collecting rocks. With his older brother George, he would scour the lime-ridge fields of the family farm in West Virginia, where the Folks vacationed every summer, picking up pretty stones. On a trip to Kelleys Island in Lake Erie when he was seven years old, he collected a large fossil coral, which he successfully identified, and which sat for decades on his desk at the University of Texas. He earned his bachelor's degree in geology, and eventually his master's and doctorate, all from Penn State. Limestone was the predominant rock surrounding State College, Pennsylvania, and he studied it and related carbonates throughout his academic career. After getting married in 1946, he worked briefly in the Texas oil industry but soon returned to academia.

In 1952, he walked in off the street in Austin, with his fresh Ph.D. in hand, and landed a job teaching structural geology and sedimentology at the University of Texas. His family became comfortably settled in Austin, spending weekends at a rustic cabin in the Hill Country. "I was allowed to teach pretty much whatever I wanted," he recalls of his early years at the university. "I could talk all I wanted about kurtosis of frequency distributions, characteristics of volcanic quartz, petrography of ostracods without interference. Thank goodness in those days promotions did not depend on how much grant money one brought in; I would never have been promoted under today's crass rules of tenure." Yet he was promoted and soon enough began publishing important papers and even pulling in grant money, while still being voted one of the best teachers in the department in survey after survey.

Every summer since 1973, he had done university fieldwork on hot spring travertines and other rocks in central Italy. Here, he felt far from the large academic department that had grown up around him. Thanks to a travel grant that had come with his endowed chair, he could invite a graduate student to come with him every summer. This time, the student was Noble, who had just begun working toward her Ph.D. With her dark tan and jet-black hair, she could have passed for a Viterbo native. The two of them had just arrived that morning.

In the hot springs around Viterbo, calcium carbonate in the water seems to precipitate as aragonite where the water is hottest, close to where it emerges from the ground, and as a calcite where it has cooled slightly. The white mounds that encircle the bubbling pool at Bagnaccio are composed of almost pure aragonite. For more than a century, geologists have explained the formation of all travertine as the chemical reaction of water laced with calcium carbonate coming into contact with the air. The water loses carbon dioxide molecules to the air, the theory goes, concentrating calcium carbonate in ever-greater amounts. At some point, when the concentration becomes great enough to result in what is termed "supersaturation," the mineral precipitates out, much as rain precipitates from a swollen cloud of water vapor. Many researchers had verified this explanation for the formation of travertine (and, for that matter, most cave formations) in experiments going back a century.

However, over the previous decade, Folk and other geologists had been finding that this simple chemical exchange didn't always hold up in nature. All crystals (not just those in travertine) form around a template, or seed crystal, which dictates the pattern for growth. Even in a supersaturated solution, crystallization cannot begin except in the presence of a seed, which leads to the chicken-or-egg paradox of which element actually starts the process. Under the microscope, Folk had observed that many travertines were thick with fossilized microbes. Often the structure of the rock seemed directly related to the type and abundance of bacteria. Some travertines looked as though they had been shaped by countless layers of bacterial colonies, much as the limestone of the El Capitán reef had been built by generations of living coral, each growing atop the last. The water associated with these travertines often lacked the high levels of calcium required for crystals to be formed by the exclusively chemical process as it was understood. Something had to be helping the precipitation along.

With a colleague named Henry Chafetz, who taught at the University of Houston (and who had earned his Ph.D. under Folk in 1970), Folk had published a landmark paper in 1984 in *The Journal of Sedimentary Petrology*. In it, they stated, "To our own astonishment we have gradually become convinced that bacteria are directly and/or indirectly responsible for the origin of the material comprising some, but not all, of the travertine accumulations" found in the hot springs of Italy and the American West.

"At some sites," Folk and Chafetz said, "bacterial action may be responsible for the precipitation of 90% or more of the framework grains comprising the deposit." The paper had been somewhat controversial but largely accepted by the geological community because of the wealth of evidence it contained. Most of the bacteria Folk and Chafetz had observed appeared to be rods just under 1 micron long, with a diameter of about 0.2 micron—near the low end of common size ranges for bacteria. But these organisms were not ubiquitous. Some sections of the travertines they had studied appeared completely devoid of fossilized cells under the microscope. These sections, the geologists presumed, must have been precipitated inorganically, as dictated by established chemical models.

Shortly after the paper was published, one of Folk's students, Victoria Pursell, wrote her master's thesis on the involvement of bacteria in the precipitation of aragonite in the hot spring travertine at Yellowstone National Park. Rod-shaped organisms called "cyanobacteria" were already known to flourish in Yellowstone's thermal pools. This was a fairly recent name for the organisms formerly known as "blue-green algae." Advances in genetic analysis had enabled microbiologists to prove what many had long argued: blue-green algae were not algae at all and did not even belong in the plant family. They were instead a form of primitive bacteria capable of plantlike photosynthesis. In fact, plants were capable of photosynthesis only because early in their evolution they had somehow incorporated whole cyanobacteria into their cells. Every plant, from the simplest algae to the tallest red-wood, harbored in each green cell hundreds of swimming organelles called "chloroplasts." They drew energy from the sun for their hosts and colored plants green.

The chloroplasts still carried some of their own DNA, separate from the DNA stored in a plant cell's nucleus. This genetic fingerprint showed that chloroplasts were cousins of their free-living bacteria counterparts. When this fact was discovered, it presented a problem to evolution theorists. They had taken for granted that photosynthesis was one of the earliest prerequisites for life, yet the cyanobacteria were merely one branch of a wide variety of ancient bacteria and by no means the most ancient branch. Many competing types of bacteria, the new DNA evidence had begun to suggest, had lived happily for billions of years before the first plant cell came along—far longer than the 500 million or so years in which plants have existed.

Theoretical debates on life's origins were of no concern to Folk. He believed, and hoped to demonstrate, that bacteria—not cyanobacteria—were the organisms helping to precipitate the aragonite found in Italian hot springs. An obscure Italian paper Pursell had cited in her thesis mentioned Viterbo, one of the few places in Italy containing hot springs that Folk had not yet visited. Folk's goal for the summer of 1988 was to find bacteria in the Viterbo travertine and compare them with Yellowstone organisms.

He pulled his 1950 Argus C-3 field camera from his pack to photograph the ancient baths, and then he and Noble continued down the path to Bagnaccio. On a bright summer morning, it is not at all unusual to find a few tourists milling about Viterbo's historic springs. But as the two descended from the ruins, they were shocked to see a busy crowd ringed by blue-suited policemen. A phalanx of young men in black T-shirts and tight-fitting jeans ran about, rigging a bewildering array of lights, ladders, cameras, and microphones. They waved huge foil-covered reflectors, sending squares of light dancing across the swimming-pool-sized circle of milky blue water.

Folk approached one of the policemen, who introduced himself as Roberto and explained that the very beautiful film star Ornella Muti was about to shoot a scene. He pointed toward a trailer that had somehow been maneuvered past the ruins to the edge of the springs. Roberto invited the Americans to stay and watch the filming, assuring them that they could make geologic collections afterward. However, he explained, the movie crew had just begun setting up; they would occupy the springs for at least several more hours.

"Perhaps," he said in Italian, clearly delighted to have met an American as fluent in the language as Folk, "you would be willing to pass the time by accompanying me to my country villa for lunch? It is only a half hour away, and I was about to go home and eat anyway."

Folk and Noble gladly accepted, climbing into a boxy Italian police car with Roberto. They ate on a patio overlooking a green-sloped volcano and talked about American and Italian films. The concrete walls of his house and garden were decorated with fossilized oysters and ancient pottery shards, all of which Roberto had collected at the site. Roberto served them homemade pasta accompanied by his homemade wine, which was distinguished by bottle tops sealed in the same local concrete with which he had built his villa. Folk explained some of the work he had done on travertines in the region and talked of how impressed he had been with the aragonite dams he had photographed that morning.

Two hours later, Roberto returned them to Bagnaccio, where filming was finally set to begin. He escorted his new friends past the taped perimeter to the area occupied by the camera crew. As the professor and his colleague looked on, Ornella Muti emerged from her trailer in a fuzzy blue bathrobe, as stunning as Roberto had advertised. She carried a baby, whom she handed to a young nanny before walking toward the spring. She paused at the edge of the steaming pool, angling her head up to face the sun as she waited for a sign from the director. When he signaled her to begin, she stepped into the water until it reached midcalf. She let her bathrobe drop behind her and walked slowly into Bagnaccio, wearing absolutely nothing.

"I've got to get this," whispered Folk. He lifted the Argus and began snapping photos. He eased closer, turning the camera sideways. Ornella began covering her exposed body with gleaming fistfuls of white aragonite mud. Folk snapped pictures even more furiously at this, spiraling ever closer toward the water's edge.

Someone in the crew chuckled. The camera kept rolling. Paula Noble stepped away, evidently trying to place as much distance as possible between herself and this crass American paparazzo, whom she didn't know from Adam. Roberto smiled and rolled his eyes.

Folk lowered his camera, and looked down the shore to where his student stood blushing.

"God, I love this country," he shouted.

Later, the scene finally shot, the last trailer only a receding dust cloud in the slanting afternoon light, Folk and Noble began sampling the sediments of Bagnaccio. Everywhere before them they found evidence of carbonate minerals recently deposited by the springs. Even bits of trash left by previous bathers—a soft drink bottle, a strip of aluminum foil—were covered with layers of fresh aragonite. These promised to be very rich samples indeed. Folk hammered and pried loose mineral chips, which he placed in sterile bags. Noble carefully drew water into a graduated container for chemical and biological analysis.

Months later, at the start of the fall 1988 semester at the University of Texas, Folk would discover under the weak, wobbly beam of his department's decades-old electron microscope that these samples were indeed loaded with bacterial forms, the most he had yet collected. It was unlikely that any of these organisms had come from the naked lady, as the water temperature was sufficient to kill most human-associated germs on contact. Undoubtedly, this was why wounded centurions were once sent to Viterbo to bathe; battle gashes immersed in the hot pools would have been less likely to fester. A microbiologist in England would eventually confirm that some of the live specimens Noble and Folk had collected that day were in fact sulfur bacteria, while others were nonphotosynthesizing, very poorly understood organisms then known as "archaebacteria." Folk would record dozens of photos of tiny fossils in the aragonite. Some of these he would paste on the oversized bulletin board in his cluttered office, where they would sit for years amid images of other stones, Italian scenery, former students, and one small print of Ornella Muti clothed in white mud.

As with other samples he had retrieved in Italy, Folk would find that the aragonites from Bagnaccio and Bullicame contained puzzling areas completely free of visible organisms. If bacteria were responsible for only *some* of the aragonite, he would once again wonder, why were these blank sections so clearly part of the same layers that had been deposited by bacteria? Perhaps the organisms were releasing an unknown chemical metabolite into the water that somehow caused precipitation. Or perhaps he and Chafetz and dozens of other experienced researchers had been wrong. Perhaps all of the travertine was formed inorganically, and the myriad colonies of bacteria that filled them were merely opportunistic hangers-on, looking for new real estate. Still, such a conclusion went against everything he had learned about travertine over the past decade. However travertine was precipitated, it had become increasingly clear that the springs bubbled forth amid a wide variety of strange life.

Perhaps the exact role of that life in creating calcite and aragonite would be clear in a few months, when the University of Texas was scheduled to receive a brand-new JEOL TSM-330A SEM, which would allow Folk to examine the blank spots in the rock at a higher magnification than ever before, up to 100,000 times. He had, of course, no idea that when the new machine was up and running in March 1989, what he would see inside those blank spots from Bagnaccio would become the driving force of his professional life for the next decade.

Back in Italy, not knowing what he held, the distinguished professor of geology dropped into a plastic bag the one chunk of rock that would lead him to discovery. It would make him for a while the source of international scientific ridicule, and yet might still propel the geologist into contention for a Nobel Prize in medicine. He and Paula Noble checked the seals and labels on their samples before shoving them into their field packs. Only a bit of daylight remained. The springs and the ruins were deserted. They began the long hike back to Viterbo. After a couple of miles, Folk saw an outdoor cafe attached to a motel and insisted that they stop for a drink. He plopped down at a picnic table, setting his pack on the grass.

As they waited to be served, Folk noticed an infant in a portable windup swing. He walked over to the bright-eyed, cooing baby.

"*Buon giorno,*" he said. He held out a finger, and she grabbed it.

"I see her mother coming," said Noble. "Guess who."

Folk turned as Ornella Muti scooped the baby from the swing.

"These are tourists," she said to her daughter, one dark eyebrow raised.

"No, we're not tourists," Folk explained. "We're geologists. Call me Luigi."

"*Buon giorno,* Luigi," she said.

Ornella Muti carried her baby into the motel, and he never saw the star again. Luigi and Paula finished the walk to town, stored the samples in their rooms, showered, dressed, and went to dinner. By chance, the place they walked into was listed in *The Guinness Book of World Records* as serving more types of pasta than any other restaurant on earth. So ended what Folk would later call "the most amazing field day of my entire life."

THREE

1992

It is sometimes important for science to know how to forget the things she is surest of.

—Jean Rostand

Presentations

Salem, Indiana

Most of the annual weeklong convention of the National Speleological Society (NSS) is devoted to reports of caving expeditions in the United States and elsewhere, rope-climbing contests, cavelike obstacle courses, and occasional loud parties. But some science always manages to take place in quiet auditoriums and seminar rooms, where a small fraction of those attending the convention listen with rapt attention to the discoveries of their peers. The biology session chair of the 1992 convention was Dr. Norman Pace, a hard-core caver who ran a microbial research lab based at nearby Indiana University. Five years earlier, Pace had received the NSS's coveted Lew Bicking Award, given to those who have proven their underground mettle by discovering and mapping large, technically challenging virgin cave systems. Despite his fame in pushing tough Mexican caves, few within the caving world were aware that Pace's day job was heading a team that had begun redefining the relationships, or *phylogeny*, of virtually all life on Earth.

Pace was one of only two NSS cavers who could claim membership in the prestigious National Academy of Sciences. He had become heir apparent to the work begun in 1977 by Carl Woese at the University of Illinois: the use of DNA identification techniques to map out the genetic kinship of all living things. Examining evolutionary changes in particular genes allowed Pace and others in his lab to deduce which organisms evolved first and which came later. Every living cell contains small protein factories called "ribosomes." Ribosomal RNA (often abbreviated as rRNA) is the chemical that creates specific proteins as instructed by an organism's DNA. When Woese had begun the genetic approach to phylogeny, he had spent months of painstaking analysis in search of the entire genetic code, or *genome*, of each organism that he studied. Pace had convinced Woese that the same genetic relationships could be ascertained more easily by focusing on a particular sequence in rRNA called the 16-S subunit. This sequence was useful for comparison between organisms because it appeared to be carried by every living thing on Earth and mutated at a known rate. By tracing back the degree of mutation, one could reconstruct a rough evolutionary clock, putting a date to the appearance of any particular organism. Already, the data gathered by Woese and Pace had all but wiped out "the five kingdoms of life" that had been taught in biology classes since the nineteenth century.

Instead of five kingdoms consisting of plants, animals, protists, fungi, and bacteria, evolutionary kinships suggested that there were what Woese called three "domains" of life. All three were predominantly microbial. The plants, animals, and fungi had all developed as very recent offshoots (relatively speaking) of a single small twig at the end of a branch of one of these three domains, the eucaryotes (pronounced "you-carry-oats"). The other two domains were the bacteria and something new to science, a vast class of life Woese named the archaea, after the Earth's most ancient geologic period. The heat-loving, deep-dwelling organisms of the archaea seemed the closest to the root of life's tree. They had been quietly evolving and adapting for billions of years before the first single-celled algae began to give off oxygen and make larger life-forms possible; they are evolving and adapting still. Pace and others were beginning to believe that the whole business of life on Earth began in the hot cauldron of a sea-floor volcano, as opposed to the calm tidal pool envisioned by Darwin.

Pace had used the research submarine *Alvin* to personally sample archaea steaming from "black smokers" in the Pacific, volcanic geysers distinguished by smokelike clouds of microbes and minerals that continually billowed up from them. The mineral mounds that typically built up around the black smokers became the habitats of bizarre crabs and tubeworms, which were able to survive in such extreme environments by means of symbiotic archaea that lived inside their tissues, converting hot minerals to food. Fittingly, however, it was an archaic organism from Yellowstone National Park that had made his current work possible.

When first developed, DNA analysis was a very slow and painstaking process, but the operation had been supercharged in the mid-1980s with the invention of a technique called "polymerase chain reaction," or PCR. Making copies of genes in the lab requires repeated cycles of heating and cooling the genetic material that is to be copied; unfortunately, DNA typically starts to break apart at higher temperatures. In 1983, a biochemist named Kary Mullis had patented a new process based on his realization that thermophiles in Yellowstone National Park replicate their DNA at high temperatures as a matter of course. From a Yellowstone archaean called *Thermus aquaticus*, which lived at temperatures of up to 170° Fahrenheit, Mullis extracted an enzyme which he named Taq polymerase ("Taq" is an abbreviation of the species name). This enzyme could keep any DNA from breaking down when exposed to heat. The science of genetic engineering grew from Mullis's observation, for which he eventually received the Nobel Prize in chemistry. By 1992, worldwide sales of Taq were worth an estimated $300 million a year.

Through their use of PCR in examining various microbes, Woese and Pace had begun to challenge many of the precepts regarding the orderly evolution of "higher" life forms from "lower" ones originally put forth by Darwin. From traditional microbiologists, who had been taught to classify organisms not by kinships but by shape, size, and metabolic strategies for survival, Woese faced harsh resistance to the elevation of the archaea to a separate domain of life. There was very little difference between the archaea and the bacteria by such standards. Scientists who had spent their lives collecting and culturing organisms resented having centuries-old classification systems erased by someone who had only studied dead organisms chopped up in a blender. But Pace's lab continually published new evidence that Woese was right, identifying scores of new microorganisms along the way, many of which could never have been collected and cultured by traditional means. Most microbiologists grudgingly began to accept the three-domain structure of life. The previous year, Pace had authored a controversial, groundbreaking essay in the prestigious journal *Cell* on the subject, entitled "The Origin of Life: Facing Up to the Physical Setting."

Around cavers, however, Pace tended to converse about current leads in Mexico, leaving the science to others. To him, spending several days following the course of a raging subterranean river was a welcome escape from scientific and academic pressures. At the Indiana convention, Pace had organized a symposium on cave biodiversity at which others would do the speaking. Among those he had assembled was Serban Sarbu, a Romanian completing a biology doctorate at the University of Cincinnati. Sarbu had been in the news lately for his discovery of a small, partially flooded cave in Romania called Movile, which was full of floating mats of sulfur-eating bacteria. These created acid that seemed to be enlarging the cave, and they released hydrogen sulfide that gave the cave a poisonous atmosphere, with very little oxygen. Yet the bacteria fed a diverse array of larger species, all of them new to science, including eyeless spiders, worm-sucking leeches, wingless flies, and carnivorous centipedes.

Also speaking were Horton "Beep" Hobbs, a legendary cave biologist, and Larry Mallory, an acquaintance of both Hobbs and Pace. A microbiologist, Mallory had discovered numerous (and totally unexpected) microbial species in Mammoth Cave. Rounding out the microbiology speakers was a team of six scientists who had been investigating insect and microbial life in

Lechuguilla Cave. Among the latter was a somewhat timid science librarian from the University of New Mexico named Diana Northup, who had recently concluded that Lechuguilla Cave harbored a limited—but interesting—population of microbial life.

Mallory, a slim, good-looking man with dark hair and lively green eyes, addressed the assembled cavers with the enthusiasm that had won him a number of teaching awards at Memphis State University, a school he had just left in order to begin teaching at the University of Massachusetts, Amherst. "First off, you should know I'm not a caver," he said. "I've never had any particular interest in caves. But I am interested in microbial life below the surface. How far down do things live? What do they eat? How is life down there different from life on the surface? Basic questions." In 1987, Mallory explained, the U.S. Department of Energy had drilled a deep hole near Georgia's Savannah River nuclear facility as part of its ongoing research into the possibility of storing nuclear wastes underground. The agency had invited microbiologists to apply for grants to answer the question of what was living at the bottom of the drill hole, if anything. Mallory had applied for one of those grants but had been turned down.

> So I thought, okay, I can't drill down to this stuff. How else can I get underground? Well, caves go underground. So I went to the literature to see what other microbiologists had found in caves. All I could find was a twenty-year-old study cited in all the reference books. According to the study, there were only five or six types of bacteria in caves, and they were all common species of soil bacteria.

Mallory curled his lower lip and nodded in exaggerated acceptance of this idea, then screwed up his face in a pantomime of confusion.

> But then this struck me as a little odd. We know that bacteria are very good at adapting to specific environments, and caves present a very different sort of environment than the soil. The water, the food, the atmosphere, and other conditions are nothing like soil conditions. And I knew from years of collecting and growing

microbes that the techniques microbiologists use in the field can be self-selecting. In other words, you go looking for soil bacteria, that's probably all you'll find. There may be lots of other stuff there, but you'll miss it because it takes different techniques to find it. You might only find the soil bacteria that you brought in on your boots, or that was carried in by occasional surface drainage, without getting a true picture of what's there.

So I started going into caves with a wide variety of sampling techniques. I'd done some rock climbing and a little recreational caving, so it wasn't too hard for me to come up with a sampling kit that would survive in a cave pack. Well, what I found in Mammoth Cave was that the standard reference book was, to put it mildly, wrong.

Mallory described an enormous range of previously unknown species he had found in several sites in Mammoth, suggesting that a fairly large and diverse microbial population existed there, and perhaps in all limestone caves.

Later that same day, Diana Northup described her efforts in Lechuguilla. She began by citing the same reference Mallory had used regarding soil bacteria in caves. In Lechuguilla, she said, many of the organisms, as predicted, could be identified as common soil bacteria. But she had identified at least a few chemoautolithotrophs—rock-eating cave bugs—unique to Lechuguilla.

Mallory approached Northup after her talk and told her frankly that she was wrong, that she had almost certainly missed *most* of the microbial species in her test site and had probably collected primarily "contaminant" organisms brought in from the surface by cavers. "What collection methods did you use?" he asked.

Northup described the containers her samples had been gathered in, explaining that the cave was so technically challenging she had entrusted cavers to do her sampling for her. She admitted to a fear of heights; collecting from Lechuguilla required one to rappel down (and later climb out of) quite a few pits. "But I made sure they knew how to avoid contaminating the samples," she added.

"Let me gather some samples for you, and I'll show you what's really there," Mallory offered.

"Gosh, I don't know," said Northup, who never made any decision, especially scientific ones, lightly. "I'll have to think about it and get back to you."

After the symposium, Mallory joined Pace for a tour of his lab at Indiana University, which had already become famous in microbiology circles. Mallory noticed a red-and-white Campbell's can on Pace's desk, which some waggish postdoc had altered to read "Primordial Soup." After the tour, the two went to Pace's house for drinks in the backyard, where a troupe of young trapeze artists—friends of Pace's wife, a circus buff—were putting on a show. As the performers wheeled and spun in the air, the conversation turned to the ideas introduced by a paper Pace had recently approved, along with Carl Woese and one other scientist, for publication in the *Proceedings of the National Academy of Sciences*. The paper was entitled "The Deep Hot Biosphere," and its author was Thomas Gold of Cornell University.

Gold had long been a proponent of a controversial theory favoring a nonbiological origin for petroleum deposits. He believed oil was created by very deep planetary processes as opposed to dead dinosaurs or decaying Jurassic swamps. Gold justified this belief by pointing to astronomical evidence of petroleum on Saturn's moon Titan and other planetary bodies—places unlikely to contain the deep, stagnant pools of water favored by standard models as the origins of petroleum. A nonbiological origin could explain the high level of helium concentration found in natural petroleum, Gold felt. The radioactive decay of uranium and thorium was known to create widely distributed bits of helium inside deep rocks. Gold believed that liquid petroleum driven up from great depths in the Earth's mantle would sweep up this scattered helium, concentrating it to the levels he had routinely measured. The problem with Gold's theory was that every known oil deposit was chock-full of biological molecules.

At the deep, hot levels from which he believed petroleum

came, none of these biomolecules would have survived. It then occurred to him that no one had ever seen petroleum at those great depths, but only at the much shallower depths that modern oil drills could reach. What if, Gold had wondered, the biological component of petroleum is *added* at the drilling depth or slightly below? What if all liquids below the surface were inhabited by microbes to a depth of, say, three to eight miles? This viewpoint had not been considered, Gold explained, because an immense quantity of microbial life would have to exist in domains where absolutely no biology was expected.

Studies in oil wells going back to the 1920s had shown petroleum deposits aswarm with living microbes, not just dead remains. However, such findings had been uniformly dismissed as surface contamination. Critics claimed that bugs from around the drilling platform had gotten into the hole and multiplied. The reason this explanation had always been accepted was that observations starting at the surface and going down through normal soil had shown a drastic decline in their biological content. Extrapolation of this rule led to the belief that no biology could exist at all below the levels that had already been studied.

But Gold was aware of the thermophiles recently found in Yellowstone and in mid-ocean volcanic vents, where the temperatures approached 240° Fahrenheit. Perhaps, he reasoned, there was a dead zone just below the surface, as soil microbiologists had long maintained. But as one looked *deeper* into the Earth's warm crust, one would find an environment more conducive to widespread microbial life. If this environment were fully inhabited, Gold argued in his paper, the living mass and volume below would exceed that of all surface life. And if rock-eating, heat-loving bugs could live far below sunlight on Earth, they could, and probably did, live below the surfaces of a great many other planetary bodies.

To test his theory, Gold had initiated a very deep well-bore project in Sweden. Some microbial debris was found in oil in purely granitic rock at a depth greater than three miles—the deepest subsurface life ever found. He then invited distinguished microbiologists from the Karolinska Institute in Stockholm to take samples and see whether they could culture them. According to Gold's paper, this was entirely successful. Two strains of previously unknown bacteria were discovered. Both were thermophilic and anaerobic, meaning they could only survive under high temperatures and in the complete absence of oxygen. It was unlikely that these organisms were contamination from higher levels in the drill hole because of the cleanliness of the drilling method, which avoided using surface mud as a lubricant. While Gold's ideas about nonbiological petroleum were still hotly contested, Pace told Mallory that he thought Gold's microbiology, at least, was very good indeed; there was a whole new world down there.

"You're preaching to the choir," Mallory said.

As the two men discussed the possibility that life had first evolved underground in a deep ocean vent, Mallory became distracted by the woman sitting next to him, who was shouting encouragements while her sixteen-year-old daughter climbed the ladder to the trapeze. He stopped talking long enough to watch the girl perform. She swung back and forth, building up speed until at last she leapt for the other swing. She grabbed at the bar and missed, falling backward to the net. As the girl bounced slowly to a stop, she let loose a string of invective that would have given any movie an R rating.

Her mother turned to Mallory and said, "Ah, the very flower of womanhood."

CINCINNATI, OHIO

The Geological Society of America's annual convention was a far more staid affair than that of the NSS, yet this was the meeting where Bob Folk decided to air publicly the startling conclusions he had drawn from his study of Viterbo travertine. Knowing all too well how grandiose ideas are received in the sciences—especially those which overturn all established wisdom—Folk nervously approached the podium to present a paper arguing that he had found a new type of very small bacteria. What he had first discovered in the Viterbo travertines had led him to examine a wide variety of other minerals. In many of these he had also found extremely small objects which appeared to be biological.

He explained that these organisms, which he proposed to term "nanobacteria," had escaped notice because previous electron microscopes had lacked the resolving power to identify them. He then proposed that nanobacteria were the principal agents of precipitation not just of hot spring travertines but of all mineral and crystals on Earth formed in liquid water, including aragonite, gypsum crystals, and calcium carbonate—basically every cave and spring formation and many other rocks to boot. Moreover, he argued, they were also the agents of the oxidation of all metals on Earth; whenever iron rusts or aluminum corrodes, it does so because these organisms are eating it. And finally, to top off his speech, he presented evidence that nanobacteria were abundant not just in rocks but also in many biological specimens, including humans. He claimed to have easily found nanobacteria in his own dental plaque and excrement. He also described growing large cultures of nanobacteria simply by placing sterile aluminum stubs in Austin tap water for forty eight hours. Nanobacteria, he concluded, are everywhere, and although invisible are probably the dominant life form of the planet.

He was not terribly surprised when the auditorium responded to his paper with what he later described as "a vast and stony silence."

COLORADO SPRINGS, COLORADO

The Rocky Mountain Speleo-Seminar at the University of Colorado, Colorado Springs, was not particularly well attended, but those who were there were eager to discuss the latest theories accounting for the bizarre mineral formations cavers continued to find in Lechuguilla. Most of these, the thinking went, could be tied to the cave's H_2S speleogenesis—that is, to Lech's formation by hydrogen sulfide–charged waters rising from deep petroleum deposits. Of course, this process had happened in the distant past, and the sulfuric waters had long since receded. The best-known cave where this type of speleogenesis seemed to be actively occurring was the remote and dangerous Movile Cave in Romania, studied by the biologist Serban Sarbu. The Romanian government tightly controlled access to Movile, and negotiating the dangerous cave required technical diving skills, so work there proceeded very slowly.

Thus the talk given by Dr. James Pisarowicz, an environmental scientist and a longtime caver, drew a fair amount of attention from speleologists. Pisarowicz claimed to have found another cave that was actively releasing hydrogen sulfide, which bacteria were actively converting to a strong acid that carved new passages. The cave was located in the southern Mexican state of Tabasco.

Each spring, Pisarowicz explained, just after Easter, the residents of the village of Tapijulapa dress in white and travel by boat to La Cueva de Villa Luz, the Cave of the Lighted House, to give thanks for the fishes. The festival is called La Pesca de la Sardina. It is marked by the rapid beating of Mayan drums and the birdlike trilling of wooden flutes. No matter how bad the drought or famine of the surface world, the troglodytic fish, a species of molly, are always so thick that villagers can scoop them up with cupped hands.

The fish appeared to Pisarowicz to feed on insect larvae, which were always present in the cave. The insects, in turn, appeared to feed on a snotlike slime coating the cave walls and dripping from the ceiling. On his first visit in 1986, Pisarowicz had been surprised to discover that his clothing was literally dissolving off his body at the end of the trip. He learned that the cave's ubiquitous slime was composed mostly of H_2SO_4, sulfuric acid, at a solution level similar that of a car battery. It not only dissolved clothing; it also caused minor skin burns. In some passages, the hydrogen sulfide made the cave air highly poisonous to breathe.

He found large deposits of sulfur and gypsum similar to those reported in Lechuguilla. The acid in the system was clearly dissolving new passages. What Pisarowicz assumed could only be microbes hung pendant from the ceiling in complex symbiotic colonies that swayed like stalactites of gray Jell-O; the highest concentrations of acid were found in the water droplets hanging at the tips. He had decided to name the formations "snottites."

Pisarowicz had obtained samples of the cave's gypsum and sulfur. Geologist Kiym Cummingham had analyzed them with X-ray fluorescence at the laboratories of the U.S. Geological Survey. The results were similar to levels found in samples from Lechuguilla and Carlsbad Cavern, in that sulfur in both minerals was "isotopically light." Pisarowicz interpreted this to mean that isotopes had been fractionated, or dispersed, by sulfur-reducing bacteria. Of course, he concluded, this was only an interpretation. No one had yet attempted a microbial study of the hanging snottites or other suspected microbes in the cave.

He hoped that such a study would be attempted soon. As things turned out, five years would go by before a microbiologist would examine Villa Luz.

FOUR

1993

A new scientific truth does not triumph by convincing its opponents and making them see the right, but rather because its opponents eventually die, and a new generation grows up that is familiar with it.

—MAX PLANCK

VALEDICTORY

It was a beautiful June evening in southern Arkansas. The loud-speaker echoing her name through the brightly lit stadium, Anne Elizabeth Taunton approached the podium, her hands shaking. She was used to being the center of attention here at Memorial Stadium. She had been the El Dorado High School band's drum major for both her junior and senior years. During eighth and ninth grades, she had been drum major in the same stadium for the junior high band. Her parents, Charlotte and Charles, still pulled out the video of Anne's first junior high halftime show for visiting relatives, or worse, for Anne's dates. No matter how loudly she groaned, there she was in green tights and white gloves, directing a marching medley from *Phantom of the Opera*.

She had never felt terribly nervous before a halftime show—or, for that matter, before her starring roles in *Annie* and *Little Shop of Horrors* on South Arkansas Arts Center's stage—but she felt so now. She squinted at the bright lights, trying in vain to find her parents and her two older sisters in the crowd. There was Mike Strange, the easygoing science teacher, who had let her make foul-smelling sulfur bombs in her senior chemistry class, and Dean Inman, the mock-trial coach, who had tried to talk her into considering law school, but her family was lost somewhere in the glare. *Oh well, better get on with it.* She smoothed her notes on the podium. Valedictorian of a class of 271. A 4.0 g.p.a.—4.56, if you added in the extra points for honors classes. *Okay,* she thought, *you can do this.* She raised her gaze and smiled.

"In Michael Crichton's novel *Jurassic Park,* he speaks of sacrifice." Her voice bounced back to her from the empty visitor bleachers across the stadium behind her. She ignored the echo and plowed on. "Whatever we seek, we have to put in the time, the practice, the effort. We must give up a lot to get it. While we're doing this, while we're going through this period of sacrifice, we are gaining maturity, strength, and discipline." Saying the word "sacrifice" caused the brief and unexpected image of her childhood hero, Christa McAuliffe, to flash through her mind. She fought against the image; she was close enough to the edge of emotion, to losing it, as it was.

She had been in the fourth grade when the *Challenger* exploded, and she still became upset at seeing the TV image of those streaming trails of smoke in the Florida sky. That was the year she had made a poster for Ms. Mock's science project on NASA and careers in space—it had started: "The solar system is an exciting place to learn about. You can learn things that you probably thought were impossible." Somewhere in her room, buried among the Beatles and Prince CDs, she still had a yellowing letter on NASA stationery. Anne had been so excited that someone there had actually answered her, had suggested courses of study for young people who wanted to work in space. Now that she no longer dreamed of flying the Space Shuttle, she wondered where she wanted to go in life. She had a full scholarship to the University of Arkansas, but she hadn't a clue as to where she wanted it to take her. Not that any doubt showed on her face as her voice boomed through Memorial Stadium.

This discipline gives us a form of self-control, so that we don't abuse our newfound strength. Crichton uses the analogy of a karate master. Many young boys begin karate lessons with the purpose of learning how to hurt people. They want this power, and they think obtaining it will be easy. But by the time they *have* obtained the ability, the ability to kill with their bare hands . . .

She paused to look at the crowd, warming to her role, getting into the rhythm of the speech she had written that afternoon with the help of her honors English teacher, Beverly Allen.

they have also matured to the point where they won't use this ability unwisely. They respect the power they now possess.

The same is true for the graduating class of 1993. Since the first grade, we have wanted the power that comes from independence, and we thought this freedom could be easily obtained. But as we come here tonight, we realize that it wasn't easy.

In fact, for Anne school *had* been easy, something that came naturally (with the possible exception of eighth-grade algebra, the only B she had ever earned).

Through our sacrifice in the past twelve years, we have gained the power of education, and it can't be taken away. It resides in us. We respect this power. And with this power comes responsibility. Like the karate master, we must be mature and disciplined enough to use our education wisely.

She could hear her father's voice in the words she had chosen. A chemical engineer, he had asked every Christmas since Anne was little for "the gift of world peace." He had taught her and her two sisters always to take time out to help others, no matter how busy life happened to get—a lesson her mother always reinforced. Where were they sitting, anyway?

We have already shown some of that discipline. Tonight, by graduating, by earning our high school diplomas, we have done what twenty-nine percent of the nation hasn't been able to do, and the sacrifice we made in yesterday's classrooms now gives us the power and maturity for the future of tomorrow.

The last words echoed into the faded sunset. She lifted her eyes and beamed. There were Mom and Dad and her sisters Jennifer and Sarah, sitting toward the back, applauding along with her grandmother, her Uncle Jerry, her Aunt Maryann, and everyone else in the stadium. Silently congratulating herself for not breaking down, only now letting a tear creep out, Anne headed back to her seat.

Almost over, she thought, *and then it's time to party.*

FIVE

1994

The Lord hath created medicines out of the earth: and he
that is wise will not abhor them. Was not the water made
sweet with wood, that the virtue thereof might be known?
                                                —ECCLESIASTICUS

COINCIDENCE

Larry Mallory was hiking along the Western Borehole with Jason
Richards, a resource manager with the U.S. National Park Service. The rest of their group was far behind them in the mile-
long natural tunnel that forms the main highway to the western
third of Lechuguilla's known passages. Navigating the Borehole
is about as easy as caving ever gets. The wide, smooth passage is
broken by occasional short hills. The ceiling and walls often
reach out of sight and seldom constrict to anything smaller than
an airplane hangar. It's like walking through a rock quarry at
night. Mallory and Richards were trucking right along, unlike the
rest of their scientific team.

Although the Western Borehole presents very easy going, the
passages one must negotiate to get there do not. At least, they are
not easy for novices. The rest of the team consisted of a number
of first-timers, some of whom had been pretty wiped out by the
climbs and crawls they had traversed the day before on the way in.
Among them were four assorted Ph.D.s in biology and geology and
a couple of support cavers to keep the scientists out of trouble.

While the first-timers took a rest day and prepped gear at the team's base camp, Richards and Mallory had decided to check some microbe traps Mallory had placed at the far end of the Borehole on an earlier trip. Both men were accomplished cavers at the top of their form, and both had made a number of trips into Lechuguilla during the previous two years. In a few months, they would lead Chris McKay, Larry Lemke, and Penny Boston, experts on Mars from NASA's Ames Research Center, through Lech. These scientists practiced a brand of science so new that it went by several different names, prominent among them *exobiology* and *astrobiology*. They wanted to look for terrestrial analogs to possible life-sustaining environments on Mars; they believed Lechuguilla might fit the bill. Some evidence gathered by NASA's Viking spacecraft suggested that Mars had once harbored thermal springs much like the one believed to have formed Lechuguilla. The NASA crew in Lech would be joined by the famed mountaineer Jon Krakauer, who was writing about exobiology for *Smithsonian Air & Space Magazine*.

The slow pace of the scientists had tried Larry and Jason, so they hiked along, happily conversing, glad to be moving once more.

As they rounded a famous landmark in the cave, a white pillar named the Leaning Tower of Lechuguilla, Richards asked Mallory what good his research would do, toward what practical purposes it might contribute.

"Beats me," answered the scientist.

"But don't we get useful products from microbes?"

"Sure," Mallory said, "but I don't 'do' useful. I'm just curious about these things." But then he couldn't resist launching into his standard undergraduate lecture on the wonderful benefits of microbes when they are employed by those who "do" useful. This medicinal and industrial tally carried the two men through several hundred feet of cave.

"So," said Richards, "you're saying there could be a cure for cancer right in front of us, a cure for AIDS?"

"Could be."

Richards paused and looked at Mallory as though he were regarding a very primitive life form. "And you're not going to do a damn thing about it?"

Mallory shrugged. "It's not what I'm good at."

But Mallory thought a lot about the conversation over the next few days. Things were not going particularly well at the University of Massachusetts, where once again he had been head butting with his dean, who had long been urging him to give up the exotic cave bugs and do some "significant" work. He had been exploring a realm of unknown life, which offered him enormous excitement, but he did sometimes worry whether others would consider it "significant." He knew he faced a tough tenure fight ahead, and although he had some powerful allies, including Lynn Margulis, the famed creator of the Gaia theory of evolution, he was beginning to worry that he might not make it. *Caves got microbes, so what?* seemed to be the response of many of his peers. He had brought his wife, Carolyn, to Amherst from her native Memphis, along with their three children. The night before he went into the cave, he had called Carolyn and learned that a fourth was on the way. They had bought a house. This was not a good time for a protracted tenure battle.

On the day he returned, tired and bruised, from his week with the NASA scientists in Lechuguilla, Mallory found a phone message waiting for him from a Dr. Miles Hacker, who identified himself as a pharmacologist teaching at the Vermont Cancer Center. Hacker had been looking for some months for a microbiologist who collected cave organisms, he explained, because he wanted to try a basic test against cancer cells to see if there might be any reason to investigate cave life further for the drug industry. "It's one of the few areas I don't think anyone's checked for potential drugs," he said.

Although Mallory normally would have considered such a request an intrusion, he merely smiled and shook his head. "I think God is trying to tell me something," he said. He described his conversation in the cave with Richards. "So the answer is, sure, I'd be happy to help out. What do you want?"

A few days later, Mallory selected living cultures of five cave bugs from his growing collection and five cultures of ordinary soil bacteria. He put these in coded containers and sent all ten to Hacker without explaining which was which.

Hacker would place all ten samples in the vicinity of living breast cancer cells to see if any of them attacked the cancer. "Hits are graded on a one-to-five scale," he had explained during their phone conversation, "with five being the strongest. If we get a one or two, it may not mean much, but if one of your samples gets a three, it definitely means there's something here worth looking at."

"What if we get two or three hits?" Mallory had asked. "What if we get a four?"

Hacker had laughed. "If that happens, you need to quit your day job."

A few days later, Hacker called and asked him to reveal the code, to tell which samples were which. Mallory did. Hacker whistled, then asked if Mallory could drive to Vermont.

"I take it we got a hit?" Mallory asked.

"You just need to come up here. We'll talk then, but I can tell you now that this is the most exciting thing I've seen in fifteen years of drug research."

Intrigued, Mallory drove to the cancer center. Hacker was a tall, heavyset man with unkempt hair and a bemused smile. He spoke with the confidence of someone who had ushered not one but two major drugs through the arduous, expensive process from laboratory to patent to testing to FDA approval to use on actual human patients. He welcomed Mallory into his office and closed the door. Of the five control samples of ordinary soil microbes, he said, one had given a level-two hit, about what you'd expect from any five random samples. The five cave samples, however, produced four hits: three of them were at level three and one at an unprecedented level four.

"I wasn't joking," said Hacker. "You need to do this full-time. Both of us do. We need to quit our jobs right away and devote all of our time to this. Four hits at once, with four unknown natural products from an unexamined environment . . . well, I've never seen anything like it. This could be very, very important."

The two men talked long into the night, and by the next morning a new company had been born.

SIX

MARCH 1996

The most beautiful thing we can experience is the mysterious. It is the source of all true art and science.

—ALBERT EINSTEIN

BACK TO THE GARDEN

I first heard of subsurface microbiology in February 1996, when Emily Davis Mobley, a noted cave explorer and longtime friend, called to suggest that I should get myself invited on an upcoming science expedition to Lechuguilla. In the fall of 1995, the National Park Service had closed the cave to exploration to allow a yearlong study of its microbial communities while the cave recovered from years of heavy caving traffic. Emily hinted that some of the microbes now being collected there were very new and very strange, probably worthy of a magazine article. She said that the microbiologist leading the trip, Diana Northup, was looking for evidence that cavers such as ourselves were unknowingly wreaking environmental devastation on tiny habitats of bizarre life. And she mentioned that Larry Mallory, another microbiologist who would be at Lechuguilla, was searching for a cure for cancer among the cave's bacteria.

I agreed that it seemed to be a good story. I convinced Northup to accept me as slave labor for her collection work, then found an editor who would pay my way to New Mexico. I was to assist Northup's team in three days of underground collection over a large general area, while Mallory's team would make shorter day trips to particular medical research sites. Northup was working under a Lindbergh Foundation Grant, which awarded researchers just over $13,000, the exact price of the *Spirit of St. Louis* when Charles Lindbergh bought it in 1927. Her goal was to collect direct, living evidence of how human activity may have changed Lechuguilla's unseen universe.

Two weeks after getting her to let me tag along, I flew into El Paso, rented an Eddie Bauer Ford Explorer, cranked up the stereo, and drove east toward the Guadalupe Mountains, or the "Guads" as they're commonly known to cavers. There's always a stiff wind blowing across the desert. The speed limit is high. Every distant hill seems to hint at hidden caves. The combination of these three factors causes me to weave all over the highway every time I drive from El Paso to Carlsbad, especially when my rental happens to be a souped-up sport-utility. Nevertheless, I made good time and arrived intact at Carlsbad Caverns National Park headquarters at sunset, just as the team was getting ready to head off the mountain and into town for dinner. Emily jumped into the Eddie Bauer, and we followed the others to Lucy's, a Mexican restaurant popular with the caving crowd.

As we stood on the sidewalk, waiting for Larry Mallory to show up in his rental car, I asked Diana about the odd diagram on her T-shirt, which appeared to be three branching lines emerging from a single point. She explained that it was the tree of life as drawn by the Pace Lab, the research center started by Norm Pace. I knew the name; I could recall reading a decade earlier his first-person account, published in the *NSS News*, of what seemed to me almost suicidally dangerous caving in Mexico.

"We humans are here," Diana said, pointing to a little tip of one of the three branches above her right breast, "with the eucaryotes." She pointed out what the Victorians called the "three kingdoms of life"—the plants, the animals, and the fungi—all out on the same little twig with humanity.

Diana was short, of medium build, forty-seven years old. There was something kindly and gentle about her voice that made me think of my son's kindergarten teacher. "All the rest of the tree," she continued, "including the biggest part of our branch and all of the other two branches, the archaea and the bacteria"—she waved her hand over the shirt—"is microbial. Everything alive belongs in either eucaryotes, the bacteria, or the archaea."

These taxonomical relationships, she explained, were based on a subunit of ribosomal RNA. Each separate line of related organisms was called a *taxon*; collectively, they were called *taxa*. Just then Larry Mallory arrived, and before we were fully introduced, he jumped in on the explanation. He was wearing jeans and a knit sports shirt, but something about his clean-cut looks and quizzical demeanor suggested that he would have been more comfortable in a lab coat; he looked like every scientist in the educational films I had seen in elementary school. He and Northup evinced the excitement of streetside evangelists addressing a potential convert. I nodded and tried to take notes.

As we finally walked into Lucy's, Emily turned and said, "See? What'd I tell you?"

"Emily, I owe you," I said.

"You owe me big time."

The lecture continued as we waited for margaritas. "If I wanted to collect a redwood tree, a tiger, and a trout," Mallory explained, "I'd be collecting much more closely related organisms than many that live in a single water droplet hanging off a single helictite in Lechuguilla. There's an incredible diversity underground. In a given pool, you might find one community that lives in the film on the surface, another on the edge of the water, another on the bottom, and maybe another that stays suspended in the middle. Each of these communities might have dozens or even hundreds of separate taxa. They've been evolving and adapting for a very long time and are very different from one another. That's one reason they're hard to collect: You need several different techniques for each site, or you're going to miss most of what's there."

I asked whether any of these weird bugs could hurt me. Might some Andromeda Strain be down there waiting for us to stumble onto it?

"Not likely," said Larry. "Parasitic relationships require a close shared evolution between host and parasite. Only familiarity can breed disease."

Over dinner, Diana explained how Larry had convinced her she was wrong about her methods for collecting microbes in Lechuguilla after their first meeting at the Indiana NSS convention. He had collected samples for her that November, using the techniques she had instructed him to use, and had gathered others with the methods he had developed in Mammoth. "Only a few things grew from half of the samples he brought me, but the other half had all sorts of bugs I'd never seen before. I mean it was *crawling* with colonies. I called Larry and said, 'Fess up, you used your methods, didn't you?' He said, 'How'd you know?' I said, 'Because there's all this stuff growing here that I've never seen before!' He convinced me the only way I could get results like that was to go in and study each site individually, and to sample it myself. So I've been trying."

"And getting pretty good at it, too," Emily added.

"I may as well tell you now so you'll be ready for it," Diana said. "I'm very slow at pits. I don't like them. I wish I didn't have to do them, so I always take my time and make sure I'm safe. The last thing I want is cavers having to pull out an old lady scientist with a big rescue."

Emily and I exchanged knowing grins. "Well, we sure don't want another 'spring break' on our hands," she said.

Eight years had passed since my swim in Castrovalva, nearly five since my last Lech trip in March 1991. That one had made international headlines when, deep inside a side passage off the Western Borehole, a loose rock fell on Emily's leg and broke it. I had been with another survey party at the time, but we had encountered Emily's team not long after they had called out the rescue effort. Extracting her from the cave had taken four days and more than two hundred volunteers (most of whom eventually got an "I Survived Emily's Spring Break" T-shirt). The park superintendent had alerted the press to the massive rescue project, and by the second day, the Carlsbad parking lot was choked with satellite trucks. My throat became raw from giving dozens of interviews to reporters. Emily's final haul to the surface, during which she sang rock songs, made all the evening network news broadcasts. She became a caving celebrity of sorts, appearing on talk shows and giving speeches at conventions.

Once we were back at the park's expedition huts, after dinner Larry and I each drank a shot of bourbon as we discussed the trip ahead.

"This is probably not the best thing to drink before you go into a cave where people get dehydrated," I said.

"You're absolutely right. But it's our last chance for the next few days."

After saying good night to Larry, I went through my gear one last time to make sure everything was ready for my return to Lech the next morning. What I remembered of the '91 trip with shame was not the media circus up top. It was the hours I spent vomiting below. A common mistake made by Lechuguilla cavers is the one often made by desert hikers, and the one I made on that 1991 expedition: the failure to drink enough water. In the excitement of keeping up with a fast-moving survey team, of finding and mapping virgin tunnels, and then of learning that the biggest cave rescue of all time was in progress around me, I had failed to stop and drink. By the time I began to experience the actual symptoms of dehydration, I was already so nauseated that I couldn't keep anything down. This only aggravated my condition. My trek out of the cave took far longer than it should have. I lost count of the number of rescue squads that passed me, rushing in and out while rigging various pulley systems for Emily's stretcher as I hunched to one side of the passage and tried to catch my breath. Accompanied by Bob Addis, another big guy who had failed to drink and was nearly as exhausted as I was, I somehow found the energy and mental focus to clip in properly and climb each rope en route to the surface. At the top of several, I had collapsed in the trail, heaving morsels of Gatorade and granola into the native food chain. Only when safely resting on the surface was I able to hold down small amounts of water. Within twenty-four hours, I was back to normal. My four earlier trips to Lechuguilla had all gone much better. I tried to concentrate on them when I finally crawled into the sack.

At ten the next morning I once more leaned against a climbing rope tied to a gnarled desert tree. "On rappel!" I shouted.

"Rappel away!" came Emily's voice from below.

I savored a long last look at sunlight, then stepped backward into the pit. I looked over to Mark Bonwick and Jane Michie, two Australians waiting to follow me down. Like me, they were volunteer labor for Diana's expedition. "See you guys at the bottom," I said.

I spun slightly as rope buzzed through the aluminum brake bars of my rappel rack. My feet touched bottom, and I quickly unwound the rack. "Off rope!" I shouted up to Mark and Jane. Down a short climb a few feet away, Emily unlocked the steel door to a vertical metal culvert installed through the jumble of loose rocks at the site of the original Lechuguilla dig. As the door creaked open, wind howled from below. With its many miles of isolated passages, the barometric pressure inside the cave was always greater or less than the changing surface pressure at its sole entrance. Whenever the door was open, the culvert blew or sucked air at speeds sometimes approaching 70 mph.

Emily and Diana descended the wind tunnel, each closing the door behind her. Cavers in Lechuguilla keep it open as little as possible to prevent excess air movement from changing the natural growth patterns of formations or microbial life. Mark and Jane were the only two members of our team who had never been here before. As soon as Jane reached the bottom of the entrance drop and could see the alcove where the culvert was hidden, I removed my backpack, opened the door, and stepped back into the narrow tube.

My feet found metal rungs leading downward. Once my shoulders reached floor level, I hoisted the pack over my helmet, letting gravity guide it down onto me. I grabbed the handle of the heavy door, and it fell shut with a resounding clang.

"Okay, let's stop for lunch," said Emily an hour later. "Mike, drink water." I had promised her that if she managed to get me signed on as a collection assistant, I would stop and drink water every twenty minutes or whenever she told me to, no matter what. It was a promise I intended to keep. I obediently pulled out a Nalgene bottle. So far, I felt terrific.

We had worked our way down a series of pits and rock faces from the entrance. The longest rappel was down Boulder Falls, the 145-foot drop before Glacier Bay. The pit was named for the loose rocks that sometimes rained down it. The room below was named for the massive blocks of white gypsum that leaned from a central mass like icebergs falling from a calving glacier. Because of the many formations decorating the main passages, cavers traveling through Lechuguilla follow narrow trails marked by survey tape. Each time a new passage is explored and mapped, new trail is laid. Thus while the gypsum on the trail through Glacier Bay had been ground to a yellowish powder years earlier, most of the floor remained white and pristine.

Diana had been scouting the main trail for places that came into frequent contact with human skin. She'd found, for example, a smooth slab of tilted rock down which cavers would routinely slide, their sweaty T-shirts riding up. She dubbed it "the sweaty rock" and was now flagging a portion of it for later sampling.

She walked up, and I passed her the canteen. She took a sip and began to describe the constant environment of the cave, unchanged over thousands of years until cavers had come along. "Now picture a cloud of living cells falling off you everywhere you go," she said. "People can leave behind ten thousand skin fragments just by passing through a room."

In addition to sampling high-contact sites such as sweaty rocks, camping areas, and yellow-flagged urinals, Diana wanted to see whether any human-associated bugs had migrated to seldom-visited portions of the cave. Specifically, she would test for *E. coli* and *Staphylococcus aureus*, two of humanity's most persistent calling cards.

In my long-ago swim across Castrovalva, I had swallowed hundreds of thousands, perhaps millions, of organisms, representing many hundreds of uncatalogued species living in complex interdependence. Some of the species identified in a single drop of Lechuguilla water are far more distantly related to each other than I am related to corn. Organisms that I may not have swallowed were certainly affected by their sudden introduction to exotic and perhaps, to them, toxic food sources—not just powdered Gatorade and sweat, but hundreds of thousands of my shedding skin cells. And I surely released some of my own microbial flora: approximately 1×10^{14} independent bacterial cells live on and in the average human. This population is ten times the number of much larger human cells I contain. In other words, my resident bacterial population (like yours) far outnumbers my own cells; it is 10,000 times greater than the number of humans on Earth. Millions of these freeloaders had surely jumped off during my swim. They may have been joined by such hangers-on as the tiny mites who frolic—despite the American passion for cleanliness—among human eyelashes, scalps, and pubic hairs. Of course, these creatures in turn ferried along their own microbial flora.

The newfound life had caught the attention of cavers who continued to explore Lechuguilla's ever-lengthening branches. They—we—were at last facing the possibility that the very act of discovery presents a threat to unknown species. Slowly, through the plodding experimentation and confirmation that scientific method demands, Diana, Larry, and other scientists were learning that many of the spectacular mineral formations unique to Lechuguilla had been deposited not by chemistry alone, but by chemistry spurred through the metabolic action of microbes. Moreover, it seemed entirely possible that the deep microbial metabolism of sulfur had produced much of the sulfuric acid that first etched the cave out of limestone. The greatest cave in the United States may quite literally be an artifact created by living beings. Some bugs, as I soon learned researchers call microscopic unknowns, residing in Lech's walls and pools may have descended from the very bugs that carved their home, via millions of gallons and millions of generations of toxic excrement.

While Jane and Mark set up to take some photos of the trail, Diana, Emily, and I found comfortable rocks. We pulled out jerked meat, granola bars, cheese, nuts. Virtually every crew passing through Lechuguilla stopped to eat at this same spot, the EF junction. We spread plastic sheets beneath us to trap the crumbs. Just beyond where we sat, the cave's three main branches intersected. The largest and, to me, the most impressive branch was the Western Borehole, which still lay several hundred vertical feet below us. That was where we were headed.

Diana recorded two locations she intended to sample as we climbed back toward the surface the day after tomorrow if all went well. Our lunch finished, we continued downward.

As supper bubbled on an alcohol stove set atop a plastic sheet, I spread out a plastic ground cloth and unrolled my Thermarest camp mattress in a broad, sandy room 1,000 feet below the surface. We would sleep at the Lake Louise Camp, one of two designated sleeping areas along the Western Borehole. We were perhaps a mile away from Lake Castrovalva.

Emily walked over. "Mike, drink water."

"Yes, ma'am," I said, although I had Gatorade.

"And, Mike," she added. "You owe me."

I had drawn water to make the drink from one of several pools we had passed as we had worked our way downward. During the early years of exploration, cavers routinely dipped empty canteens directly into watering holes. Each dunking left behind new traces of mud and sweat. Now plastic siphons and spigots were installed in the most frequented pools to keep foreign dirt and microbes out. No water at all could be removed from the less frequented pools.

Larry had convinced me not to worry about personal danger from the many species I surely gulped with each injunction from Emily. Lechuguilla water was perfectly safe, its inhabitants much too far removed from humanity's twig on the tree of life to have developed the bad habits of, say, *Giardia*. After a comfortable night's sleep, all of us better outfitted for cave camping than anyone had been in 1988, we set out to take samples from several common water sources and from a pool that was almost never visited, Oasis, which lay at the very end of the Western Borehole.

Sampling a highly populated rock face proved a four-person operation.

As Emily recorded the site and sample number in a data book, Diana removed a sterile rayon swab and rolled it against a particular region of the chosen rock. She then held the swab just above an open test tube Jane had removed from a padded tray. I clipped the swab with a sterilized Leatherman tool such that only the head plopped into the solution inside. Jane sealed and labeled the tube, while I dipped the Leatherman tool into a bottle of alcohol, burned it clean with a butane lighter, and readied myself to clip the next swab. The tubes from some samples were next placed in a pot of hot water atop a camp stove, where they were cooked for a prescribed time and at a prescribed temperature in order to force some of the organisms into a spore state and kill the rest.

Larry Mallory, in contrast, was placing his samples in petri dishes full of highly specialized nutrients, in an attempt to bring live colonies of organisms out of the cave and into the lab. He would rub a sterilized loop of very fine wire lightly against a rock, then scratch the wire over a waxy agar medium in the dish, inoculating it with invisible life. He had spent years perfecting recipes for different types of agar to use in caves. One of the things he had learned was that microbiologists often hold back special tricks when they publish papers, just as your grandmother might hold back the key ingredient when sharing her recipe for pineapple upside-down cake. Once he had tried repeatedly to grow a particularly fickle organism, with no success. Finally he called Orvin Mundt, the recognized expert on the bacterium and one of Mallory's former professors. Mundt had asked, "Did you remember to put carpet tacks in your medium?"

"Carpet tacks?" Larry asked.

"Yeah, they won't grow at all without 'em."

He went to a hardware store and bought a box of carpet tacks. Sure enough, his colonies prospered.

One of several things that Larry had learned about Lechuguilla's bugs was that you had to try to maintain their temperature and humidity after you took them out of the cave. He kept his petri dishes in white PVC tubes that not only protected them in transport through the cave but also locked in cave air with the samples and prevented any inadvertent exposure to daylight. Months later, he would pull the dishes out to see what was growing.

By chance, I would be in his lab in May when he examined some of the samples collected from this trip. The lab was located in a musty basement that had once been divided into cattle stalls for the college of agriculture. The petri dishes had lain inside their tube in a cool, dark closet since his return. (Although he had resigned his teaching post the year before, Larry's new company, Biomes, had leased lab space from the university through the end of 1996.) As he pulled out the dishes, I could see that most displayed several white or yellowish circles, each of which represented a different organism.

Especially interesting to Larry were areas where the circles of two different species came close to each other. A clear zone in between them was a sure indication that bacterial warfare was taking place, perhaps via a novel antibiotic. "Where there's warfare, there's weaponry," Larry said. He found a dish containing several visible battles and opened the lid. Immediately, I was hit by a distinct smell I would have known anywhere: the smell of Lechuguilla, the smell of caving. What I had always assumed to be the odor of rocks and gypsum flour was in fact the heady aroma of dark life.

While Diana chose the next site back in the Western Borehole, I studied a loose, rustlike corrosion on the limestone slab beside me. Cavers had given the granular black and brown deposits occurring throughout the cave the colorful name of "gorilla shit." Although several geologists had attributed the slow decay of Lechuguilla's walls and boulders to a chemical reaction involving upwelling air currents, Mallory, Northup, and other biologists believed the gritty substance resulted from a biological process. They thought that the corrosion residue might in fact be an accumulation of microbial waste products. Diana said that the jury was still out on whether the biologists or the geologists were right. She suggested that they might both be right, in that the corrosion could come from a chemical process dependent on biology, or from a biological process based on chemistry. Sometimes science made my head hurt. I flamed the Leatherman and clipped the next swab.

Diana obtained three samples from each individual site. Often when we stopped to collect she would select several sites at once, so it was a laborious process. During these pauses, I drank water. I didn't feel at all nauseated; but late in the day we came across a site that was, in its own way, sickening to any Lech caver.

"I can't believe this," Diana said. "Someone must have stumbled on this while they were camping."

"This is no accident," Emily said. "No one who would camp this far in could make that sort of accident."

"This" was a ruined collection site, apparently destroyed by a caver angered over the closing of Lechuguilla to exploration. Sometime after November 1995, one of a group of glass slides placed in the Huapache Highway campsite, located atop an immense flat boulder on one side of Hard Daze Nights Hall, had been stomped flat. The collection area, about a meter square, had been flagged with striped survey tape. A sign warned, "HUMAN IMPACT STUDY SITE—DO NOT TOUCH."

I could almost hear the unknown guilty caver muttering "Study this impact!" as he reduced the slide to slivers and shards. I say "he" because the bootprints were fairly large, and because stomping slides seemed a very male, turf-defending sort of thing to do. Months later, one potential suspect would offer a convincing argument that Diana was right, that the damage was accidental, caused by sleepy cavers stumbling around a cramped camp after a lengthy and difficult survey trip. But that wasn't how it looked to us at the moment of discovery. The prints came down at several angles, as though the person who left them had danced a little jig. We knew that the vast majority of Lechuguilla explorers remained highly supportive of research and conservation. But Jason Richards, the National Park Service cave specialist who supervised exploration and research in Lechuguilla, had had trouble with one or two in the past. One caver who had been caught leaving behind unwrapped "burritos" had been quietly banned from future expeditions.

"Did you keep a set of clean polypro for Oasis tomorrow?" Emily asked me that night in camp.

"Yep, clean gloves, long-sleeve shirt, and long pants."

"And you brought aqua socks, didn't you?"

"No, but my feet are pretty tough. I can handle a little water without them. I've got polypro socks."

She rolled her eyes in exasperation. "It's not for you, you ninny, it's for the cave. You can't go into Oasis without aqua socks."

The polypropylene, I knew, was required because Diana had found that it worked better than other light fabrics—and far better than nudity—at containing dead skin cells. Emily explained that the neoprene footwear was required for the same reason: polypro socks would become abraded on rocks, leaving behind contamination. Fortunately, even though Emily's foot was a great many sizes smaller than mine, her aqua socks were expandable enough for me to squeeze into them, and she was willing to lend them to me.

"Yeah, yeah," I said, as she passed them over that morning. "I owe you."

"And don't you forget it." At least she smiled when she said it.

Emily found a comfortable spot at the entrance to Oasis to wait for Diana and me to take samples from the lower pool. "Really, I think you'll like it in there," she said as we dressed in head-to-toe dark polypro. "It's truly special."

No more than two at a time were allowed inside the delicate chamber, and then only with a specific scientific permit. Now that cavers had acquired knowledge of the tree of life, we could no longer frolic brazenly in the fountains of Lechuguilla. We were ashamed, and covered our nakedness.

Slowly, precisely, sober as a Mennonite, I dipped a sterile syringe into the pure, still waters amid some of the finest cave formations I had seen in all my years underground. The beauty of the room far surpassed that of Lake Castrovalva, let alone any tourist cave in the world. Over the past decade, I'd seen a great many photographs of Oasis, but they could never re-create the color, immense size, and variety of the room's profuse calcite formations. There was no mud anywhere, just sparkling damp minerals and, I was more certain than ever, the invisible microbial gardeners who colored and tended them. I emptied the syringe into a sterilized vial, passing it to Diana with all the care of a priest handling the Host.

Later, long after our trip was over, she would E-mail me that although some of the campsites we tested came up positive for human-introduced organisms, the several tests of Oasis had proved negative. For now, nothing lived in that pristine place that had not lived there for a very long time. For now, the foreign bugs seemed to be staying where they had been dropped.

I felt very lucky to have seen such a place once in my life. Although I hoped to return to Lechuguilla, I saw no reason to enter this room ever again. I did not swim, nor did I drink. I soaked in the view. The last sample gathered, I made my way out of Oasis, carefully choosing each step, happy in my fallen state, moving with deliberate purpose toward a surface world grown ever smaller, toward a universe alive with promise.

.✦.

THE PLUME OF LIFE

A network of highly sensitive microphones rings the world's oceans, though there is no longer much for them to hear. Miles of linked hydrophones, called arrays, form the frontline of a SOund SUrveillance System (SOSUS) maintained by the U.S. Navy. Once a closely guarded military secret, SOSUS took a decade to develop, at a cost of over $300 million. For a while, the listening network had proved highly efficient at tracking Soviet submarines. In 1990, with few submarines left to monitor, the system was made available to the world's oceanographers and geologists, provided they could come up with science projects that could benefit from undersea ears.

On February 28, 1996, James Cowen, an oceanographer at the University of Hawaii, heard exactly the SOSUS signature for which he'd been waiting years: the roar of a violently erupting undersea volcano, 100 miles off the coast of Oregon. Cowen had been studying the steady streams of microbes that rise from hot vents in the deep ocean, but he wondered whether microbial life extended into the deeper, hotter fluids that could reach miles below the sea floor. He knew that such fluids were very difficult to extract from above, but were sometimes blasted out from below by volcanic events. Cowen, a tanned forty-year-old with a bushy blond haircut out of a Beach Boys song, considered himself an oceanographer and a *biogeochemist*, as opposed to a traditional microbiologist. He had come to microbiology from his interest in the impact of microorganisms on the geochemical cycles of the ocean. He had gradually come to believe that this impact was enormous.

In many places in the ocean where seawater had once been considered nearly sterile, Cowen had discovered that very small bacteria (about 0.2 micron in diameter, just slightly larger than Robert Folk's nanobacteria) were in fact the main agents controlling water chemistry. But even more mysterious than the marine ultramicrobacteria, as the tiny ocean organisms were called, were those that poured from the deep vents lining the edges of oceanic plates in Earth's crust.

Virtually every deep-sea vent studied poured forth a visible cloud of microbes. No one knew how the heat-loving thermophiles colonized a new vent from the surrounding cold ocean. A growing theory was that they moved in from deep, water-filled cracks in the bedrock below the sea floor, as opposed to via the open sea. Oceanic ridges like the Gorda in the North Pacific are the source of Earth's continents, where new land is born from the upwelling of magma between spreading crustal plates. Cowen had been listening for a sudden, explosive eruption of lava from a ridge because such events are often accompanied by outpourings of superheated, mineral-saturated water. If the water contained a large microbial population, he reasoned, then that population must have been in place already, before the eruption. Alternatively, he knew that such eruptions often triggered a pumping effect, sucking nearby seawater underground into the hot zone, where it would become charged with minerals and boil out again, with microbes rapidly multiplying, or "blooming," after the water had emerged. Some had likened this hydrologic cycle to an engine's cooling system, in that it helped regulate the temperature of Earth's land-building machinery with circulated seawater. But the details of the process were sketchy; the easiest way to get a handle on what occurred below the sea floor would be to sample water from a fresh event. Now Cowen had such an event, as well as a research vessel loaded and waiting at the dock.

The eruption had begun at 7 A.M. Greenwich Mean Time on February 28, 1996. For the first forty-two hours, its precise location could not be derived due to the failure of the two closest SOSUS arrays. But on March 1, SOSUS operators at the Naval Ocean Processing Facility on Whidbey Island, Washington, were able to use distant microphone arrays to triangulate the seismic event in the general area of the northern Gorda Ridge, 100 miles west of Oregon.

Cowen got on the phone and dispatched a graduate student of his to join the National Oceanic and Atmospheric Administration (NOAA) research ship *McArthur* in a four-day survey of the suspected eruption area. The *McArthur* sailed from Seattle on March 7. If the NOAA team, led by Ed Baker of the Pacific Marine Environmental Laboratory, succeeded in finding an erupting plume of heated water, Cowen planned to head a second cruise to study it. The research vessel *Wecoma*, owned by the National Science Foundation and operated by Oregon State University, was equipped to measure thoroughly and to sample the size, chemistry, and fauna of the plume. Furthermore, it could follow a sudden plume across the open ocean, to see how far it carried its cargo of dark life.

The *McArthur* was able to locate an enormous plume on

March 10, with several smaller ones in the vicinity of the sea floor eruptions. Using a robotic sensing device towed beneath the ship, Baker was able to measure an emerging column of hot water half a mile thick. The plume, however, seemed to be dispersing quickly; it appeared as if the eruption may have been short-lived. The *McArthur* continued to measure and plot the event. Cowen, meanwhile, began lining up a team, as well as National Science Foundation funding, on the chance that the outpouring would continue for another few weeks. Then on Friday, March 15, SOSUS recorded the largest eruption yet, and the *McArthur* quickly found what Ed Baker called a "megaplume": a vast river of hot water more than five miles in diameter shooting rapidly from the sea floor. Cowen packed a sea bag and flew to Oregon for the departure of the *Wecoma*. He headed a crew of sixteen expertly trained scientists and technicians, including microbiologists who had developed new techniques for keeping heat-loving, oxygen-hating bugs alive.

The cruise had several goals. The first was to locate the source of the megaplume on the sea floor, establishing the spatial pattern of sea floor breakage and eruption. This information was considered critical to understanding the origin of megaplumes— whether they came from ordinary seawater somehow cycled through the sea floor by the volcanic action, from the breaching of a preexisting fluid reservoir, or from some combination of both processes. A second priority was to establish whether there had been a subsurface bacterial bloom.

Cowen believed the injection of magma into the upper ocean crust would cause sudden blooms of the subsurface biosphere as organisms took advantage of the outpouring of chemical nutrients. Since a heated column of water would cool rapidly in seawater, the population of the species resulting from the process would also rapidly diminish, making sampling of culturable species more difficult as time went by. Hence he felt a critical need to find the source of the megaplume as soon as possible. Cowen also planned to record the times at which megaplume geochemical and microbial values were measured, in order to chart the pace of changes in its water chemistry and in the structure of its microbial community. The *McArthur* had been on site at the initial time point; obtaining a second time point was essential for plotting the life cycle of the plume and the creatures within it. In addition to sampling the megaplume, the *Wecoma* would release at least a neutrally buoyant float that could trace the fluid's movement within the surrounding ocean over the course of several months. Cowen could then try to locate and resample the leading edge of the dispersed plume later in the summer. Finally, the team hoped to find outpourings of fresh lava on the sea floor and obtain samples by dredging or rock coring.

The *Wecoma* left Newport, Oregon, on April 6, sailing with a weather prediction of rains and gale force winds. The main instrument package Cowen would use was a device called a "to-yo," a steerable robot crammed with gear lowered via a long cable. Using the to-yo was tricky under good conditions, but navigating the device in a storm-tossed sea could become nearly impossible. And as the ship headed toward the Gorda Ridge, the seas continued to get worse. By the time the team reached the coordinates established by the *McArthur*, large swells were crashing over the deck. The crew tried several times to drop the to-yo into the water, only to have to pull it in because of the heavy seas. The winch that lowered the device was battered by the strain of the rolling ship, requiring several repairs, during which crewmen dangled over dangerously heaving equipment.

Finally, on April 11, the ship was able to locate the megaplume. The initial temperature reading indicated that the plume was still in place and still discharging geysers of life into a wide expanse of ocean. Cowen immediately ordered a series of camera tows, which recorded images of the milky, bacteria-laden water roiling past. The cameras also filmed several fresh lava flows. But the forecast was for building winds and seas. On April 12, the crew was forced to tie everything down and wait the storm out.

After twenty-four hours, Cowen wasn't sure whether there had been a slight improvement in the weather, but he had become so frustrated that he decided to lower a stripped-down package of minimal equipment over the side of the ship. The *Wecoma* towed this along a natural valley to one side of the Gorda Ridge, crisscrossing over the plume and one valley wall throughout the day and into the night. The last two to-yo passes revealed a plume seven nautical miles long by five across, rich with microbes—tons of them—rising from a geyserlike eruption east of a fresh lava flow. Despite the heavy seas and still-cantankerous hoists, the crew managed to retrieve a small boulder of the new lava with a dredge and also to place an underwater tracking beacon into the plume.

The storm was still building. The skipper described the seas as 40 feet. Cowen, who'd spent much of his career on the open ocean, thought they were closer to 20, 30 at the most. He intended to keep his experiments going. He didn't want to risk the safety of several million dollars' worth of government equipment, not to mention a dozen college professors, but he persuaded the skipper to once more lower the to-yos. Years might pass before a similar opportunity for measurement came up again.

Part of the process of recording data involved crossing the deck to a "radio van," an enclosed area on the fantail where radioactive isotopes used to measure water chemistry were stored. Cowen and two volunteers crossed to the van on April 15 to gather the final data before the ship turned back to port. Just crossing the deck in the high winds and tossing seas was difficult. Cowen's assistants were Melanie Summit, a microbiology student from the University of Washington, who had been attempting to sample some of the plume thermophiles, and Xiyuen Wen, a microbiology and chemistry student, who was Cowen's lab assistant at the University of Hawaii. They had to climb down two metal ladders to an exposed area, reaching the fantail via a lower portion of deck that was frequently awash in green seawater.

Once they arrived in the van, Cowen asked Xiyuen to carry some of the test material back to the ship's main cabin. Xiyuen turned to go back into the storm just as the ship slid down the crest of a wave. A strong gust of wind caught the heavy metal door of the van, slamming it on his hand. Cowen and Summit managed to usher him back into the safety of the main cabin for first aid, leaving his job unfinished.

While the ship's medical officer tended to the student's hand, Cowen headed back out into the storm alone, determined to fill several beakers with 250 milliliters of radioactive solution each, in order to complete the final round of experiments. The shelves were full of heavy, pressurized containers used in chemistry measurements—should any of these break loose, they would become deadly projectiles in the tiny enclosed space. The weather seemed to be getting worse. Cowen wedged himself into a corner of the van, pouring the sloshing liquid as the wind and waves pounded the door a few feet away. After twenty minutes, he heard a harder pounding on the door. It was the ship's mate. Cowen carefully lowered a beaker between his knees, then leaned over and unlatched the door.

"It's just too rough," the mate said. "You've got to come in."

"Ah, I can't come in. I've got to get this done." Cowen had spent enough time at sea to know that when the skipper and crew said it was getting too rough, they usually meant it. But he was focused on the job at hand. He'd be finished in an hour, maybe less.

"Well, I'm locking everything up," the mate said. "You can stay in here, we'll try to go every half hour and check on you from the little porthole. See if you're still there. But we're latching everything down, so you can't go back into the cabin through the door back here. You'll have to go all the way up to the bridge to get back inside."

"No problem."

Cowen went back to work and the mate took off. The job proved slower going than he thought it would be. It was like doing science inside a washing machine. The dark wet day had faded into night by the time he finally left the van. It was only then that Cowen realized what he had committed himself to doing. He would have to feel his way along the slippery deck without light and climb a ladder to the upper deck, which he would have to cross. He suddenly realized he had spent very little time up there; finding his way might get a little dicey.

By timing his movement with the waves, Cowen made it to the ladder without being washed overboard. Then he paused at the upper deck, trying to remember the locations of all the lines, chains, and other projections that sailors lumped together under the descriptive term "toe knockers." He took it slowly, feeling his way along until he reached another ladder. He went up into the teeth of the wind, easing himself onto yet another ladder that brought him to the bridge. He knocked on the door so as not to startle the officers, then walked in. It felt like coming home.

Cowen closed the door and leaned back against it. "That was a little tough," he admitted.

Two months later, Cowen was back over the plume with NOAA ship *Discoverer*. The float that the *Wecoma* had placed had traveled over a thousand miles in the general direction of Japan, carried in a circular current that rings the Pacific. By taking samples along its path, Cowen was able to confirm that life from the biosphere below had indeed traveled along with it. The ship recovered thermophilic organisms traceable to the initial eruption that had drifted across a vast swath of ocean. Most of the bugs had shut down in the cool seawater but could be easily revived in the lab. By computing the numbers of bugs recovered, the measured size of the plume, and the distance it had traveled, Cowen was able to calculate that millions of tons of microbes had emerged from the single eruption.

The microbes had to have been down there already. The Gorda Ridge event had shown that, at least along the ocean's volcanic ridges, vast reservoirs of hot water and microbes extended five miles or more below the sea floor. The majority of this life never came in contact with the open sea, let alone sunlight or oxygen.

SEVEN

JUNE 1996

"One *can't* believe impossible things."

"I daresay you haven't had much practice," said the Queen. "When I was your age, I always did it for half-an-hour a day. Why, sometimes I'd believe as many as six impossible things before breakfast."

—LEWIS CARROLL
Alice in Wonderland

CAN YOU KEEP A SECRET?

Anne Taunton had applied for a NASA internship only because her academic advisor, Derek Sears, had more or less ordered her to do so. An expert on meteorites, Sears edited the leading meteorite journal, *Meteoritics and Planetary Science.* He headed up the Cosmochemistry Group, a research program based at the University of Arkansas chemistry department. Sears had helped create the science of cosmochemistry, which he defined as the study of the composition of extraterrestrial materials and of chemical processes occurring in space. By minutely examining the chemical content of meteorites, cosmochemists sought to answer basic questions about the processes that had formed the solar system.

The Cosmochemistry Group employed a wide variety of analytic tools in the study of meteorites, among them the scanning electron microscope, or SEM. In January 1996, Sears had handed

Anne a flyer stating that the Johnson Space Center was looking for a summer intern who could operate an SEM. He thought she should be the one. Sears had been a real taskmaster as a teacher and advisor, as tough on her as he was on his doctoral candidates. But she respected him as a scientist. Born in Britain, he had earned his Ph.D. in analytic chemistry at Manchester University, and he knew his stuff. He was rigorous, with an intellectual tenacity that matched the bulldog looks afforded him by his old-fashioned mutton shops and close-cropped, curly gray hair. Anne took the form from Sears and brought it home to fill out.

Although the internship would have her working at the Johnson Space Center, it was actually sponsored by the Lunar and Planetary Institute (LPI), a nonprofit organization headquartered just outside JSC's eastern gate. It made her think back to that "Careers in Space" science poster she had made in the fourth grade. For the past three years she had stayed busy as an honors student, as a student government senator, and as a volunteer with a service sorority, and she liked to listen to live music and go dancing on Saturday nights. Going to graduate school, let alone starting some sort of career, were the furthest things from her mind. Yet part of her childhood dream of exploring space was still alive. The more she thought about the internship, the more excited she became. She called her dad to tell him she was applying. If nothing else, a summer at NASA would give her an idea for the topic of the honors thesis project that loomed in her senior year.

The following March, she received a strange phone call.

"Are you Anne Taunton?" a man asked.

"Yes."

"Hi, Anne. Dave McKay calling from Houston. We've been looking over your application, and I have to say we're very interested in having you come down this summer—"

"Ohmagosh! Really? That's fantastic!"

"—but first, I need to ask you something. Is this a good time?"

"Sure. Yes. Absolutely. Ask away."

"Can you keep a secret?"

"I guess so. Sure."

"The work we're doing here is highly confidential. It's bad for science if research gets out before it's published. If you want to come down and work with us, you can tell people you have an internship, but you can't reveal the details to anyone. Not your parents, your friends, your teachers, or anyone else, until after the research is published. Would you be okay with that?"

How could she not agree to such an intriguing proposition? "Sure, no problem."

A week later she was officially accepted. When Anne read a description of the projects on the intern list published by LPI, hers was almost a letdown after the buildup from McKay's phone call:

ANNE TAUNTON, University of Arkansas

Advisor: David S. McKay, Johnson Space Center

"SEM Studies of Microbes." A major goal of the exploration of Mars is to determine whether life has developed there. To help understand how potential Martian life may have evolved and whether such life might still exist in extreme environments on Mars, we will study selected samples from extreme environments on Earth. Samples of microbes are known to grow in rocks in Antarctica, in hot springs, in highly saline evaporite lakes, in arid deserts on rock surfaces, and deep in the Earth in rocks at depths of 10 kilometers or more. The intern will study representative samples of each of these materials with the scanning electron microscope (possibly supplemented by transmission electron microscopy studies of selected samples) to characterize the morphology and chemistry of the microbes, document the microbe-mineral interactions, and determine the types of fossil preservation, if any. Using published data and papers, the intern will also make a parallel evaluation of Mars's environments in terms of their potential to sustain microbial life.

Why the fuss? Cataloging microbes in rocks? Sure it could be interesting, looking for life that *might* resemble what a robot would try to find on Mars in twenty years, but it could just as easily grow old in a hurry.

In May, she drove the twelve hours from Fayetteville to Houston. McKay was off at a conference, but Anne met the other members of the team she'd be working with at a meeting conducted by Everett Gibson, a friendly, bearlike geochemist, who, like McKay, had been a JSC fixture since the heady days of the Apollo program. He'd handled his share of moon rocks. She met Sue Wentworth, the SEM specialist, with whom, Everett explained, she'd be spending much of her time. Kathie Thomas-Keprta, another meteorite and SEM expert, rounded out the crew. Sue was short, with dark hair and bright eyes that always seemed to presage a smile. Kathie was tall, slim, and blond, like Anne; she looked young enough to pass for an undergraduate intern herself. Anne warmed to both women immediately. Both worked for Lockheed-Martin, NASA's primary private contractor at JSC, but their offices were in Building 31 along with the rest of the team's. Finally, Everett explained, Anne would meet visiting scientists from Stanford and two other universities who worked with them from time to time.

Anne soaked it all in. They were all very nice, especially Kathie and Sue. Anne was a person who laughed easily and loudly, and her new colleagues displayed a relaxed humor that gave her plenty to laugh about. But at the same time they seemed to be staring at her, checking her out with an unnerving frankness. She felt self-conscious. It wasn't as though they looked at her disapprovingly, but Anne couldn't escape the feeling that she wasn't being told the real reason for the meeting or their eagerness to help her get started. Even at NASA, no one really could be so concerned about a new intern. Before she could worry over this too much, however, the meeting ended. Everett handed her a thick stack of scientific papers, which he told her to read. Sue trained her on an old JEOL 35 SEM in Building 31 for two weeks. When Sue thought Anne was ready, she took her across the complex to introduce her to Lou Hulse and his FESEM.

She quickly realized that this was a very different place from Building 31. If the conversations in the offices and labs of the

McKay team tended to be somewhat intellectual, the mood was also relaxed and laid back, as on a college campus. Here in Building 13 the dress was more formal, the manners more military. The waxed hallways and the polished shoes that echoed down them suggested flight crews and mission planners, serious people doing serious work. It was a place that bespoke "the right stuff."

The device Anne approached in the center of Building 13 sat squarely at the intersection of twin paths of scientific exploration, one looking outward, the other inward, both stretching nearly four hundred years into the past.

The outward path began in Italy in 1609, when Galileo, already famous throughout Europe for his theories of motion and gravity, pointed his newly acquired telescope heavenward. He focused on the moon, Mars, and Jupiter and its satellites. What he saw eventually moved him to put into writing something he had long suspected: Copernicus was right; Earth circled the sun. Man's place in the universe was something other than that which church doctrine dictated. To the scientific institutions of the day, challenging the wisdom of Aristotle, who had taught that the sun moved about Earth, was perhaps a greater heresy than challenging scripture. Despite Galileo's wide reputation as a pious and learned man, he was brought before the Inquisition. He was lucky to escape execution and spent the last eight years of his life under house arrest. Yet his ideas held sway, and the size of our universe continued to expand in scientific thought.

Armed with ever more powerful light telescopes, generations of observers pushed back the boundaries Galileo revealed. Eventually light failed, and telescopes that recorded radio waves and X-rays pushed the borders back further still. Our solar system became a tiny speck on the edge of an enormous galaxy of stars, and our galaxy a mite among countless others. Lenses not unlike those used by Galileo were fitted and packed in Building 13 before being loaded aboard the command module of Apollo 8. Through its windows they recorded one of the most striking—and strikingly lonely—visual images humanity has yet captured: the blue circle of Earth as it appears from the moon, spinning alone in its empty expanse of space.

The inward-looking path of science began in late August of the year 1675 in the Dutch town of Delft, when a self-educated shopkeeper and lens grinder named Anton van Leeuwenhoek saw "very little animalcules" in his homemade microscope and shook the scientific world. Few believed him at first. How could they? No one had ever conceived of organisms as tiny as those Leeuwenhoek found spinning giddily about in pond water. Nothing so small, went the thinking of the day, could possibly be alive. And unlike Galileo, the man had no credentials whatsoever. He was a haberdasher who made a little extra money from his part-time job as the janitor of the Delft town hall. But he insisted that he had observed life, and he showed that others could repeat his observations.

Leeuwenhoek went on to find microbes everywhere—in well, river, and seawater, in the guts of insects and animals, in garden soil, in outcrops of rock, even swimming over his own teeth, excrement, and semen. Eventually, no less an authority than the British Royal Society, then considered the ultimate arbiter of scientific truth, declared that Leeuwenhoek's wee beasties were real. Since the microbes couldn't be explained away, thinking changed to allow for their existence. This paved the way for Pasteur, Lister, and Koch to create modern medicine.

As with the telescope, the microscope was improved over the centuries until it at last magnified visible light to the limits of the medium. Other wavelengths of electromagnetic energy were harnessed in its stead. Better resolution was achieved with electrons beamed through a sample (called transmission electron microscopy, or TEM) or bounced off a sample (scanning electron microscopy, or SEM). A device was added to the SEM which could determine the chemical constituents of tiny sections of a microscopic object by reading their X-ray signatures. Other microscopes were developed that could "feel" individual molecules and even atoms by means of a tiny, ever so slightly movable crystalline probe. And the SEM was further improved by packing electrons into a tighter stream, resulting in the FESEM.

• • •

The machine Anne sat down to master took full advantage of recent improvements in SEM field strength and X-ray diffraction. Operating it was a pleasure after the touchy and cantankerous university machine on which Sue had trained her. She spent two weeks learning the NASA FESEM's finer points from Lou Hulse, a gruff perfectionist who loved to kid. In a movie, he'd have been played by Ernest Borgnine. He and Anne began an almost immediate banter that continued throughout her internship. He was soon advising her on cars, boyfriends, and every other problem that she brought to him.

She was also assisted on the machine in those first days by Sue and Kathie and, after he returned from his trip, by Dave. Her new boss proved to be a soft-spoken, kindly man. He was the same age as her father and reminded her of him in a number of ways. She liked him instantly. It was clear she would have no shortage of father figures and female mentors during her internship.

In addition to learning how to operate the FESEM, Anne had to become familiar with the assortment of machines she was to use in preparing specimens. Unlike the microscope itself—a gleaming, computerized device in comfortable surroundings—the coating machines and sample prep area, located back in Building 31, were crammed into a warren of cluttered little rooms. Metal bookshelves bulged with aging notebooks of moon rock data, labeled by mission number and lunar collection area. The coating machines, many of them relics of the Apollo program, were imposing cabinets of gray steel, sporting a few art deco curves and dozens of dials and meters. She had learned their various quirks. By trial and error, she had perfected her ability to judge how much acid to use to etch fossils from surrounding rock, how to dry the etched sample, and how to coat it with gold atoms in such a way as to avoid the creation of misleading metallic blobs that might be mistaken for bacteria. Now, five weeks through her ten-week internship, she wondered why her NASA colleagues continued to act so mysterious. There seemed to be nothing mysterious at all about her work.

She had read the papers Everett gave her: Folk on the SEM of nanobacteria; Chafetz on bacteria in carbonates; Chris McKay, Jack Farmer, and Michael Carr on exobiology and Mars; Imre Friedmann on the microbes of rocks in the Antarctic and the Sinai Desert. She read of living bacteria revived from ancient sediments at the bottoms of glaciers, yeast collected from the guts of insects preserved in 30-million-year-old amber, and green algae from salt domes that had last been exposed to sunlight more than 200 million years ago. She became aware of the significance of the archaea through papers by Carl Woese and Norm Pace. She was excited by Thomas Gold's paper "The Deep, Hot Biosphere."

She read a paper by E. Olavi Kajander, who led a medical research group in Finland. Kajander's team had cultured blood nanobacteria in the lab, placed radioactive markers on them, and injected cells into a rabbit, where they rapidly migrated to the kidneys, heart, stomach, and esophagus and began to multiply. These findings, although published in legitimate medical journals, had been widely ignored because they contained neither conclusive images nor complete chemical analyses of the nanobacteria. Since standard biological thought held that nanobacteria were too small to be alive, many scientists doubted the Finns had found them in blood, or anywhere else. They couldn't exist, the doubters argued, because their cells were smaller than the minimum volume necessary to hold the chemistry of life as defined in all freshman biology textbooks. At most, they were some sort of substance released by larger microbes, or parts of dead cells. At the least, they were mere artifacts of the microscopy preparation process and imagination.

But until very recently, as Anne also learned, no one had possessed adequate tools to question whether the standard definition of bacterial size might simply be wrong. The commonly taught minimum diameter for prokaryotic cells (those lacking a nucleus, including archaea and bacteria) was 0.2 micrometer (a unit of measurement more commonly called *micron*). Not coincidentally, this was the smallest object that could be resolved in a standard light microscope set at maximum magnification. The number was supposedly derived from the smallest space into which the elements of *known* organisms could be compressed.

Another interesting paper in the stack had been written by James McKinley and Todd Stevens, concerning organisms they had extracted from deep drill holes in Washington's Columbia River basalt (CRB) in a project funded by the Department of Energy (DOE) at Pacific National Laboratories. This was a sophisticated, multimillion-dollar study that built on what the DOE had learned of the deep biosphere from its 1987 drilling project in South Carolina. Stevens and McKinley had designed a special sealed capsule which they sent down shafts up to just under two miles deep, bringing back samples of fluid and rock that were kept isolated all the way to the lab. Chemical markers called tracers would reveal any sign of contamination from surface organisms. From these carefully quarantined samples, they had grown a wide variety of heat-loving microbes, including some small archaea and bacteria that appeared to survive on nothing but hydrogen and water. Many of these deep organisms exhibited an extremely slow metabolism, appearing to divide cells no more than once per century.

Part of the reason Anne paid special attention to the CRB paper was that Todd Stevens had come to Houston and given a talk to the NASA interns during her third week. He had been a funny young guy in jeans and a T-shirt. Despite the humor with which he lectured, his knowledge of extreme microbes and techniques to study them was impressive. All of the interns had come away from his talk convinced of at least the theoretical possibility of dark life beneath the surfaces of other worlds. More important to Anne's project, Stevens had entrusted several pristine samples of rock from a deep CRB drill hole to Kathie Thomas-Keprta during his visit.

Anne had gotten around to looking at one of these on a late Thursday night in Building 13. She had become quite proficient at finding bacteria in rocks, and she soon realized that this basalt chip was loaded with fossilized organisms. Although no one had ever given her a reason for it, Anne knew that Dave was especially interested in smaller bacteria and nanobacteria, those fitting into the size ranges described by Folk. She had found occasional small objects in several earlier samples, and had reported them in regular meetings with the group. During these meetings, the others hung on to her every word as she described forays into various rocks. *They're just being nice,* Anne had told herself, *showing concern for an overwhelmed student.*

When she boosted the magnification on this new CRB sample, she realized at once that it was one of the best she'd seen for nanobacteria. The stone was packed with discrete colonies of fossilized rods and filaments. Some of the apparent bugs were only 30 or 40 nanometers in diameter and 150 nanometers long. This was well below the 200 nanometers, or 0.2 microns, of standard small bacteria. Anne opened a deck of Polaroid film and began snapping pictures. She kept going until after 2 A.M., mainly because she didn't plan to shoot any more images the next day. She was driving home to Arkansas for the weekend, her first trip back since the internship started, and Kathie had said she could leave early on Friday.

No matter how late she stayed up, Anne had never been able to break the habit of rising early. So the next morning, she came in at eight and dropped off the photos on Kathie's desk.

"I found some cool things in that Todd Stevens sample," Anne said. "I just wanted to let you know, so you could take a look before I head out at noon."

Kathie flipped open the notebook of Polaroids in plastic sleeves, took a quick glance at the scale bar on one image, and immediately sat down. "Stay here a second,"she said. She studied each and every photo. "Oh, Anne, this is beautiful," she said as she flipped the pages. "This is so good. I am so proud of you. This is just what we needed. Oh, my gosh, I can't believe it." She looked up at Anne. "I'm afraid you'd better forget about going home today. We've got to call a meeting. We have a lot of work to do."

Anne didn't get it. "I've been doing this stuff for five weeks," she said. "What's the deal here?"

Kathie paused, then put on the strange smile that Anne had seen once too often. "Well, you know, we'll talk about it later."

"No, I don't know. Let's talk about it now. What's going on? What am I doing here?"

Kathie shrugged. "Show these to Dave. Maybe he'll tell you."

Anne stormed down the hall to Dave's office. He was working at his computer. She dropped the binder in his lap.

"Look at these," she ordered.

He began to peruse the notebook. He raised his eyebrows.

She sat in the chair by his desk. "Dave, I'm frustrated. Tell me what's going on. What am I doing here? Why is Kathie so excited? Why is everyone acting so weird?"

A bemused smile crossed his face. "Well, okay. Here you go." McKay closed the notebook and reached into his desk. He pulled out a glossy eight-by-ten SEM image and tossed it in front of her. "Do you know what that is?"

Anne glanced down at a group of wormlike rods. "Yeah, that looks exactly like what I just found."

"Umm, that one's from Mars."

✦

DARK LAKE

Near the geographic center of Antarctica sits a loose collection of fifty-year-old Soviet-era shacks surrounded by a plain of smooth, unbroken ice that stretches for a thousand miles in all directions. This is Vostok Station, perhaps the loneliest place on Earth. Once the coldest outpost of the cold war, Vostok is desolate even in comparison with other Antarctic bases, most of which are located near the (slightly) more accessible coasts. The scientists who huddled there, often under miserable conditions, gave the former Soviet Union an early advantage in the study of ice sheets and the climatic records stored within them.

Beginning in 1974, Russian scientists stationed at Vostok began drilling and extracting tubes of ice from the thick sheet that sits atop the frozen continent. The layers of dust and minerals in these cores provided an unbroken record of the planet's climate, stretching hundreds of thousands of years into the past. Trapped amid the ash of ancient fires and volcanoes were frozen microbes, carried from warmer latitudes by high-altitude winds.

Casually scratch your arm while hailing a cab in Honolulu, and you may launch a flight of *Staphylococcus* that will touch down six months later at the South Pole. While solar radiation destroys many of the microorganisms carried aloft, many more survive aerial dispersal and, like windblown dandelions, take up residence wherever they happen to land. When living cells have the bad luck of hitting ice, they tend to enter what microbiologists call a "shutdown mode," shrinking in size and ceasing all metabolic activity until the surroundings warm up. They can wait, scientists were learning, for a long time. Microbiologists from Russia and elsewhere had routinely revived 10,000-year-old microbes from Vostok cores. In 1988, Richard Morita, an Oregon State University microbiologist who had studied Antarctic bugs for three decades, managed to culture live bacteria from spores found in a 200,000-year-old Vostok sample.

Each summer season, scientists pushed the deepest of the Vostok bore holes a little further down, a little further back in time. By the end of the 1995–96 season, this hole was two and a quarter miles deep, into ice some 500,000 years old. At that point, the Russians shut down the drilling, a mere 500 yards above a substance that, they knew, would soon ignite the interest of the worldwide scientific community: liquid water—lots of it. Professor Andrei Kapitsa of Moscow State University had known there was water below the ice since 1959, when he had first detected it with seismic readings. But no one knew how much water was there until 1995, when data collected from new, more sophisticated seismic soundings could be combined with ice-penetrating radar by British research aircraft.

What Kapitsa's 1995 measurements told him, and what the new British data supported, was staggering: A lake 140 miles long by 30 wide, the size of Lake Ontario but twice as deep, lay trapped beneath the ice. The sealed lake was up to 2,000 feet deep in places, heated, scientists hypothesized, by deep geothermal activity as well as by the immense pressure and friction of the ice itself. What's more, precise radar altimetry measurements from ERS-1, a NASA satellite launched in 1991 to study the poles, indicated that the lake's water was fresh, containing little or no salt. It was one of the purest reservoirs on the planet, wholly removed from sunlight and atmospheric oxygen. The only sort of life it was likely to support was microbial.

The cover of the June 20, 1996, issue of the British journal *Nature* featured a map of Antarctica in psychedelic colors, a composite image based on the ERS-1 data. At the map's center was a brilliant red crescent identified as Lake Vostok. In the cover article, Kapitsa and others argued that the lake should contain a vast treasure trove of microorganisms separated from the surface for at least half a million years. The seismic data had revealed a layer of silt and sediment on the lake bottom, up to 500 feet deep at one end. If the water itself took hundreds of thousands of years to cycle through the ice into the melt zone, the sediment at the lake bottom would contain a record, and possibly actual life, extending back millions of years.

In a series of meetings planned for the coming year, an international team of microbiologists would try to come up with a plan for ways in which to sample the water while keeping surface organisms from contaminating the isolated biosphere. Scientists at NASA were interested in the problem because they felt it could help them prepare for an eventual hunt for life beneath the frozen, Antarctic-like surface of Mars.

NASA was interested for another reason as well. In the 1970s, the Pioneer spacecraft had revealed that the surface of Europa, one of the moons of Jupiter, appeared to be composed entirely of ice. Some scientists had suggested that liquid water might be trapped beneath the moon's ice—a notion that became the basis for Arthur C. Clarke's 1984 science-fiction novel *2010: Odyssey Two*. In the fall of 1996, the long-delayed Galileo spacecraft was at last scheduled to transmit high-resolution pictures of Europa which, planetary scientists hoped, might indicate that liquid water was indeed trapped beneath the ice. If their hopes were borne out by Galileo, then Lake Vostok could become a very important testing ground for devices that might one day find extraterrestrial life.

EIGHT

AUGUST 7, 1996

Extraordinary claims require extraordinary evidence.
—CARL SAGAN

THE ANNOUNCEMENT

Back at the Johnson Space Center, Anne stared at the squiggly worms in the photo, waiting for Dave to deliver the punch line. It dawned on her that he was serious. For a moment she couldn't move.

"Oh my goodness," she managed to say.

"Your project? We wanted someone who didn't know anything about this to find something that looked like it in a terrestrial sample." The idea made sense: An intern would have no preconceived notion of what to find, and no professional stake in the matter either way. They needed someone reasonably observant, unbiased, and unafraid of a high-powered electron microscope. Anne had fit the bill.

"And you did it," Dave said. "You absolutely did it. And you can't say anything about it. Our paper comes out in six weeks, and we've got a lot of work to do."

From that moment forward, she became a true part of the team, privy to its secret efforts. She was allowed to look into samples of ALH 84001, the meteorite from Mars. Anne quickly became adept at clicking off the microscope's computer monitor whenever another intern stopped by to chat. She became increasingly vague with scientists outside the team and in weekly phone calls to her parents. When her roommate in Fayetteville called to ask how the internship was going, Anne realized how much she sounded like Kathie Thomas-Keprta as she said, "Oh, you'll find out eventually. It's really interesting stuff, though."

She learned the history of the rock that had traveled from Mars to Earth. It was one of twelve meteorites collectively known as the "SNC achondrites."* The initials stood for Shergotty, Nakhla, and Chassigny, which were towns where three of the meteorites had been collected after their descents had been observed in 1815, 1865, and 1911, respectively. An "achondrite" is a meteorite lacking chondrules—small mineralized, rounded pellets commonly found in rocky (as opposed to metallic) meteorites. Most chondrites (rocky meteorites containing chondrules) appear to have originated near the asteroid belt. For several decades scientists had disagreed on the source of the SNCs; a few had suggested that perhaps they came from Mars, blasted off the planet by impacts from comets or large meteorites. Most of the SNCs were about 1.3 billion years old and thus much younger than common meteorites, which tend to be around the same age as the solar system—about 4.6 billion years. The SNCs had other characteristics suggesting they were the volcanic products of a much larger parent body. In the early 1980s, scientists identified a different group of unusual meteorites as having come from the moon by comparing their chemical composition with samples collected during the Apollo missions and now stored in Houston. The lunar meteorites had evidently been blasted off the moon by ancient impacts; this finding lent credence to the theory of Martian origin of the SNCs.

Six of the twelve SNCs were found in Antarctica, where every year teams of volunteers search regions where rising ice meets mountain ridges. Antarctica gets no more meteorites than anywhere else, but a natural phenomenon there manages to gather them and make them extraordinarily easy to find. Whenever a meteorite lands on a polar ice sheet, it is gradually covered by

---

*A thirteenth Martian meteorite was found in 1998.

layers of ice laid down over the course of subsequent winters. It begins slowly to flow with the deep ice in which it is trapped. Over many thousands of years, much of Antarctica's ice slides to the sea, but whenever a moving sheet hits a mountain range, it begins to ride up the rocky flank. If the surface is frequently scoured by strong, dry winds, the rising ice sublimates— becomes vapor without ever melting. Any heavier object carried to the surface will remain there. As more and more ice rises and sublimates, the revealed objects pile up. Other than polar researchers and occasional lost birds, the only heavy objects that land on Antarctica are meteorites. In certain parts of the continent, one can find meteorites lying there for the taking, black bits of the solar system standing in sharp contrast to the white light of a six-month-long "day."

Research expeditions sponsored by the National Science Foundation and NASA have now retrieved thousands of Antarctic meteorites. Most of these are stored at a special facility located in the Johnson Space Center. One SNC-type meteorite collected in 1979 near Antarctica's Elephant Moraine, designated EETA 79001, was found to contain tiny, trapped gas bubbles. When scientists measured the gases in these bubbles a few years later, they revealed unusual isotopes at levels that were an exact match for the Martian atmosphere as sampled by the two Viking landers in 1976. EETA 79001 had been chemically fingerprinted: it was unquestionably from Mars. By implication, so were all the other SNCs, including a potato-sized specimen collected near Allen Hills in 1984 called ALH 84001.

Even for an SNC, ALH 84001 was a strange rock. At 4.5 billion years, it was far older than the other eleven samples. That was nearly as old as Mars itself, and older than any known rock on Earth. It had been at or (more likely) just below the planet's surface for most of its history. Radioactive nuclei created by deep-space radiation showed that it had wandered in space for 16 million years before blazing into Antarctica a mere 13,000 years ago. Scientists who had been studying Viking images of the red planet for nearly two decades had found ample evidence that in the distant past Mars was a warmer, wetter, more Earth-like place. Rivers once flowed into lakes, perhaps even into small oceans. In several of the other SNC meteorites, researchers had detected trace amounts of carbonates—carbon-rich minerals— but ALH 84001 was loaded with them. Carbonate deposits filled many older cracks in the rock, and these in turn were cir- cled by unusual dark rims, rich in organic molecules.

ALH 84001 was so unlike the other SNCs, in fact, that for many years no one recognized it as one of them. It was classified as a "diogenite," a fairly ordinary type of chondrule-lacking mete- orite, until early 1994, when D. W. Mittlefehldt, a meteorite spe- cialist working at JSC, published proof that its carbon and oxygen isotopes matched those of other Martian stones. Everett Gibson, who also worked at JSC, and Christopher Romanek, a National Research Council postdoc working in Gibson's lab, were intrigued by the unusually high levels of carbonates. Rep- resenting about 1 percent of the meteorite's total weight, the level was fifty times that in other SNCs. On Earth, carbonates are often deposited by groundwater. They can be created at both low and high temperatures. At about the same time that Mit- tlefehldt determined the rock was from Mars, Romanek mea- sured isotopes in the carbonates that seemed to favor a low-temperature formation, such as would occur in groundwater.

Romanek was a geophysicist who had done work at the Savan- nah River Ecology Station, where he had been involved in the first DOE deep drilling project. To Romanek, the carbonates in ALH 84001 seemed reminiscent of those precipitated by bacteria popu- lating the water-filled cracks of subterranean basalts on Earth. In April 1994, he mentioned this to Everett Gibson, who was just then learning to operate the powerful new field emission electron microscope the JSC had purchased for Space Shuttle engineering studies. When Gibson suggested the possibility of biology to Dave McKay in June, McKay recalled a talk he had attended in 1992 at the Geological Society of America conference. There, McKay told Gibson, Robert Folk had stunned the audience by proposing that the principal agents of all low-temperature carbonate formations were a type of microbe he called nanobacteria.

At the time, McKay and Gibson filed the notion away. But

several months later, they and other scientists studying the rock at JSC had found many more elements and chemical variations, that seemed suggestive of life. Kathie Thomas-Keprta sent a sample to Richard Zare, a prominent organic chemist based at Stanford. With his postdoc fellow Simon Clemett, Zare was able to show that the meteorite contained a variety of complex molecules called *polycyclic aromatic hydrocarbons,* or PAHs. These molecules by themselves were not indicative of life, but they occurred at levels suggesting the decay of organic matter. More significantly, they occurred at greater numbers in the center of the rock than around the edges—exactly the opposite of the distribution one would expect if the rock had somehow been contaminated by PAHs from the Antarctic ice. Kathie Thomas-Keprta found tiny crystals of magnetite in the rock that were very similar to those produced by mud-dwelling bacteria on Earth. The bacteria use tiny magnets like a compass, aligning themselves with the Earth's magnetic field for unknown reasons. Although no significant magnetic field had been detected on modern Mars, it was possible that such a field may have existed in the ancient times when the carbonates were formed.

Encouraged by these findings, McKay visited Folk in Austin to learn more about nanobacteria and how to go about searching for them; Folk eagerly obliged. McKay didn't explain why he was curious about carbonates, only that he thought Folk might be pleased with the ultimate outcome of some ongoing research at NASA. One night shortly after his tutorial, McKay and Gibson decided to slip over to Building 13 and take a look into one of the Martian meteorite's carbonate rims, just to see what they might find. What they found was a very full house. Neither of them slept that night.

McKay, Gibson, and the rest of the nine-member team the two had begun building after taking the momentous photograph prepared a careful case after submitting their paper in April, which was accepted for publication in the August 16 issue of *Science.* Anne Taunton's find of wormlike squiggles in Columbia River basalt that matched those in the original image was icing on the cake. News of the forthcoming report traveled swiftly up the chain of command through JSC and NASA to the White House. Rumors and leaks multiplied, spreading so far and wide that Sherry Rowlands, the call girl engaged by Clinton campaign advisor Dick Morris, recorded it in her diary on August 2, writing, "They've found evidence of life on Pluto," according to a report published later in *The Washington Post*. As more and more reporters hounded *Science*'s editors, the magazine, which has a firm policy of not discussing forthcoming articles, agreed to allow a precedent-setting press conference. Early on the morning of August 7, Anne Taunton called her parents in El Dorado. Her mother answered the phone.

"Mom, you know how I've been kind of secretive about my project lately?"

"I've noticed it," she said. In fact, both parents had commented on this to her on several occasions.

"Well, turn on *Good Morning America*, and you'll see what I've been up to."

"What is it? What did you do? Are you going to be on television?"

"No, they decided not to fly a lowly intern up to Washington with everyone else. But you'll see what it's all about. And when they show nanobacteria from the Columbia River Basalt, I took those pictures. That's good enough for me."

As it turned out, *Good Morning America* sketched only the barest details of the story and invited viewers to tune into the live press conference later in the day. The televised announcement began with a statement of congratulations from the President of the United States at the White House, then switched live to NASA headquarters. After a brief technical glitch, during which no one could get the sound to work in a room crowded with reporters, NASA Administrator Dan Goldin beamed as he introduced Wesley Huntress, NASA's Associate Administrator for Space Science. Huntress in turn introduced David McKay and several of his co-authors, who sat at a long table. McKay and then Gibson spoke, followed by Kathie Thomas-Keprta and Richard Zare, all of them describing the two years of detective work through which they had reached their startling consensus.

At that point McKay displayed a series of slides of the carbonates and the suspected fossils within them. He ended with the most tantalizing, which showed what appeared to be a segmented tube flopped over a rock ledge. "Are these strange crystals?" he asked. "Are they dried-up mud? We believe, we interpret, that these are indeed microfossils from Mars. They are extremely tiny. The longest one is about two hundred nanometers. This is very high magnification . . . We're looking at rocks and minerals at a scale that has really not been used before. These are extremely high-magnification, high-resolution pictures. Next slide, please."

A high-magnification (although still slightly fuzzy) view of one of Folk's travertine samples collected at Bagnaccio in 1988 appeared on the screen. "Just for comparison," McKay said, "these are some tiny bacteria, nanobacteria, on an Earth rock, on calcium carbonate, the same kind of material we're looking at on Mars . . . These things are the same size and shape as many of the forms that we're seeing in the Mars sample." McKay then showed several additional slides of the wormlike features in ALH 84001. He saved his strongest comparison for last. "And finally, I want to finish up with a slide of some real bacteria, that we know are bacteria, which turn out to be about the same size and about the same shape as the things I've been showing you in the Mars sample."

Anne's slide flashed onto the screen at NASA headquarters and on television sets around the world. "These are from the Columbia River basalts from the state of Washington," McKay said. "They're from volcanic rocks, and they're buried deep within the ground. They're a couple of kilometers deep, these come from a drill core, and it turns out that within samples from this drill core, there are subterranean, subsurface bacteria, and some of them—there are larger ones—but some of these are a very small kind of bacteria."

Among the many scientists worldwide who watched the press announcement, none was more surprised than Todd Stevens, who had provided the CRB borehole sample. Like most microbiologists, Stevens was leery of the whole notion of nanobacteria, even though he had seen very small organisms in his sample that were just slightly larger than the commonly accepted lower size limit of 200 nanometers. He couldn't believe organisms below that limit were real until someone could explain how working nucleic acid could fit into such a small package. Even then, he wanted to see proof of metabolism and reproduction, not just the electron microscope images Folk had presented. Yet there was one of his samples flashed on all the networks, full of little rods they were calling nanobacteria. He wished someone had at least told him they were going to do this.

Robert Folk was working in his SEM lab when a student ran in and said, "Hey, they're showing nanobacteria from Mars on TV." Folk followed the student and beamed as he watched the slides on television.

Back in Anne's Houston apartment, the phone rang the minute the press conference ended. She knew who it was before she picked up.

"Hi, Mom," she said.

She was right.

✦

TERMINAL SIPHONS

After visiting my sister in Boulder for a few days, I drove down to Salida on August 2. It was a beautiful descent from the Front Range to the southern Colorado valley, marred only by a long delay in a small town whose main highway had been shut down by a tie-dyed throng gathered for an outdoor rock concert. Jerry Garcia had been dead for a year. For an uncomfortable twenty minutes or so, I thought I had been plunged into some sort of time warp as Dead-heads gave each other big hugs and "miracle" tickets amid the stopped traffic. I leaned out of the rental car window to ask a passing young woman with flowers in her hair what was going on. "Phish," she said, dreamy-eyed. When I said "Who?" she looked at me in a way that made me feel instantly middle-aged.

Eventually the local police cleared the highway, and I made

my way south. The boxy Winnebagos and gleaming Harleys of the tourist route gradually gave way to dented pickups and dusty horse trailers. I knew I had finally reached the site of the 1996 National Speleological Society convention when I saw that Salida's large initial "S"—made of a painted cement slab on an overlooking hill, as is the tradition in western towns—had been modified: smaller, brand-new letters "N" and "S" now preceded it. Cavers had taken over the ranching town of 5,500, swelling the population by 20 percent for a week. I quickly found the riverside campground where the registration tent was located, signed in, then drove into town to find Salida High School, site of the convention meetings that would begin the next morning.

As a longtime caver, I try to make the annual national convention at least every third year, but in 1996 I had several reasons for coming. One was a gig. Part of the reason I felt so out of it for not recognizing the band Phish was that I would be playing bass with the Terminal Siphons at the traditional Wednesday night campground party and dance, something I'd done with great pleasure at the '88 and '91 conventions. The band's name was a caving term for water-filled passages that halt exploration. The group was composed entirely of cavers, with a repertoire that included classic rock and original tunes. The founder and lead singer was an associate professor of geology at Middle Tennessee State University and a former roadhouse star. The lead guitarist was a geology master's candidate who was well known in the music scene around Athens, Georgia. The harmonica player was an environmental lawyer, the drummer the talented twenty-year-old son of geology professors who were both life members of the NSS. It was your prototypical overeducated garage band, with a warm patina of cave mud.

My other convention gig was literary: Emily Davis Mobley ran Speleobooks, the country's largest supplier of caving literature. My first book, a caving reminiscence, had just been published, and Emily had set up a signing at her booth during the convention. It was one of the few places where I could hope to sell copies without having to explain to every potential reader what the book was about. But a third, and, to me, equally important reason for attending the conference was that I knew Diana Northup, Dave Jagnow, Art and Peggy Palmer, and other Lechuguilla researchers would be presenting the results of some of their latest work. Diana had told me that she thought there would be several other significant microbiology papers presented at the convention. "The pace is really starting to pick up," she had said. Larry Mallory had told me he would be on vacation with his family during the convention, but he had asked me to fill him in on any interesting Lechuguilla news that came out in Salida.

I found Emily at sunset and helped her unpack from her crowded van cases of books, T-shirts, bat jewelry, and posters for display in a science classroom turned bookstore. I met Emily's assistant, a geology student named Penny Taylor, who was completing a master's thesis on cold-water travertine deposition in certain streams of upstate New York. Penny had put in a full career with the U.S. Postal Service, entering graduate school only after her children were grown. I mentioned to her Folk's theories regarding microbial precipitation of travertine.

"Sheesh!" she replied. "I spent all these years learning chemistry, and now they want me to learn microbiology? Forget it! The chemistry works. I'm too old to learn a whole new science!" Although Penny was joking, I had begun to suspect that hers was the serious response of a great many senior geologists who had been suddenly confronted with new bacteria during the past few years.

I had been reading up on bacteria in general and extremophiles in particular. During my flight to Denver the previous week, I had laughed out loud at parts of Bernard Postgate's *The Outer Reaches of Life*, a recent book that seemed two parts Stephen Jay Gould, one part Monty Python. Postgate, one of England's leading microbiologists and the author of *Microbes and Man*, a classic textbook, wrote with comic British understatement of bizarre bugs that thrived in cold, heat, acid, salt, and other miserable conditions, as well as of the ways people could put these bugs to good use.

Postgate also described recent findings concerning the "guests who came to stay," the bacteria bound up as mitochondria inside every human cell. After genetic analysis had shown that mitochondria and chloroplasts were indeed related to free-living microbes, a number of researchers had begun an active hunt for examples of separate species converging into single organisms. Lynn Margulis of the University of Massachusetts had emerged as one of the leaders of this research. She termed the cooperative wedding of bacteria and eukaryotic cells or organisms *endosymbiosis.* She believed that the cilia lining our breathing passages, and several other highly specialized human cells, began as independent parasites. After a long, mutually beneficial association, they were somehow subsumed into our own DNA. It began to appear that the "dust of the ground" from which God fashioned Adam was like all dust on Earth and teamed with microbes as the breath of life fell upon it.

At Larry Mallory's suggestion, I had signed up to take the standard undergraduate microbiology course in the coming semester at my university. I had already begun reading ahead in the textbook. (I had wanted to audit the class, but Larry said if I took it for credit, with the appropriate lab instruction, he could hire me as a "lab rat" for a week or two to give me firsthand experience with Lechuguilla bugs.) From the course of reading I had begun, I was learning that, as Stephen Gould himself would soon write, "on any possible, reasonable or fair criterion, bacteria are—and always have been—the dominant forms of life on Earth." I had become fascinated by the notion that should all human life vanish tomorrow, the world's microbes would flourish unperturbed, as well as by the corollary truth: if all microbes vanished tomorrow, humanity would quickly cease to exist.

On Monday morning, I sat in Emily's temporary store, signing books and discussing caving trivia with old and new friends. That afternoon I drove to the campground. On a tarp-covered wooden stage, conveniently located near the beer tent, I rushed through the band's single annual rehearsal. The lead guitarist and I jotted down chords to thirty-three songs—five sets' worth—and taped them to amps and mike stands. The band's leader sang himself hoarse, as he does during the Monday rehearsal every year, but we knew he'd be ready to go after resting for twenty-four hours. I was glad that I'd avoided any book or music commitments for Tuesday, for that was when a special all-day Lechuguilla science session had been scheduled.

At the appointed time, I filed behind a Who's Who of cave scientists and National Park Service cave managers into the aging high school auditorium. Dave Jagnow, who had introduced me to Lechuguilla with his slides in China, opened with a historic overview of the evolution of the theory favoring cave formation by ascending hydrogen-sulfide-rich spring water, and the theory's application to Guadalupe Mountain caves, including Carlsbad and Lechuguilla. He was followed by the husband-and-wife geology team of Arthur and Peggy Palmer. Based at the State University of New York, Oneonta, the Palmers have published between them dozens of significant papers on cave science. Art Palmer had appeared on the *Today* show during Emily's 1991 rescue, nervously pointing out the route on a Lechuguilla map as Bryant Gumbel peppered him with questions. In 1994, Art had received the prestigious Kirk Bryan Award from the Geological Society of America, in recognition of his contribution to cave geology. That same year he and Louise Hose, another well-known speleologist, had organized a conference in Colorado Springs with the tongue-twisting name of "Breakthroughs in Karst Geomicrobiology and Redox Chemistry." The conference was significant in that it brought together for the first time NASA exobiologists; the principal theorists of hydrogen sulfide cave formation, Donald Davis and Carol Hill; the travertine experts Folk and Chafetz; the microbial geneticist Pace; the Palmers, Louise Hose, and a dozen other scientists who had studied caves influenced by hydrogen sulfide.

Art and Peggy were also widely respected for their volunteer work within the caving community. Warmhearted and unassuming, always enthusiastic, the two of them had once seen me making a mess of a Mexican buffet I had agreed to cook for two hundred cavers attending a weekend event in upstate New York. Without my asking, they immediately set to chopping onions and garlic. They didn't leave until the last vat of refried beans had been consumed and scrubbed clean. At one time or another, they had similarly helped out many of the cavers I knew. I liked them both immensely.

"Here we have the map of Lechuguilla Cave," Art began his talk, "which, as you can see, looks like the web of a particularly angry and demented spider."

After the crowd finished laughing, Art began enumerating the unusual minerals in the cave and the places where they were located. He listed the famous gypsum sprays of the Chandelier Ballroom as well as the far more delicate gypsum hairs—thin strands of the mineral up to twenty feet long that swayed in the slightest breeze. He described the cave's "rusticles," stalactites of iron-rich minerals named after the formations that the ocean explorer Bob Ballard had found curling from the sides of the *Titanic* in the deep ocean. As on the sunken ship, the rust formations in Lechuguilla were packed with fossil microbes, suggesting they might be a product of iron-oxidizing bacteria feeding on a mineral deposit in the cave.

Also endemic to Lechuguilla were formations called subaqueous helictites, pasta-like fingers of calcite that formed just below the waterline in certain Lechuguilla pools. Before these had been discovered, helictites were thought to form only in cave air. Although first identified only in Lechuguilla, Art mentioned that they had now been found in two other desert caves in Asia. He also showed slides of formations called "pool fingers," first recognized in Lech, which look like normal cave soda straws, except that they are connected by loops of calcified material which geologists also suspect were deposited by microbial growth.

One of the recent findings Art discussed was that all the sulfur in Lechuguilla appeared to occur near layers of sandstone that interbedded in the limestone in which the cave was formed. Many of the yellow minerals that cavers had long assumed to be sulfur, however, had proved not to be sulfur at all, but metatynyamunite and other unusual minerals produced by chemical reactions with small amounts of uranium. With this observation, Art set the stage for a later talk by Cyndi Mosch, a geology graduate student, who presented experimental evidence that metatynyamunite, a canary-yellow powder that dots certain passages in accumulations that resemble small daisies, could form only in the presence of microbes. She explained that the mineral was created when uranium, carried upward by the flow of former springs, was oxidized in the presence of pyrite and potassium. She theorized that in the cave environment, the potassium would most likely come from microbial action.

To test the theory, she had placed sterilized jars containing cave air and the raw materials for metatynyamunite in a Guadalupe Mountains cave passage. Some of the jars were sealed, but others had very small holes that would allow for the passage of microbes. When she retrieved the jars six months later, all of those with holes displayed bright clumps of the target mineral, whereas those that were sealed contained only the dun-colored raw ingredients. "I was all in favor of a strictly inorganic production mechanism," she concluded, "but the results are as you see. This is, without a doubt, a biological process."

Even more interesting biology was yet to come in a later science session where Diana Northup would present work she had done not in Lechuguilla, but in a Kentucky cave called Parkers. In 1993, Diana took a vacation from the University of New Mexico in order to take a course in microbial diversity at the Woods Hole Institute in Massachusetts. Early in the course Norm Pace had given a lecture on the genetic study of microbial diversity. Diana had actually met Norm at a meeting of an Illinois caving club in the early 1970s, when he had just begun work in Carl Woese's lab. When she had seen Pace again at the 1992 NSS convention, she had not been at all convinced that interesting microbiology was taking place in caves, but after meeting up with Larry Mallory, that was no longer the case. She had met Emily at the '91 convention; through Emily's encouragement and the caving tutelage of Jason Richards, a cave specialist at Carlsbad Caverns National Park, Diana had become one of the most active scientists working in Lechuguilla.

"Could you," she had asked Norm at Woods Hole, "arrange to sequence some samples from Lechuguilla, and see what we get?"

Pace had agreed, and Diana and one of Pace's postdocs, who was also working at Woods Hole, had tried unsuccessfully to extract useful DNA from small Lechuguilla samples. However, Pace was aware that Parkers Cave in Kentucky had an active vent of hydrogen sulfide near a warm spring that emerged in the cave. Slimy white filaments of organic material had accumulated in the water, and Pace suspected these were sulfide oxidizers. He and Northup sampled one of these mats and succeeded in sequencing a number of thermophilic bacteria, as she was now prepared to report at the Salida convention.

All of the organisms but one were unique, she said, only distantly related to known microbes. "The one that we could identify is actually the closest living relative to a sulfur-oxidizing, symbiotic bacterium of a deep-sea polychaeta worm, which produces food for the worm in exchange for a safe home and a constant flow of sulfur-rich water." Diana smiled and added, "The interesting question, of course, is how did this primitive deep-sea microorganism get into a cave in the middle of Kentucky? I don't begin to know the answer."

How indeed. It was a question I pondered on Wednesday afternoon as I copied the set lists and ran one last time through various chord progressions by Petty, Clapton, Hendrix, and the Terminal Siphons's geologist-songwriter founder, Albert Ogden. But it was a question I ultimately filed away as, just before the dance party was to begin, Emily stopped by the stage and asked, "Did you hear the news? NASA just announced that they found fossil microbes from Mars."

I was dying to know more, but Albert gave us a wink and said, "Okay, let's go, 'Locomotive Breath.'" With that we were off. My ears were ringing and my finger blisters had long since burst when, hours later, I found a convenience store with a newspaper headline touting the year's biggest story.

I stood reading in the fluorescent light, amazed.

✳

VACATION

Sixteen miles due north of the White House, in the quintessentially suburban town of Rockville, Maryland, sits the white two-story colonial of Dick and Nancy Mallory. The couple built the rambling, comfortable home with their family in mind in 1991, the year Dick retired from public school administration. Bedrooms are tucked in everywhere. The finished basement has its own kitchen. A first-class swing set in the backyard overlooks an inviting wooded path running along a creek. Next door lives George, the colorful bachelor handyman, straight out of central casting. The Mallorys' strategy had worked, as first one and then another of their grown daughters returned to the nest, bringing in tow two spouses and three grandchildren.

The big house was therefore packed when Larry and Carolyn Mallory and their four children came to visit during the first week of August 1996. Larry was eager to fill his parents in on the progress of Biomes, Inc., the drug development company he had formed the year before with Miles Hacker and two other partners. The name came from the scientific term "biome," used to describe a regional or global biological community, such as a grassland or desert, that can be characterized by its dominant forms of plant life and prevailing climate. Dick Mallory, who was fond of puzzles and word games, had jokingly suggested that the company name was actually an acronym for "Buy into Our Money-Earning Scheme." In fact, he had been one of the company's first investors and was tremendously excited by its progress, not only because Larry was his son but also because he could grasp the science behind it and was proud that it had been initiated by one of his star pupils.

For many years, Dick Mallory had been a high school chemistry and biology teacher in Fresno, California, where he had taught Larry in both subjects. Dick had educated his children in science from an early age, taking summer jobs in the national parks where the kids would study nature and geology firsthand. Once, he had helped Larry manufacture a green smoke bomb in the high school chemistry lab as a special effect for the halftime show at a home football game. The bomb had worked perfectly, but the choking green cloud became trapped in the bowl-shaped stadium, emptying the stands and delaying the second half of the game as the haze lingered on.

The news that Larry brought with him from Massachusetts was good, and he shared it amid the noisy interruptions of seven kids and a rambunctious black dog named Terra. Biomes had been operating under what was called a phase I grant from the National Cancer Institute, a division of the National Institutes of Health (NIH). The grant was part of an NIH program supporting innovative research by small businesses that could lead to products or services benefiting the public. Innovation and the probability of commercial success were the primary criteria for funding. Upon its completion of the phase I grant, the company was to file a report that could allow it to receive a phase II grant, which meant a substantial increase in government support. So far, the Biomes results looked sufficient to justify the bump-up in funding. This was important not only for the research support it guaranteed but also because it would suggest legitimacy to potential investors within the pharmaceutical industry. One of the things Larry had learned was that finding a new drug was easy compared to actually bringing it to market. A useful natural chemical had to be isolated, synthesized in the lab, and patented (a process that alone could take several years and millions of dollars) before actual drug testing could begin. Hacker, who had successfully brought other new drugs to market, had warned Larry that the testing process could cost up to $70 million before the first prescription had been written. It was thus impossible for any small company to introduce a new drug without substantial support from major investors.

Fortunately, one of the four Biomes partners was James Theroux, a business professor at the University of Massachusetts with a worldwide reputation for growing small technology companies into major concerns, a process he had successfully completed with his own cable company before he had entered academia. One of the deep-pocketed investors Theroux had been able to woo with the initial test results was Jerome Lemelson, a modern-day Edison who held more than 500 patents for a range of inventions relating to the VCR, camcorder, fax machine, cordless telephone, robotics, and machine vision. After winning a decades-long lawsuit awarding him a substantial percentage of the royalties from all bar-coding devices, Lemelson had become an advocate of individual invention and creativity. Like the NIH, Lemelson had cautiously offered a token amount of support for the moment, enough to help pay for collection equipment and Larry's airfare to the caves, with the hint of greater investment should the early promise of the initial tests be borne out. Unlike the NIH, however, Lemelson had personally requested that Larry keep the financier's involvement with Biomes secret. Until Lemelson's support ended upon his death a year later, Larry never dropped the name with any investor other than his father.

The company's future was largely in the hands of its third partner, Jim Bigelow, a chemist who worked with Hacker at the Vermont Cancer Center. Bigelow was, by coincidence, an NSS caver, as well as a deeply committed humanitarian. "I like separating things, I like to cure cancer, and I like to cave," he said. "With Biomes, I can do all these at once." Bigelow had detected several potential antibiotic and anticancer chemicals in Larry's cave bugs.

"Once you know what kills cancer cells," Bigelow explained in an interview with a reporter from *National Wildlife* magazine, "you have to isolate a chemically pure bacterial product, figure out how it works, what else it kills, how it moves in the body, how long it remains effective, how much of it you need. These steps are all part of the long road of drug development. You want to kill the cancer but not the patient." In addition to a lab full of sophisticated and expensive equipment, making those chemical determinations would require large quantities of sample—that is, lots of bugs.

For that reason, Larry had been flying around the country, collecting bugs in Lechuguilla; at Mammoth Cave National Park; and from caves formed in volcanic rock called lava tubes in Hawaii Volcanoes National Park. He gathered samples only from public lands because an important part of the future patenting process would be Biomes's ability to prove the provenance of source organisms; that the company had proper access to them; and that specific organisms could be precisely located. The permits provided by the park service thus became legal documents that would reassure potential investors. The controlled access and detailed mapping common to caves in national parks ensured that Larry could return to find specific organisms at a much later date, even if their only known habitat was a certain small puddle.

Serban Sarbu invited Larry to sample microbes from Romania's Movile Cave, but Larry had then received a contract from the Romanian government claiming 70 percent of gross sales of any product resulting from a discovery in the cave. The unintended effect of such a provision would have been to keep any large investor away. If a sample from Lechuguilla or Mammoth eventually did yield a valuable chemical product, Larry wanted there to be no possibility that the Romanian government (or, for that matter, the owner of an American cave on private land) would challenge its ownership. So he scrupulously avoided entering any cave that was not publicly owned. Larry explained to his father that finding a new cancer cure underground was a chore akin to baking Henny Penny's bread: No one wanted to help find the bugs, extract the chemicals, win the patents, or test the drugs for FDA approval, but many seemed willing to lay claim to any money a successful drug might generate.

With each sample Larry collected, he first tried to culture organisms. He then had to define the cultured bugs in terms of their size, shape, and mobility (whether by use of flagellar swimming appendages or by means of a mysterious gliding motion microbiologists call "motility"), as well as their ability to carry out various chemical reactions. He checked for fermentation reactions such as those performed by the microbes that give the world its wine, beer, pickles, cheese, and yogurt. He observed whether they possessed the ability to digest glucose and other sugars. He calculated the organisms' average life spans and recorded their times and methods of reproduction (cell division, sporulation, etc.). So far, he had done this with nearly 3,000 novel cave microbes.

Of those, sixteen seemed to show the ability to kill cells associated with a particular type of breast cancer without harming healthy cells or other cancers. Why would cave bugs be capable of such a thing? Barring divine intervention (which Larry didn't discount entirely), his best guess was that in order to protect their scant underground food sources from invading fungi, the organisms had evolved powerful toxins to attack an enzyme associated with a particular fungal growth phase. Like us, fungi are highly evolved eucaryotes. It seemed quite possible that some unicellular cave fungi employed a growth mechanism similar to the one that causes malignancies to blossom.

Moreover, as Larry had explained to me, caves are *oligotrophic* environments, meaning they have low available nutrients. Organisms who have adapted to oligotrophic life can't afford to waste energy wiggling around looking for something to eat. They become adept at sticking tightly to surfaces in places where the food will come to them, via the slow trickle of water or other chemicals through rock. It turns out that sticking tightly to surfaces is one of the attributes one looks for in anti-cancer drugs. Once it has found a good piece of real estate, an oligotrophic bug must closely guard it from invasion. In food-rich *heterotrophic* environments like pond scum or your mouth, bugs that even bother to battle each other do so with much ineffective flagella waving and molecule spitting. Cave bugs, in contrast, employ quick, deadly weapons, powerful molecules that allow them to avoid the energy-draining effort of traditional microbial warfare.

The trick for Biomes was to find such natural weapons that could be aimed at specific diseased cells. A few of Larry's Lechuguilla samples seemed amazingly proficient at killing any kind of adjoining cells—animal, plant, bacterial, fungal, diseased, or healthy. He quietly filed these organisms away, firm in his belief that humanity had already mass-produced all the killer toxins it needed. (Miles and Jim joked, nervously, of the CIA breaking into their lab à la *Three Days of the Condor*.) Of the sixteen best hits that selectively targeted breast cancer cells, four appeared especially strong. Three of these came from isolated pools in Lechuguilla, the fourth from a few thimblefuls of drip water in a basin inside a Hawaiian lava tube.

•   •   •

Larry had earned his undergraduate degree in microbiology
with high honors from the University of Maryland, and he still
kept in touch with several of his former professors. On the third
day of his vacation, he went to visit one of them at the Center of
Marine Biotechnology (COMB), an independent research center in Baltimore with a commitment to developing practical
applications for microbiology. Larry's professor described a
small-business initiative that COMB had begun, which he
thought would be ideal for a company like Biomes. A typical collaboration would provide the company with office and laboratory space, but would allow Biomes to retain the lion's share of
any profit arising from the agreement. Moreover, a collaborator
with Larry's experience could also be hired as visiting faculty,
providing him with a salary while he continued his research.
Larry agreed to think about the offer, explaining that he had
tentatively agreed to a similar deal in Amherst. His former university was sponsoring the construction of a new low-rent science center that Biomes planned to move into later in the year.
The construction had been delayed several times, however, and
the cost to Biomes for space in the new structure kept rising, so
Larry agreed to keep COMB in mind. For the moment, his lease
on the moldy office and lab in the basement of the Stockbridge
School of Agriculture had been paid through December.

Not that he got on well with the landlord, his former dean,
whom he had frequently criticized while on the faculty. As Larry
had feared, the man had led a successful fight against Larry's
application for tenure the year before, arguing that his cave
research lacked substance (even as NIH approved Biomes's phase
I grant) and that Larry lacked a significant number of publications. By working with a university office dedicated to furthering
joint ventures with entrepreneurial technology companies, Larry
had wangled a lease at UMass and the use of the university's lab
space and equipment, despite objections from his former adver-
sary. The dean had let him know, however, that the lease was for
one year only. Come January, Larry would have to pull his cave
bugs from the freezer and find them a new home.

When Larry described to his father the various options open to him, Dick Mallory was predictably enthusiastic about COMB. "You could move in with us," he said. "There's room in the basement for you and Carolyn and the kids. You could keep your Amherst house on the market until you got a good price for it and take your time finding a nice place down here."

Larry smiled and shook his head, picturing how well *that* would go over with Carolyn. "Honey, how would you like to move in with my parents and my two sisters and their husbands and kids?" He had told his dad thanks, but no thanks—until the afternoon of August 7, when the telephone rang.

"Larry, it's for you," his teenaged niece shouted over the din.

He picked up an extension and was surprised to hear one of his former UMass colleagues on the line.

"What's up?" Larry asked.

"I hate to interrupt your vacation, but you'd better get up here, pronto," his friend said. "A moving crew is dumping your stuff in the hall. Files, equipment, everything—they're just stacking it up in the hallway. I got them to put the live cultures back in the freezer for now, but they say they've got to go, too." Larry's friend explained that the department had hired a new faculty member, promising him Larry's space. The dean had approved the department head's decision to make room for the new faculty.

"He can't do that! I've got a paid lease."

"I think that's why he waited for you to go on vacation."

They talked for several more minutes. His friend agreed to gather the colonies of live cave organisms and store them, as they were Biomes's most valuable asset. Larry decided to let the rest of his family stay in Maryland and enjoy their vacation, while he drove up to Amherst to see what he could salvage. In fact, his lease had been made with the university economic development office. That office had made a temporary arangement with Larry's department when the construction of its new lab space had been delayed. Larry thus had no recourse against the department itself–he had to find new digs, quick.

He hung up, already composing the case he would present to

Carolyn. If he couldn't get back into his lab, he realized, they were going to have to go ahead and do it: for the sake of science, they were going to have to move in with the folks, just for a while. *The horror, the horror.*

He walked into the living room, scarcely noticing when his father mentioned there was something on the television about fossils from Mars.

NINE

THANKSGIVING 1996

This would be the biggest story of my career, bar none—
bigger than the landing on the moon by a long shot, but a
different kind of story, a story that was probably going to
come out in dribbles and drabs.... So you may be covering
the biggest story of your life and you will not be sure until
after you are gone that you did indeed cover that biggest
story. Those things are going through your mind. You do
not want to miss the first installment on the biggest story
of your career.
> —JOHN NOBLE WILFORD
> on covering ALH 84001 for *The New York Times*

SYMPOSIUM

The Space Policy Institute, a D.C. think tank established by
George Washington University in 1987, conducts research on
space policy issues; organizes seminars, symposia, and conferences; and offers graduate courses. It was a natural choice to
host the first public symposium on ALH 84001, which it had
scheduled for Friday, November 22, 1996, with the title "Life in
the Universe: What Might the Martian Fossils Tell Us?" Vice
President Al Gore had called for a "space summit" in December
to discuss future NASA plans in light of the life-on-Mars
announcement; this symposium was billed as the public pream-
ble to the private summit.

As I found the lecture hall on the George Washington campus, I was glad I had applied early for my press pass. The turnout was clearly higher than expected, and anyone without an advance reservation was being sent to a larger auditorium to watch the proceedings on closed-circuit television. I checked the registration sheet and saw that Larry Mallory was listed in the overflow group. I placed my briefcase across a couple of folding chairs in the press gallery to hold them, hoping to sneak Larry into the main room when he arrived. In the center of the semicircular hall sat a glass case containing a piece of the Martian meteorite. A dozen photographers hovered over it like moths about a streetlamp. To the left of the rock stood the speaker's podium. To the right, a large poster described the upcoming Mars Pathfinder mission. A life-sized model of Sojourner, the mission's rover, was parked in front of the poster. I walked up to it, marveling at its small size—it could have been one of the riding toys that my two-year-old twins used for scooting down the hallway. It seemed an appropriate physical emblem of the downsized, post-Apollo NASA: a shrunken version of the lunar rover that had captivated me on television as a child. I wondered whether the little go-cart would make it to Mars. I suspected that many in the room wondered the same. A highly publicized Russian mission to the red planet had crashed into the Pacific just a few days earlier; NASA's previous Mars orbiter had lost all contact with Earth just before reaching its destination.

The crowd began settling into its seats, and I went back to the door to check for Larry. At 10 A.M., it had already been a long day. I had missed a connection in Atlanta late the night before, spent the night in Georgia, caught a sunrise flight to National Airport, and cabbed it directly to the university. I had been able to stash my luggage in the corner of a pressroom set up just outside the lecture hall, where telephones had been set aside for *The Washington Post, The New York Times*, and several other brand-name media. I ducked into the pressroom now for one last cup of bad coffee, stepping out just as Larry walked in. The doors of the lecture hall were about to close, which was probably a good thing, as the students charged with checking credentials were busy guiding latecomers to the overflow auditorium, and I was able to usher Larry to the spot I had saved.

David Brandt, the program director of the National Space Society, opened the symposium by explaining that Carl Sagan had originally agreed to keynote the event, but that the famed scientist was unable to attend due to complications from a rare bone-marrow disease he was battling. Brandt explained that the idea for the symposium had actually come from Dwayne Day, a graduate student who had been the Space Policy Institute's representative at NASA's August 7 press conference; Day stood up to take a bow. At last Brandt introduced Kathie Thomas-Keprta, who took the podium to review the story of ALH 84001. Tall, blond, and wearing a surprisingly short skirt, she looked nothing whatsoever like my preconceived notion of a NASA electron microscopy expert. No one in the audience could have known it from looking at her, but she was several months pregnant with her first child, having learned of her condition just after the original press conference.

"What we have here is a scientific detective story," Thomas-Keprta began. "Let me review some of the lines of evidence in that story." She described the original National Science Foundation collection in Antarctica, David Mittlefehldt's identification of the rock as Martian, and Chris Romanek's observation of the carbonates within it. She discussed the analysis that proved the carbonates had formed at low temperatures conducive to life and then displayed slides of the "Oreo cookie rims" that ringed the carbonates and contained organic chemical signatures. She went through several slides of bacterial fossils from ancient Earth rocks before showing the by now familiar image of the segmented wormlike rods from Mars. This was followed by Anne Taunton's images of the Columbia River basalt nanobacteria.

She described Bob Folk and his work, and then said, "Since the August announcement, I have been looking more closely at these Columbia River basalt samples, and I've brought with me today several images not yet seen in public." The crowd murmured appreciatively as a series of side-by-side slides appeared on the screen. Those on the left were from ALH 84001; those on the right, from the CRB samples. In one series after another, the left- and right-hand images were nearly identical.

"As compelling as these images are," Thomas-Keprta cautioned, "more evidence is needed before we can say without a doubt that they represent biological forms. Ideally, we would like to find evidence of cell walls, cell division, or both. Toward that end, I'm working on developing techniques by which I can use acid to extract the CRB fossils from their surrounding matrix and then attempt to cut them in half in order to look for cell walls or other cellular structures." She concluded by reviewing the still-raging argument over PAHs and discussing several new studies that original team members were undertaking.

Next up was John Grotzinger of MIT to discuss the ongoing scientific debate. "This is the sort of thing that will take years to sort out," Grotzinger said. He argued that the issue would probably not be settled until pristine rock samples had been brought back from Mars and examined for fossils. The oldest fossilized multicellular life on Earth, he pointed out, was about 550 million years old. He compared ALH 84001 to rocks bearing older fossil microbes on Earth that had been discovered fifty years ago. Until then, common wisdom had held that seven-eighths of the planet's history had been sterile, with life appearing only relatively recently. Skepticism that the fossils could be older than 550 million years held sway for decades, until better samples had been found. Eventually, when cyanobacteria preserved in 3.5-billion-year-old chert had been shown to be virtually identical to living cyanobacteria, science set back the clock for the beginning of life on Earth. Chert, Grotzinger explained, preserves much clearer fossils than carbonates. "So long as we have only carbonate fossils to examine, the issue of whether or not they *are* fossils is likely to remain open."

Grotzinger was followed by a pair of impassioned speakers from the National Space Society and the Planetary Society, both of whom argued for a renewed U.S. commitment to send manned expeditions to Mars. As Robert Zubrin, a podium-pounding evangelist for the Martian cause, described how to make inexpensive rocket fuel from components in the Martian atmosphere, Larry passed me a document from his briefcase. "What do you think of this?" he whispered.

The paper was entitled "Recovery of Microorganisms from Underground Biotic Zones on Mars—a Proproposal" and was attributed to Biomes, Inc. I skimmed through an introduction summarizing the most likely underground habitats for extant microbial life and found at the heart of the paper a section labeled "Cave-Navigating Robots." "Designing a robot capable of traversing a cave environment is very challenging," it read. "Caves contain pits and steep slopes, boulder-strewn floors, and tight irregular passages." To overcome these challenges, Larry proposed to load miniature microbial testing packages on robots based on the designs of Dr. R. A. Brooks at the Massachusetts Institute of Technology. The robotic cavers would be called SPIDERS, for Self-Propelled Independently Directed Exploratory Robots, and would operate untethered from a larger Mars rover parked near the cave entrance. They would pour out of the rover on little mechanical legs, staying in contact via a series of miniature radio relays dropped every few meters like Hansel and Gretel's breadcrumbs.

"They would be used in concert under Earth control to carry out the project objectives," the paper explained. "The loss of one or even most of the robots would not doom the mission objectives."

Alternatively, Larry proposed using a group of small robots tethered to the rover by up to a kilometer of fiber-optic cable, sheathed in lightweight power conduit, for each SPIDER. These tethers would transmit power to the SPIDERS and data back from them to the rover. While miles of cable would present enormous opportunities for tangles in the typical cave passage, the fact that the SPIDERS were being directed in concert "could mitigate the potential problem of a snagged or broken tether by either freeing the snagged tether or splicing a broken one. Again, the loss of a single robot would not doom the mission." The proposal suggested that NASA or NASA subcontractors would design and build the robots, while Biomes would collaborate in testing "the robots' abilities to navigate various underground environments and would aid in designing appropriate micro-bial-sampling and culture procedures to be employed on Mars."

I immediately pictured a group of mechanical arachnids crab-bing their way down the Western Borehole two or three years hence. It would be fun to watch, anyway. Of course, as the pro-posal was careful to point out, before you could explore Martian caves, you had to find Martian cave entrances, which no one had yet done. But Viking data suggested the existence of several types of cave entrances: basaltic lava flows on Mars resembled the types on Earth that always create lava tubes, while ancient streambeds that appeared to emerge whole from canyon walls suggested cave springs. Perhaps the upcoming Mars Global Sur-veyor—which was scheduled to map the entire planet in high resolution—would be able to pinpoint definite entrances. The paper also addressed the problem of preserving viable microbes during the long exposure to harmful radiation they would endure while traveling from Mars to Earth. It suggested a series of tests of different shielding material that could be performed on Earth-orbiting satellites prior to the actual Mars mission.

"Where are you sending this?" I whispered.

"To some of the folks at Ames who went to Lechuguilla," Larry replied, meaning NASA's Ames Research Center. I wished him luck; it seemed like a reasonable plan to me.

A reporter next to us, a bearded man who held a small tape recorder and took assiduous notes, glared at us, so I hushed up and turned my attention back to the stage. At last the pleas for new manned spaceships wound down. Peter Caws, University Professor of Philosophy at George Washington University since 1982, rose to address the issue "How will we know that the Mars findings are valid?"

His wool suit and wild scientific hair fit perfectly with his commanding British accent, which seemed custom-made for BBC nature documentaries. Caws gave a brief discourse on the etymology of the word "knowledge" and the semantic shadings of what it is to "know" a thing, then turned to scientific knowl-edge in particular, speaking with an eloquence and a conviction that had me wishing I could enroll in one of his classes.

"Where do we get our theories?" he asked, leading up to the meat of his talk.

The short answer is: out of our heads. They belong in here with us, not out there in the world—a point I sometimes drive home by saying the stars are indifferent to astronomy. A theory is best thought of as a kind of inspired suggestion that we look at a bit of the world in a particular way. Most theories do not arise at all simply out of observations, they arise from thinking about the results of observations. One quick way of characterizing science is to say that it is "imagination controlled by evidence": the theoretical imagination goes to work, but it has to accommodate itself to the observational evidence.

How sure can we be that we have got the imaginative part right? That is the bottom line with respect to the issue of interpreting the ALH 84001 findings as evidence of life on Mars. The theoretical conjectures we are dealing with, that the meteorites came from Mars and that the fossils are of biological origin, are driven, it is true, by observation—the composition of the trapped gases, the microscopic signatures. But making the claim does involve boldness of imagination, and confirming it calls on many parts of the complex structure. . . . The thing is that different parts of the structure are more or less well entrenched. The most solid part in this particular cluster of theories is celestial mechanics—which is still Newtonian!

We do not have to worry about Einstein and Company, not for macroscopic objects in the solar system anyway. Such objects are too big for quantum corrections and too small for relativistic ones. So the rocks really could have come from there to here. But rocks could also go from here to there—so they might have gone from here to there and back, picking up a bit of Martian atmosphere on the way; or from somewhere else to there to here. Chunks like this only get thrown up by relatively big planet-smashing events, like the one thought to have caused the extinction of the dinosaurs.

That is the kind of challenge data of this sort have to face, quite apart from the contamination challenge and all the rest.

And yet there is something tremendously special about these data. How do we account for this? There have been many reports of organic material in meteorites, so it cannot be just that. The excitement lies I think in the convergence of small clues, in the elegance of the careful work that has gone into the findings, and finally in the possibility that at last we may have a bit of real evidence about extraterrestrial life. For if science is imagination controlled by evidence, we have to admit that so far, where life elsewhere in the universe is concerned, imagination has had the field to itself—hence science fiction. The only bit of whatever looked like evidence up to now was what Percival Lowell and his people thought they saw in Flagstaff, Arizona, at the turn of the century. Not that we have not been looking for evidence, with moon shots, Mars landers, probes—it is just that they have so far drawn a blank. And now it looks as if the evidence may have been in our backyard all along.

It is still pretty slim. I am reminded of Mark Twain's remark about science. You remember that he was struck by the fact that the Mississippi kept getting shorter because it cut through bends, and he worked out that it was losing about a mile and a third per year. "Therefore," said Twain, "any calm person, who is not blind or idiotic, can see that in the Old Oolitic Silurian Period, just a million years ago next November, the Lower Mississippi River was upwards of one million three hundred thousand miles long, and stuck out over the Gulf of Mexico like a fishing rod. And by the same token any person can see that seven hundred and forty-two years from now the Lower Mississippi River will be only a mile and three quarters long, and Cairo and New Orleans will have joined their streets together, and be plodding comfortably along under a single mayor and a mutual board of aldermen." And he added: "There is something fascinating about science. One gets such wholesale returns of conjecture out of such a trifling investment of fact."

What are the implications of the findings, if they do test out, for the popular question that has been highlighted by the media? Finding some polycyclic aromatic hydrocarbons in a bit of Antarctic rock is one thing; finding that we are not alone in the universe quite another. One thing that may be worth noting is that we are alone anyway: the existentialists pointed out long ago that each of us is sufficiently different from everyone else for our nearest and dearest to count as alien life forms. But on the question of life forms and their proliferation, there is still a lot we do not know about life on earth, let alone on Mars. A new third biological domain, the archaea,

Upon this comment, Larry Mallory and I simultaneously nudged each other and perked up.

is currently being added to the two old ones, the bacteria and eukarya. It is beginning to look, given the evidence from deep ocean vents, as if the old cybernetic claim—that combinatorial possibilities in energy-rich environments lead necessarily to the emergence of ordered structures—was right. If these structures include transcription mechanisms they may be self-reproducing, and there you are: life.

Where it goes from there will involve some variant on a basic natural-selection scenario—proliferation, competition, elimination—and on what Buckminster Fuller used to call the "critical path," the series of chances that mean the difference between survival and extinction as much for organisms as for ideas. Given all this, it would be surprising if there were not life forms elsewhere. But we have to wait for the evidence, and have only scratched the surface. From one point of view science knows a lot; from another point of view it knows almost nothing. Mention of Bucky Fuller reminds me of the recent discovery of buckyballs—they were around too for millions of years but nobody noticed. The chances that if there is advanced life anywhere—and PAHs on the whole make poor conversational companions—it will actually intersect with us remain marginal. Yet it matters to us very much. Exactly why that is would take a philosophical inquiry of a quite different kind, one belonging to the human rather than to the natural sciences.

One final word: I have been discussing the assigned question with an emphasis on the future tense—"How will we know the findings are valid?" One obvious answer to the question posed in this way is: we will not know for sure until we have done a lot more work. If knowing matters as much as I think we are agreed it does, that is a powerful argument for doing the work, in particular for going to Mars and checking things out on the ground. It is generally true of scientific work that each step you push the frontier back costs a lot more than the previous step, and in a society governed by the bottom line that can lead to cold feet. . . . It is expensive to go to Mars, and not that easy. The political leader who had the vision to commit national resources to going to the moon was shot in Dallas thirty-three years ago today. It would not be a bad memorial to him and to that vision if our current leaders made a commitment to see this one through as well.

It was as fine a lecture as I had ever heard. I turned to Larry and said as much.

But nine more just as memorable were to be given before the day was over. First, noted experts on religion examined the tenets of Christianity, Judaism, and Islam and claimed to find nothing in them which would make faith in God difficult to reconcile with the existence of extraterrestrial life. (Quite to the contrary, Islamic scholar Abdul-Monem Al-Mashat cited numerous passages from the Koran which seemed to insist that creation encompassed many inhabited worlds beyond Earth.) The *New York Times* science reporter John Noble Wilford addressed the media response to life on Mars; the science-fiction author Kim Stanley Robinson considered the red planet from a literary perspective. As thoughtful and entertaining as these talks were, as the symposium progressed Larry was clearly disappointed at the lack of in-depth technical discussion of upcoming tests of ALH 84001 or possible life-sampling missions to Mars. He was somewhat mollified late in the day, however, when Bruce Murray, a planetary geologist from the California Institute of Technology and former director of the NASA/Caltech Jet Propulsion Laboratory in Pasadena, spoke on "Developing a Mars Exploration Strategy." The talk laid out several broad guidelines for robotic searches for evidence of past and present life. Many of Murray's points seemed to favor the sort of plan that Larry hoped to pitch for Biomes.

If Peter Caws had been the day's most eloquent speaker, the most engaging was the last to appear. NASA Administrator Daniel S. Goldin entitled the closing talk "We Will Go to Mars." Goldin had been in the news a great deal over the previous months as the champion of the space agency's new "smaller, faster, cheaper" mandate. Critics and proponents alike agreed that the upcoming Pathfinder mission to Mars would be the first test of the streamlined, businesslike approach Goldin had brought to NASA upon taking over the agency in 1992.

Goldin looked every bit the hard-nosed businessman in his gray corporate suit; his demeanor and features suggested Robert De Niro playing a Wall Street financier. But then he opened his mouth, spilling forth with warmth and humor in a heavy Queens accent:

> . . . Now, America is a bold nation. We are visionary. We are explorers of the frontier. Our ancestors settled the East Coast of America and we explored the West. We explored the poles, and we have been to the moon. But we really have not left Earth orbit (after all, the moon orbits around the Earth), because it is tough and it takes a determination to do more than undertake an intellectual experience.
>
> We are getting ready to leave Earth orbit. There are three things I believe we need to do in order to make that happen. First, we need a vision. We had a vision for the moon and we accomplished it. I think the vision for Mars has to be broader than the vision for the moon. . . . We need to have sustained presence, and this needs to be part of a broader vision.

Goldin explained that his "broader vision" was articulated by NASA's newly announced Origins Program, which would use multidisciplinary science and exploration projects to find the beginning of everything:

> We want to understand how we started with the big bang and the helium and hydrogen that was produced by that big bang

and that later transitioned into stellar clouds rich in organic material. We want to understand the evolution of the planets and the stars, the conditions that are conducive to the start of life. We want to trace the evolution of life, both here on Earth and on other planets in our solar system, and on planets in solar systems not our own. We also want to know if life of any form, single-cell or higher, carbon-based organisms, is unique to our own planet. We think we know, but we are not sure. We want to know where the environments are that are conducive to all forms of life, and what conditions lead up to life's emergence. Are there resources in the solar system that we could benefit from?

We will do this with robots, and people on the ground, and people in space. My anxiety is with the announcement that we possibly might have identified fossilized life that could be 3.6 billion years old, some are already suggesting that we should add money to the NASA budget and rush off to Mars. Now, I am obviously not against going to Mars, but I am terribly, terribly concerned about a feel-good, quick adrenaline rush instead of doing something in the context of a total Origins program, using all the tools available to us.

Second, we have to identify what challenges we have to over-come. If we want to send human beings to Mars . . . there is not one challenge that I can think of that is not solvable. But before we do that, we need to develop a credible plan for the President and the American people so we can have a contract with them.

Third, we have to help the American people recognize the cornucopia of benefits that would flow from Mars's exploration. We should not tell the American public, "Let's go to Mars and solve cancer," but rather "Let's go to Mars and learn and bring back tools for use on Earth."

Weather predictions come out of the space program, as does direct broadcast TV, a whole brand-new industry in America. NASA started working on direct broadcast satellites in 1971. You could go back to newspaper criticism of NASA, "Why are you working on such a silly thing?" Well, NASA needed it for telemedicine, but now America has a multibillion-dollar industry.

Goldin enumerated several other NASA commercial successes: KA band telecommunications, Teflon, Velcro.

Articulating a vision, addressing solvable challenges, and identifying a cornucopia of benefits—that is what we need to do.

Let us take stock and see where we are relative to the vision. This last year has been unbelievable. We have found planets around stars not our own. We think we have identified fossilized life on Mars. Three years ago, it would have been impossible to take that rock and make the measurements we made, had we not been doing the microelectronic, micromechanical, or information systems technology we had been working on for the prior decade. It did not happen by accident—some rock got found and all of a sudden we found life. The discovery was the result of intense technological and scientific activity.

We have made findings on our own planet about the robustness of life. We now think we have found life on Earth that is 3.87 billion years old. Earth, we believe, was formed a little over 4.5 billion years ago. For their first 600 million years of existence, Earth and Mars were pounded by comets and asteroids, and temperatures were well above the boiling point of water. Yet at the first point in time where there were conditions conducive to life, in a geological millisecond, if you will, life formed. We have found anaerobic life under the oceans that is close to the boiling point of water and does not need oxygen. The first forms of life on Earth were anaerobic, we believe.

We have identified potential life zones in the solar system. A life zone is a place where we have—and I will very broadly define it—liquid water, some form of energy source, electromagnetic or chemical, and some transport mechanism to support life. We used to think that maybe Earth and Mars were the only places in our solar system conducive to life. But now if we go back in time, it looks like Mercury may have at one point in time been in the life zone. It looks like Europa—a moon of Jupiter—has a very good chance to be in the life zone.

In December 1996, the Galileo spacecraft will be snapping some pictures of Europa, and we might be able to validate the hypothesis that there could be a liquid water ocean underneath an ice crust on Europa, and that the moon has a warm solid core. Titan could have pre-biotic conditions for life. These things have happened in the last year. What a great time to be alive! Let us not just concentrate on a Mars rock. There is a broad set of disciplines involved.

Goldin then addressed the challenges of Mars exploration: the monetary cost of getting material out of earth orbit; the problems of providing food, water, and air for extended manned missions in space; the eight- to forty-minute delay between the time a signal leaves Earth with a command and the feedback from Mars is received; the variability of the Martian atmosphere and weather; the dangers of interplanetary radiation to humans and machinery; and the potential dangers of Martian microbes. "So for all of these reasons," he said, "we now have eleven robotic missions planned to Mars, two or three every launch opportunity. These missions were designed before the findings of life on Mars, and I think we need to restructure them. I am hoping some restructuring will take place within the next year or two." He suggested several ways in which planned missions might be modified to provide more information on the possibility of extraterrestrial life.

We are going to reshuffle the budget to build a new cadre of bright young students in biology, physics, and chemistry and convert some of the graybeards to work with them. The astrobiology budget must be significantly increased if we are serious about leaving Earth orbit, because we have no ground truth that we understand. . . .

The last point that I want to make is: all these challenges are solvable, but we need to take the time to plan how to address them; we should not now throw billions of dollars per year at exploring Mars. We should throw the beauty of the human mind at it. But most important, when we decide to do it, NASA, the aerospace community, and the university community must do what they say they are going to do.

Goldin went into lengthy specifics on funding and mission planning, detailing the process to the point that he began losing some of the audience who had sat in the stuffy lecture hall all day, listening to speech after speech. He had already lost Larry, who had headed for home in Maryland right at the start of the talk, trying to beat the five o'clock D.C. traffic. But then Goldin finished with a bit of his own science fiction that played directly to the crowd. It was pure emotional hokum, and I think we all recognized it as such. Yet it nonetheless worked magic on every dreamer in the room.

NASA has a new tool; we can go all the way into the future in cyberspace. We obtained the log of one of the first astronauts who landed on Mars, and I would like to read to you the thoughts and feelings of this astronaut:

"We have landed on Mars. We are here. In seconds, we'll step out of our lander and onto the surface. My hands are trembling. My heart is pounding. A thousand images flash through my mind, a footprint in the dirt, the beams of a fledgling structure, a neat row of seedlings in red soil, a child on her way to school under a cloudless pink sky. A thousand other possibilities flood my mind: the knowledge we'll gain; the resources we'll find; the science; the fossil; or God willing, a pale green, pea-sized discoloration inside a rock.

"Finally, we open the hatch. In a dream, I hear my boots crunch down on the rocky soil and feel the strange stiff pull of gravity. In a dream, I look out across the flat, barren terrain. It has been 261 days since I saw Chuck smile or felt Sarah's chubby little arms around my neck; 261 days since I felt the sun on my face or had a moment alone to replenish my soul or my humanity.

"I've experienced the terror of solar flares. I've been rationed on water. I'm thirsty and dirty. I've lost a crewmate. I've been lonely. I've been very afraid. And now, I'm looking out on a red landscape studded with crags that are sharper and more forbidding than anything I've ever seen on Earth. It should be awe-inspiring, but it isn't. I'm tired and I am numb. I'm standing on the surface of Mars seeing what no human eye has ever seen before, and I feel nothing. And then something flickers at the corner of my eye, and I turn to see my crewmate straightening up.

"I catch my breath as the chiseled escarpments at the base of Olympus Mons sweep into view. In front of them, gaily, boldly a bright scrap of color flutters gently in the thin atmosphere. It seems to promise something. It seems to throw out a dare, somehow a challenge full of laughter and hope. I want to capture this moment for history. I want them to know what this looked like, felt like. I adjust the knobs of my camera to focus, steady now, steady. But it's no good. The sweet familiar red, white, and blue blur and swim together as I am suddenly aware of the stark, fierce beauty of this place and the Creator who fashioned it."

Thunderous applause followed. Those of us left in the seminar room stood, ready to enlist for the next mission to Mars.

✦

DINNER

That night, I joined Larry and his wife, Carolyn, for dinner at a Maryland crab house. The next day, at their invitation I drove out to the Mallory household in Rockville for a traditional Thanksgiving spread. The holiday was actually five days away, but Larry had offered to cook his extended family a turkey dinner on Saturday, because on Monday morning he was flying to Albuquerque to meet with Diana Northup. Diana had become a Biomes contractor, and Larry planned to spend a day conducting business at her lab before heading down to Lechuguilla for a collection trip. While the rest of America watched football and tried to squeeze in one last slice of pumpkin pie, he planned to be deep inside the Northwest Territory, a tangle of newfound passages north of the Western Borehole.

I pulled a rented hatchback into a driveway crowded with cars and an idling John Deere 170 lawn tractor. A cheerful gray-haired man shut off the tractor's engine, looked at me, and said, "You must be Mike Taylor."

"This must be the place," I said.

"Oh, this is the place, and what a place it is." He stuck out a hand. "I'm Dick Mallory, and welcome to my used-car lot." He led me up a flagstone path to the porch, which was decorated for the season with a bale of hay and colorful ears of Indian corn.

Larry emerged from the kitchen wearing jeans, an oxford shirt, and an apron. He led me through a family room dominated by two blue leather recliners. He listed the resident crowd of eight adults and nine children, introducing me to those present, waving in the directions of those elsewhere—all of whom would be joining us for dinner.

"I was just starting to chop vegetables," he said. "Why don't you come give me a hand, then I'll give you the grand tour later."

The well-appointed kitchen overlooked a backyard crowded with children playing soccer. Several pans simmered on the stove. On the island counter stood a tall bottle of Filippo Berio Extra Virgin Olive Oil, three kinds of bottled pepper sauces, and mounds of fresh produce. Four uncooked pies sat on a small table near the phone, awaiting space in the basement oven, where one of two turkeys was roasting.

"Cooking is my primary form of relaxation," Larry said. He nodded toward the noise in the yard. "Around here, I tend to cook a lot." He handed me a cutting board, a well-honed knife, and some green peppers. As I began chopping, he described his current arrangement at the Center of Marine Biotechnology in Baltimore, an hour's drive away.

"I'm using the office quite a bit," he said. "But I don't have much in the lab yet, because at this point most of the lab work is being done by Jim Bigelow up in Vermont. He's extracting chemicals and running assays, and meanwhile we're still pitching to potential investors every few weeks."

The back door flew open, and Larry's towheaded four-year-old son Jonathan burst in, crying in a manner that suggested his nap time was nigh. "Christie won't let me play with her!" he wailed.

Christie, Larry explained, was Jonathan's five-year-old cousin and housemate. Larry tried unsuccessfully to interest the boy in a quiet indoor activity until Carolyn came to the rescue.

"Why don't you come shopping with me," she offered. Jonathan nodded, stifled his tears, and allowed her to scoop him up. It was a ploy I recognized, having used it myself on a number of occasions: the instant this kid hit the car seat, he'd be out. To Larry, Carolyn said, "I'll just be gone a half hour or so. I need to find out what the heck a Turbo Builder is, because it's all Matthew's talking about for Christmas." Larry assured his wife that dinner would be at least another hour.

As he juggled pots on two stoves and settled disputes that continued to arise among the remaining children, he enlisted his mother, Nancy, to give me a tour of the house. She was clearly proud of the pale blue dining room. Copenhagen plates displaying the birth year of each Mallory child circled the room on a wooden ledge just above eye level.

"The war years were especially hard to get," she said, "but they're all there."

As we wandered through the house, I noticed framed Lechuguilla photographs adorning several walls. When Larry's father came in from his yard work, he saw me admiring a shot of a small Lech pool I recognized because of a particular crystalline formation it contained.

"Larry doesn't want the name of the pool getting out," he said, "but right here"—he pointed to a spot at the pool's edge— "is where he got his best hit. That's the home of the bug that eats breast cancer cells in a single gulp."

When Larry had put the last dish into the oven, he made a round of cocktails for the adults, then asked me to join him in the basement while he made a phone call to Diana and Emily Davis Mobley, who was staying with Diana over the holiday. Larry's cave gear hung from the rafters, still bearing a faint aroma of the cave. Larry handed me the phone and I said hello to Diana and Emily, feeling terribly disappointed that I wasn't going along with them in a few days. I took solace in the knowledge that, although I wouldn't be in Lechuguilla, I did in fact plan to get underground the day before Thanksgiving. My family would spend the holiday with Lee and Sharon Pearson, longtime caving friends living in Tennessee. On Wednesday, the husbands would go caving and the wives would hit the malls, while the kids of both families played together in a program at Knoxville's West Side YMCA, which Lee directed.

After Larry's phone call ended, we went upstairs to the pale blue dining room for a feast that lasted two hours. All seventeen family members, George the next-door neighbor, and I crowded the long formal table, digging into a bewildering array of dishes as Larry's sisters and parents regaled us with stories of the scientist as a child. Over dessert, Larry mentioned his wife's patience in letting him gallivant off not only to Lechuguilla but also to Hawaii on a regular basis. In fact, he planned to be collecting on the Big Island for most of the month of January.

"Need an assistant?" I asked.

✦

STUDY

A thousand miles away from Washington, in Fayetteville, Arkansas, Anne Taunton studied for an exam she would take the following Monday morning before tackling the now familiar twelve-hour drive to Houston. She planned to get in a few days' SEM work, then head back home to El Dorado for Thanksgiving Day with her parents and some visiting relatives. After the fun and celebrity of September, the semester had really snuck up on her. First she had presented her internship talk to a room crowded with senior scientists who fired hard questions at her. Several times, Dave McKay had risen to her defense, reminding the audience to ask questions related only to his intern's SEM work on terrestrial samples. She was twenty-one years old after all, he cautioned his peers, and she had conducted none of the chemical analyses on PAHs nor had she studied the carbonate formation temperature or isotopic signatures of the Allen Hills meteorite that the audience seemed so eager to discuss.

Back at school, Anne had been profiled in the campus paper and by local media and had been written up in the magazine of the college of arts and sciences. At the urging of her advisor, Derek Sears, she had given a presentation on her NASA work to the department. Sears had also tried to get her to attend a major scientific conference for the same purpose, but Anne had insisted she wasn't ready for that. She'd seen the sort of questions skeptics threw at Dave and Everett, who were senior scientists; she could just imagine what they'd do to a nervous undergrad. Even during the presentation on her home turf, several members of the biology department had sneaked in to ask tough, unanswerable questions about nanobacteria and the minimum necessary cell size to sustain life.

While Sears was clearly proud of his student's involvement in such highly public research, he also believed the McKay team had engaged in little more than wishful thinking. The McKay et al. paper was, he told her bluntly, poor science. He suggested to Anne that her NASA colleagues had conditioned her to find life where there was none. At best, perhaps they had found in ALH 84001 some organic contamination from the Antarctic ice; at worst, they had seen fossils in bits of mineral and microscope coating material. Either way, the team's visual evidence was weak, as was whatever visual support for that evidence Anne might find in terrestrial samples. He began pressuring her to create a senior honors project that would objectively bear out the fallacies he thought inherent in the team's work.

She made several proposals during the first few weeks of the semester, all of which he had rejected. Finally, another student suggested a project both could agree on: Anne would examine some of the lunar meteorites which had been retrieved from Antarctica—and which virtually all scientists agreed had originated on a truly, absolutely lifeless world. Lunar meteorites ought to be completely free of objects resembling the sort found in the Martian meteorite. If she could locate tiny rods or worms in pieces of the moon using the same NASA equipment that had uncovered the purported nanofossils from Mars, then McKay and his team (and the rest of the scientific world) would be forced to acknowledge that what they had seen in ALH 84001 was either Earthly contamination or nonliving minerals.

Whether or not one thing "looks like" another is, of course, a highly subjective judgment, so Anne had agreed to let a group of disinterested experts make the call. First she would try to obtain several photos of objects that *might* resemble biological remains in the moon rocks. If she succeeded, she would send them along with an equal number of ALH 84001 images to a test group of legitimate microbiologists without indicating which photo was which. She would ask them to classify the images, without giving them any further instructions or criteria. If the microbiologists she surveyed proved unable to separate Martian nanobacteria from unknown lunar squiggles, then the bias of the original investigators would be revealed. On the other hand, if a group of random microbiologists had no trouble identifying biological signatures in the Martian carbonates and failed to do so with nonbiological lunar objects, the study would support the validity of the original team's findings. Anne had refrained from emphasizing this possibility to her advisor.

The only problem with the project was that Anne still had a number of classes to complete for her degree and didn't see how she could put in the necessary time with lunar meteorites before the spring semester. So far, she had spent several weekends searching through hundreds of cracks and crevices in lunar meteorite samples she had been able to acquire from the JSC collection but had found nothing more biological-looking than occasional round spheres of the gold-palladium used to coat the samples. She had tried hard but still didn't have a single lunar image to use in the survey she planned. On the other hand, within thirty minutes of looking into a fresh section of ALH 84001 carbonates, she had easily found scores of rodlike objects, taking several new images that were every bit as enticing as McKay's original photos. Still, she had promised Derek she would find the best lunar match, and she felt that she would be able to do it. The experiment demanded that she succeed.

She would have a full two weeks over Christmas break to spend at JSC, but she doubted that would be enough time.

Assuming she did eventually find suitable fossil-like objects in the lunar meteorites, her survey of microbiologists would probably take several additional months. On top of everything else, she had fallen so far behind in a couple of classes that, for the first time in her college career, she had dropped them in order to preserve her high grade point average. Anne had reached a decision, which she planned to break to her parents over Thanksgiving: she wouldn't graduate in May. She would accept the second summer internship that NASA had offered her for 1997 and graduate in the fall of 1998. That would give her not only another summer at JSC, during which she could polish her project, but also a chance to decide what she wanted to do upon graduation.

She had never planned to go to graduate school; she had always planned to find a job, buy a car, have some fun. She knew now that she could easily land a technician position at JSC. But Sue Wentworth, Kathie Thomas-Keprta, Everett Gibson, Dave McKay, and several other scientists whom she admired tremendously had each pulled her aside to tell her the obvious—any real career in the research Anne had begun would depend upon her graduate education, and she was ideally situated for acceptance into the top graduate programs. The research was truly exciting. She wanted to stay with it.

The problem was that she had no idea of what to study at the graduate level—chemistry? microbiology? geology? At Princeton and two or three other schools, she knew, there were newly created departments of geomicrobiology, a field dedicated to the study of microbes in rocks. This was certainly closest to her current interests, but acceptance into the new programs was tough. And if she did get in, she would face difficult course work in a variety of disciplines, starting with a full year of undergraduate microbiology before she could even enroll in her first graduate class.

Thinking about these things made it a chore to concentrate on the literature exam she faced Monday morning. She opened her book and tried.

✦

SUNSHINE

Although I was no scientist, I had begun to play among them.

I had been granted a one-course teaching release at Henderson State University in order to enroll in a basic microbiology class. Halfway through the semester, I felt as though I had developed a knack for some of the techniques I had seen Larry and Diana employ. At least, my cultures tended to flourish under incubation, which was more than what could be said for the petri dishes inoculated by some of the less attentive of the nursing students who predominated in my class. At the dinner table, I would present my colored-pencil drawings of E. coli after Gram staining, or I would describe the surprisingly strong smell that rose from a forty-eight-hour culture of *streptococcus* I had sampled via a cotton swab shoved down my lab partner's throat. These nightly show-and-tell sessions inevitably delighted my five-year-old son just as they inevitably elicited stern looks from my long-suffering wife.

I learned that up to 15 percent of people admitted to hospitals acquire nosocomial infections—that is, they're infected by microbes living in the hospital. According to the Centers for Disease Control, about 20,000 people die from these infections every year, and the number is expected to rise drastically as various bacteria become resistant to traditional antibiotics. Larry's work took on new meaning when I realized that the discovery of novel antibiotics—such as those he hoped to extract from Lechuguilla—could give humanity another few decades of lead time against deadly bugs that had all but defeated penicillin and its derivatives.

I read the essays of Koch, Lister, and even that cantankerous Dutch lens grinder Anton van Leeuwenhoek. In October, I spent hours on the Internet studying new Galileo images of Europa as soon as they were posted: The moon was covered with broken plates of ice that had clearly rafted over a liquid surface, much like pack ice in the Arctic Circle. I read the analyses of these new images in the journal *Science*. Some felt the images indicated that liquid water might exist beneath no more than a few kilometers of ice. In the journal *Nature*, I followed the evolving plans for studying the lake beneath the Vostok research station in Antarctica. I read one *Scientific American* article on the Columbia River basalt organisms, another on the new evidence of a warmer, wetter Mars in the distant past, and I tracked down the suggested reading listed at the end of both pieces. I followed with some interest the acrimonious debate over the existence of nanobacteria that raged in the *Science* letters column.

I used interlibrary loan to obtain the reports of research teams that had extracted heat-loving, iron-eating bacteria from oil company drill holes up to a mile deep in Colorado and Virginia. Most of these bugs were obligate anaerobes, meaning they died when exposed to oxygen, so they could not have come from or survived at the surface. Yet genetic analysis showed that, despite the hot depths at which they lived and the wide geographical distance between them, the iron eaters in Colorado and Virginia were closely related to one another, much like Diana's bug from the Parkers Cave microbial mat and its relative that lived in the gills of deep-sea-vent worms.

And as I learned, I gradually crossed the line from detached observer to active participant. I no longer wanted to *write* about research into the subterranean biosphere; I wanted to *do* it. I wanted to find dark life, to design experiments that might reveal its secret nature. I wanted to collect new bugs not only in Lechuguilla but also in Movile, Villa Luz, and the ice caves of Mars. I wanted to look inside the many travertines I'd seen during years of travel to karst areas for evidence of nanobacteria. If I found it, I wanted to learn once and for all whether the nanobacteria were living organisms or something else. I'd lie in bed at night creating methods for culturing nanobacterial colonies visible to the naked eye, or running them through fine filters to extract their DNA. Even as I was learning the tenets of scientific objectivity, I began to toss journalist objectivity aside: I wanted in, personally, on the fun of what I had begun to perceive as a great turning point in human knowledge.

All of this hit home on a stunning fall day as Lee Pearson and

I scrambled toward the entrance of what I'll call Sunshine Cave, although that is not the name that appears on maps. We hiked past a pioneer cemetery, following a flank of the Cumberland Plateau in central Tennessee. We had been to the cave some years before. Even though it was listed in a number of popular guidebooks and had been visited for decades, we had found a series of short pits that led to what appeared to be virgin passage. The entrance lay at the base of a spectacular mountainside sinkhole perhaps 130 feet deep. A waterfall poured over the top of the sink, falling free of the undercut cliff to crash onto gigantic boulders that lay strewn about the floor. The resultant stream splashed into a large horizontal cave entrance.

Although it was possible to free-climb down one side of the steep sink, Lee and I had brought enough rope to rappel from the high side, gliding through 130 feet of empty space adjacent to the waterfall merely for the fun of it. Inside, the passage branched to the left and right. The left-hand tunnel petered out quickly, but the right led to a ledge about 10 feet above the floor of a large chamber—slightly too high to climb down without a rope. A passage off this chamber in turn ended at a pit of about 20 feet, at the bottom of which passages branched in several directions, including one slanted tunnel that led to additional short pits.

Lee had found a map of the cave prepared by a Tennessee cave club decades earlier; it had shown only a small portion of these deeper passages. What was more interesting, however, was that the large stream thundering into Sunshine vanished completely in the cracks and crevices of a breakdown pile just inside, never reappearing in any known branch of the cave. Somewhere beyond the rocks, without question, the water emerged in an active stream passage that could lead to many miles of new cave. Lee and I hoped to find a way to reach it.

On our previous trip, we had failed to carry sufficient rope to try all of the little pits. This time we had brought along more than enough. We worked our way down to the point where we had been previously forced to turn around. I began rigging a nylon static line to a boulder in order to rappel into a pit that looked no more 30 to 40 feet deep. As I did so, Lee noticed a dark hole high on the wall of the irregular chamber in which we stood.

"Why don't you check out the pit first," he said. "If it goes, I'll come down with you; but if it's a dead bottom, I want to check this little lead up here."

"Works for me."

I clipped my rappel rack on to the rope and stepped over the ledge. The pit was circular, perhaps 20 feet in diameter, with beautifully fluted sides that indicated occasional waterfalls. I bounced twice against the wall, then touched down gently in soft mud, sinking up to my ankles. Except for the marks made by the rope and my landing, the surface was smooth and unbroken. Either this was a virgin pit or recent water and mud had completely erased the evidence of any cavers who had preceded me. There was no obvious drainage outlet, but there were several low, tight openings around the perimeter, the largest of which was of slightly less than human proportion. I squatted for a closer look.

Sharp blades of limestone roofed the opening, but the floor was thick soft mud. I poked my finger into cool earth and became more convinced that the passage was truly virgin. The outer surface displayed a slight sparkle of mineralized crystals that was absent from the interior. Such layering could be an indication that cave soil had remained undisturbed for many years, perhaps centuries. I had noticed this sort of "virgin mud" many times in caves, but for the first time I wondered whether microbiology might have something to do with the sparkling surface. In cross section, the layers of lighter and darker lines near the mud's surface resembled a photo I had seen in my microbiology textbook of layers of various algae that inhabit the mud of tidal flats.

"There doesn't seem to be any passage down here," I shouted up to Lee, "but there's some really cool mud."

"Thanks, but I'll pass," he yelled, his voice echoing oddly through the pit. "I'm gonna check out this little climb."

"I'll see if I can scoop aside enough mud to get into the one crawl here, but it doesn't look too promising. Why don't you check your lead, and we can meet back at the rig point."

"Sounds good," he said.

I switched off my battery-powered lamp for a moment, watching the flickering glow of Lee's carbide light retreat from the edge of the pit and vanish. I stood for a while in the silent darkness, savoring the proximity of dark life, which I felt surrounding me. I thought of Larry, at that moment deep in Lechuguilla. At last I switched on the light, dropped to my belly in the mud, and began scooping the buttery stuff to the sides. I swam forward over the cool damp path as I cleared it, following the faint impression of an old watercourse. Four or five body lengths away from the pit, the passage became too small for easy excavation by hand. Coated in mud and unknown organisms, I wormed my way back to the rope. I used my rappel rack like a scraper, peeling the outer inches of mud from my nylon coveralls. I pulled my still-clean ascenders from my pack and climbed the rope.

Lee was nowhere in sight. I assumed his opening must have led to something, so I shed my mud-covered climbing harness, hauled up and coiled the rope I had just used, and worked my way into his tunnel. Ten minutes inside, I heard the muffled thump of footsteps in a large room somewhere ahead.

"Anyone home?" I shouted.

"We got no caves, now git!" said Lee, in the voice of a backwoods landowner.

I knew this response meant he had discovered something interesting. "What you got?"

"Oh, it's a pretty nice big room. Doesn't seem to do much, though. There's a low crawlway back behind you with a real interesting sound in it. But before I show you the crawl, you ought to come and see this room. Not that we're the first ones here."

As he said this, my head popped out from the tunnel and I saw what he meant. The irregular floor of the house-sized chamber was coated in several inches of thick mud, over which a single set of boots had previously wandered. We speculated as to which of several Tennessee cavers we knew might have happened upon the chamber during the past few years or decades. We both realized that the chance of additional passage here was slim, because anyone who could find their way to such a room could probably find any passage that lay beyond it. If a "going" lead had been there to be found, the room would have been crisscrossed with multiple prints from later survey trips. Still, we had to see for ourselves. Water dripping from the few stalactites hung here and there had carved tiny wells in the mud floor.

Looking over the chamber with new eyes, I saw that each drop-carved hole was ringed by tiny dots of gray fuzz that could only be fungal colonies. There were darker gray and black spots clinging to the drops of moisture on the limestone walls. These also evidently were colonies, but of a different type than those clinging to the mud spatters—probably mixtures of fungi, bacteria, and perhaps even archaea. On closer inspection I saw even smaller white dots that appeared to be aragonite and might well have been precipitated by bacteria.

To investigate even this single room thoroughly, I realized, would yield enough data for a microbiology dissertation. A sort of subterranean Walden, remarkable for its natural beauty and complexity, lay hidden in this dark cavern. I touched my index finger to one of the gray dots, smearing the tiny circle of greasy material with my thumb. I held it to my nose. It gave off a faint aroma not unlike the smell that had risen from Larry's Lechuguilla cultures in his Amherst lab, an aroma to which I could now assign a name. I whispered to the darkness, "*Actinomycetes.*"

I was beginning to see dark life everywhere. Just before driving to Tennessee, my wife, Kathy, and I had driven with the kids to Hot Springs for an afternoon of Christmas shopping. We hit several of the specialty shops that stand across the street from the row of historic bathhouses lining Central Avenue. As we walked out of the Toy Chest, where all three boys had spent an hour enthralled by a large display of wooden trains, the twins professed an immediate need of a public rest room. The closest one was across the street in the Fordyce, a circa 1915 bathhouse that serves as the national park visitors' center. The ranger at the information desk in the lobby directed us down a narrow staircase to the basement.

Just outside the rest rooms was a large glass window looking onto the bubbling, rock-lined pool over which the bathhouse had been built. After nature's calls had been answered, we took a few minutes to inspect the display spring. The pool was perhaps four feet by eight and two or three feet deep, enclosed by a well-lit tiled room. Large faceted quartz crystals lining the water's edge were clearly not native to the site; they had probably been brought in from one of the crystal mines near Mena, about thirty miles to the west. The spring's evident source was a crack less than a foot wide that extended downward and back into the hillside. The overflow poured from the pool into a mineral-encrusted iron pipe.

I noticed a white scum swirling on the surface, which at first glance looked to be composed of tiny Styrofoam spheres, such as those that would rise from a discarded, slowly dissolving coffee cup. I wondered how some careless visitor had been able to litter the pool through the sealed glass window, but then I saw two or three of the floating spheres pop up from within the crack. Whatever the little balls were, they were emerging from underground, along with the spring water. I looked more closely at the scum and realized that what I had first thought were spheres were actually discs, thin white circles a millimeter or two in diameter that rode the surface tension of the water. Every few seconds a few more floated up from the depths.

Excited, I returned to the information desk upstairs. While I waited in line behind a group of retirees with questions about bathhouse tours, Kathy took the boys out to the broad tiled porch. I watched them trying out the comfortable wooden rockers that had been conveniently placed there by the park service. At last I was able to ask the ranger about the floating white dots.

"Yes, those are very interesting," he agreed. "A geologist in Fayetteville studied them a couple of years ago. They're composed of a type of calcium carbonate called aragonite. When the springwater hits the air, it loses carbon dioxide, which causes crystals to precipitate out. The crystals are light enough to float on the surface tension."

"If hitting the air is what makes them form, why are they rising from below?"

"I guess the water starts losing carbon dioxide a few feet before it hits the actual surface."

"What makes them float?"

The ranger shrugged. "I'm not really sure. They must have small gas bubbles trapped inside."

"Could bacteria be involved somehow?"

"Oh no, it's strictly a chemical process," he said confidently. "There's some unusual algae and other organisms that have colonized the park's surface pools, but the springwater is actually sterile. It's heated by the natural radioactive decay of rocks deep underground to a temperature high enough to kill any bacteria. Here, you can read more about it in this brochure." The ranger then turned his attention to another group of visitors.

"Uh-huh," I said. "Thanks."

I walked out to the porch and unfolded the park's "Official Map and Guide." Under the heading "What's Special About This Water?" I found a paragraph that began:

> The most important thing about Hot Springs' thermal water is that it is naturally sterile. For this reason, the National Aeronautics and Space Administration chose this water, among others, in which to hold moon rocks while looking for signs of life. Even during the many early years that the springs were uncovered, the absence of bacteria in the water helped prevent the spread of disease.

"Yeah, right," I said, grinning broadly at this. I read it aloud to Kathy. "'Sterile.' I bet that water's about as 'sterile' as warm spit. If there's anything in it that really prevents disease, it's probably some kind of bacteria. Maybe a thermophile in there knows how to zap your garden-variety warm-spit bacteria, which is probably all they've ever tested for here."

"Could we give the bacteria a rest?" Kathy asked. Alex, our five-year-old, was rolling in hysterics at my "warm spit" analogy, to the clear amusement of a tourist couple nearby. She had a point.

"I guess I have had a one-track mind lately," I admitted, "but I'm continually amazed at how little anyone knows about this stuff. There's so much left to learn. It's truly frontier science."

•   •   •

So much to learn, I thought as I stood in Sunshine, smearing one of the cave's white dots across my finger, *so much to learn.* I touched the finger to my tongue, smiling as I tasted the unknown.

Lee interrupted my bacterial musings. "So do you want to see my interesting crawl?" he asked "Or would you rather stand around eating mud?"

"Lead on," I said. I followed him to a low opening not far from the lip of the small pit I had rappelled. It was bound top and bottom with smooth limestone. The opening was only a few inches tall but very wide.

"Scoot in there a few feet," Lee instructed. "Then be quiet a minute and tell me whether I'm hearing things."

I wriggled flat on my belly between the unyielding floor and ceiling. After a few feet, I lay still, closed my eyes, and heard what had excited Lee: the unmistakable rumble of water thundering over rocks, coming from somewhere ahead. Beyond this crawl lay the lost stream passage and glory.

"It's there all right," I said. "You weren't hearing things. But this passage doesn't look exactly passable." It stretched ahead as far as I could see, getting gradually smaller.

"I didn't want to get in there alone," he said. "But now that you're here and can grab my feet to pull me out, let me see how far I can push it."

"Be my guest." I backed out to let him in.

Lee is tall and big-boned, but he's always been thin. He soon snaked and grunted his way a good thirty feet inside the claustrophobia-inducing space. Having been in such places myself, I could tell when he reached the point where he had to exhale to gain any forward progress. With a full breath, the air in his lungs expanded his rib cage to the point where it hung him up. Exhaling created as much as two inches of wiggle room. He blew out, pushed a few inches forward with his toes, took a couple of shallow breaths, and then repeated the process.

Lying flat out to watch him, I could see that the passage eventually got too small even for Lee's determined effort. The stream was down there, somewhere, but this crawlway wouldn't be the way into it. Eventually Lee agreed. It took him half an hour to back out of the low spot into which he had wedged himself. Once he did, we left Sunshine, pausing at the entrance waterfall to rinse off some of the mud. I pictured millions of bugs pouring from me, carried by the stream back into the cave, where they would establish new colonies somewhere along the banks of a river that might never experience human presence or a single photon of light.

"Let's go back to Knoxville and watch some football," I suggested. "And next year, let's bring a shovel."

TEN

January 1997

We came at last to torn and ragged deserts of scorched and blistered lava—to plains and patches of dull gray ashes—to the summit of the mountain, and these tokens warned us that we were nearing the palace of the dread goddess Pele, the crater of Kilauea. . . . If you stand on the brink and close your eyes it is no trick at all to imagine that you are sweeping down a river on a large low-pressure steamer, and that you hear the hissing of the steam about her boilers, the puffing from her escape pipes, and the churning rush of water abaft her wheels. The smell of sulphur is strong, but not unpleasant to a sinner.

—Mark Twain
at the Kilauea caldera, 1866

Volcano

The tropical trade wind shoved me over a jagged, desolate landscape. Volcanic steam curled from a dozen holes in the surrounding plain, a rocky no-man's-land ringed by 200-foot cliffs that receded in the distance. I smelled a strong sulfur tang. Squinting in the bright sunlight, I could just make out a discreet white-on-brown National Park Service sign: "CAUTION—Thin Crust Area, Stay on Trail."

"Okay," Larry said, "this is where we leave the trail."

I look at him dubiously. "Thin crust. Meaning, you step on it and fall through?"

"More or less. Could happen. The lava here hardened around big gas bubbles, so it's hollow in places." Larry was already well off the trail, hiking toward a landmark he had picked out on a remote cliff. I followed cautiously.

Behind me walked Joel Aycock, a bearded telescope technician who worked at the nearby Keck Observatory. He and I were to be Larry's helpers for a week of collections in Hawaii Volcanoes National Park. Although Joel had done almost no caving beyond assisting Larry on an expedition the previous year, he was a longtime resident of the Big Island. He'd hiked nearly every square mile of its massive shield volcanoes—the closest thing on Earth to Olympus Mons, the great dead volcano of Mars. For Joel, this was a pleasant afternoon stroll. I, however, felt awed by the enormous barren bowl of the caldera that surrounded us. Crusted black lava crunched underfoot like so much broken dinnerware. The wind shoved me onward.

After twenty minutes off the trail, we reached an entrance pit perhaps 20 feet deep, a skylight leading down to a subway-tunnel-sized lava tube meandering beneath the surface. Scant decades ago, this tube had carried a vein of red lava from Kilauea's beating heart. Now the passage seemed solid and substantial, much like a limestone cave millions of years old. We worked our way into darkness over blocks of breakdown, watching for the telltale shift of boulders that would signal unstable footing. Groundwater percolated from the surface in drips and drops. Traversing the cave was like walking through a rain forest after a storm. Until the volcano flowed this way again, the cave's nutrients, temperature, and darkness would remain constant. This unchanging environment, poor in many of the minerals common to limestone caves, made the species that lived here extraordinarily fastidious. Traces of sulfur and iron provided the principal food sources.

Using the methods he had developed in Lechuguilla and Mammoth, Larry had created specialized—and secret—techniques to keep the shock of removal from killing all his samples. Earlier researchers who had examined fresh volcanic rock and similar low-nutrient environments for microbes often recorded the presence of "VNC" organisms—microbiological shorthand for "viable but nonculturable." In other words, live bugs were there, but they always died before anyone could get them into the lab. (This was why Carl Woese and Norm Pace had been able to revolutionize two hundred years of microbial classification: recently killed bugs could be run through a blender for rRNA analysis just as easily as live ones.) Through trial and error, Larry had become adept at easing lava-munching microbes into healthy captivity. Like a naturalist tracking a snow leopard or mountain gorilla, he learned to avoid the sort of direct assault that could harm his quarry. The tricks were fairly simple—but Larry knew them, and no one else did. At least none of his methods had appeared in the microbiology laboratory workbook I had completed in December. Before allowing me to join the expedition, Larry had asked that I not reveal the exact nature of how he kept the bugs alive. It was a condition to which I readily agreed. (Likewise, I had promised Bobby Camara, the natural resource manager for the Hawaiian Volcanoes National Park, that I would not divulge the name or precise location of any of the caves I visited. Because so many Hawaiian caves are culturally sensitive burial shrines, access to all of them is tightly controlled; fortunately, none of the caves where Larry was conducting his work contained cultural artifacts. These caves were much too young for ancient Hawaiians to have used them.)

We poked along in darkness, playing the beams of our cap lamps over black lava that seemed to swallow light. We were seeking a ribbon of orange survey tape. At last Larry spotted the study site, the first of two in this particular cave. We pulled petri dishes, slides, a sterilization kit, and other gear from our packs. Using a flame-sterilized pair of pliers, Larry carefully removed collection traps placed during a previous visit.

"You know," said Larry as he worked, "people will think I'm a nut and an idiot for spending all my time on this stuff. But then I'll get a critical hit, and I'll suddenly go from an idiot and a nut to this person who's been withholding vital information from the scientific community and has thus hurt all mankind."

"Sounds about par," I agreed.

Joel and I snacked on dried cuttlefish and macadamia nuts as Larry performed the bit of the voodoo that would turn VNC specks on the traps before him into colorful thriving colonies, preserving their warfare and weaponry intact.

"I see your observatory has been getting a lot of press for finding new planets," I said to Joel.

"It's a hot field right now," he agreed. "I think we're going to see a bunch of new planets over the next few years. You can't actually see the planets with the telescope, of course. What you see is the very slight wobble that the planets cause in the stars they orbit."

Joel listed several astronomers he had helped to launch planet quests in the thin air atop Mauna Kea, although the only names I recognized were Geoff Marcy and Paul Butler, probably the best known planet hunters. I had read that in November 1995, Michael Mayor and Didier Queloz of the University of Geneva made the controversial announcement that they had detected a Jupiter-sized planet in close orbit around Star 51 in the constellation Pegasus—the first "extrasolar" planet ever identified. Although other astronomers doubted the find at first, over the past year the twin Kecks and several other large telescopes had confirmed not only the planet at "51 Peg," as it came to be known, but also a half dozen others around additional stars. So far, astronomers had been able to detect only gas giants the size of Jupiter or larger. Even so, evidence was mounting that the formation of planets around stars was a routine event.

If planets were in fact common throughout the galaxy and if dark life could thrive beneath the surface of many kinds of planets, then life itself might pervade the universe, though perhaps not intelligent, technological life like us. Fussy as we are about oxygen, the climate, not getting pelted by giant meteorites, and other planetary luxuries, our kind might be exceptionally rare, at least in theory. But converging lines of astronomy and biology had begun to suggest that evolution's wet, chaotic engine could quite easily be chugging away around most of the stars that lit the night sky.

"Planets aren't the only thing Joel and his buddies find," said Larry, who had finished prepping the samples and was now stowing his gear. "Tell Mike about the spy satellites."

Joel laughed. "That was just some fun I had a while back." As we hiked down the tunnel toward the next site, Joel told the story. "I used to work on Maui with the NASA Lunar Ranging Experiment—LURE for short. My job was to bounce a three-gigawatt laser off reflectors that Apollo astronauts had left on the Moon and off special satellites launched as part of the program. The goal was to determine the exact distance, within a centimeter or so, to the targets.

"Across the road from LURE was the Air Force ARPA telescope and laser facility. Their job at the time was to track Russian spy satellites and photograph them for intelligence analysis. We shared the same watering hole in Haleakala. One night, I got to talking with a guy from across the street. He told me the story of an irate phone call, from the Russian consulate to the U.S. government, complaining that the U.S. had tried to destroy a Russian 'weather satellite'—wink, wink, nudge, nudge—with a high-powered green laser while it was passing over the Pacific. Now, the ARPA lasers were red and infrared and much lower power than our green laser."

"So you guys were zapping the Russians?"

Joel nodded. "That was the only reasonable conclusion. Three hippies with a high-powered laser managed to spark an international 'near incident.' Consider the fantastic odds. A beam packet with a diameter of twenty-four inches and a length of only two inches, fired in a burst that lasted less than two billionths of a second, happens by chance—by chance—to strike a small object floating in the near infinitude of orbital space."

"You think the Air Force just tried to pin the blame on you, that they did it themselves?"

"I don't see how. We had the only laser in the Pacific with that kind of power. If they'd had one like it at ARPA, I would have known about it."

We passed a skylight to the surface and continued deeper into the cave.

"By the way," Joel said. "It gets a bit hot ahead. You might want to run some of this over your glasses to keep them from fogging." He handed me a bar of soap and a paper towel.

A few hundred yards down the tube we reached a junction. Larry stooped into a branching passage, where the temperature immediately shot up. We pressed forward into a steam cloud. It was exactly like walking into a wet sauna. My cave clothes were instantly soaked. Even with soap on the lenses, I couldn't see through my fogged glasses. I was grateful for my helmet as it cracked loudly against the low ceiling. We hunched over, trying to spot the orange flagging as we knuckle-walked along. The ground became slimy with steam-loving bacteria.

"Look on the left wall," Larry said. "It's down here somewhere, but in these conditions we might walk right by it."

At last I spied a fuzzy orange line. "Over here," I said, unpacking gear as quickly as I could manage. A person couldn't stay in a room like this for very long. The steam carried just the faintest whiff of sulfur. It reached into my lungs, reminding me of the smelly humidifier my mother used to run when I had a cold.

"Time me," Larry said, flopping out his gear. "This is going to be a record for fast collection."

I timed him: We were repacked and moving again in under six minutes. Joel led the way—not back out, but further in.

"There's a back door ahead," he explained. "I think it'll be quicker."

A few minutes later, we emerged from one of the steaming vents I had viewed in the distance from the surface trail. The trade wind dried our sweat, and we crossed the caldera to make another collection before lunch.

What is it with microbiologists and Thai food?

When I had first visited Larry Mallory in his Amherst lab, he took me to lunch at his favorite restaurant, a spicy Thai place just off the college town's picturesque central square. When I had landed to a pink Honolulu sunset at the start of our current expedition—extra jet-lagged due to a two-hour ground delay after boarding at LAX—I had fought my way through rush-hour traffic to the University of Hawaii. I found the oceanography department and eventually located Jim Cowen's office. After exchanging several E-mail messages regarding the Gorda Ridge microbial plume, he had invited me to stop by and see him on my way to the Big Island. He immediately suggested that we eat dinner at his favorite restaurant, a Thai place.

Cowen had been busy since his Gorda Ridge adventure. Loihi, a seamount off the eastern coast of the Big Island that will one day break the surface to form the newest real estate in the Hawaiian chain, had been the source of a tremendous seismic event in July. For two weeks it had rumbled with earthquakes and small explosions; it had been venting lava and hot water ever since. "I'll tell you about it over appetizers," he said. "I could really go for some *kai nai ko koey.*"

I followed his car out of the university parking lot, becoming hopelessly disoriented as he led me through a labyrinth of shabby back streets that I vaguely recognized from chase scenes in episodes of *Hawaii 5-O* and *Magnum, P.I.* I had not yet checked into my hotel, a budget high-rise where I planned to grab a few hours' sleep before a predawn flight to Hilo. I wondered how I'd ever find my way to it after Cowen and I had parted company. We parked in a gravel lot behind a deserted filling station and walked into a small, family-run restaurant that smelled of paradise.

Like Larry, Jim Cowen was tall and slender, with the sort of chiseled looks one finds in *Esquire* clothing ads. But if Larry's pale skin and dark hair hinted at an affinity for the underground, Jim's beach-boy tan and sun-flecked hair bespoke the open sea. "So tell me what you're doing on the Big Island," he said as we sat down.

I described Larry's work with Biomes and the sort of collections he had done in Lechuguilla. Larry had already been on Hawaii for two weeks, I explained, collecting from a state preserve on the island's southwest coast. For the portion of the expedition I would join, he planned to focus on caves in the national park, with perhaps a one-day excursion to a long, newly discovered cave in another state preserve near the center of the island.

As I talked, Cowen's eyes brightened. "Any other time, I'd force you to take me along," he said, "but I'm tied up with lectures and grant meetings all week. It sounds like great fun, and Larry sounds like someone I'd love to compare notes with."

I tried to talk him into playing hooky and coming along anyway, without luck, as we ordered a variety of spicy and sweet coconut dishes. "So tell me about Loihi," I said.

In July, Jim explained, the Loihi seismic event was recorded on the Hawaii Volcano Observatory's seismometer grid. The effects of oceanic volcanic eruptions and collapses can range from increased carbon dioxide emissions to tsunamis and landslides that destroy all life in the surrounding sea. In quick response, the National Science Foundation had funded a cruise, much like the one that had observed the Gorda Ridge event. This had been followed by extensive NOAA-funded research in September and October.

Cowen and a number of his colleagues had found that the southern part of Loihi's summit, shaken by swarms of sea-floor earthquakes and the sudden withdrawal of magma, had collapsed. A crater nearly a mile across and a thousand feet deep had appeared. For this to have happened, as much as 100 million cubic meters of volcanic material had to have plunged downward. A four- to five-square-mile area of the summit had been transformed, strewn with bus-size volcanic rocks, some precariously perched along the rim of the crater. "Pele's Vents," a much-studied hot-water source on the southern rim of the volcano, previously considered very stable, had disappeared. In its place was an enormous steep-walled black hole, now named "Pele's Pit."

"So naturally I got into a tiny submarine and went into Pele's Pit," Jim said.

"Of course," I agreed. "How could you not?"

"The diving was a little dicey," he admitted.

"How dicey?"

"There was so much bacterial matter, mats of it flying everywhere, that you couldn't really see the sides of the pit, so the sub pilot had to kind of feel around it as we went. A couple of times we felt our way into cracks that we had trouble backing out of."

• • •

Seawater was flowing down into the newly formed pit, where it percolated through the volcanic structure, mixed with minerals and deep bacterial matter, then flowed out over a lip on Loihi's western edge. Jim and his pilot encountered vents fairly early in the dive but decided to wait for a better vent field deeper down before starting to sample. But the sub kept getting stuck at dead ends. An hour before the scheduled end of the dive, the sub brushed against an unseen wall, crushing one of the thrusters. The two men inside couldn't back up. "We were wedged underneath an overhang with one thruster gone. We had to kind of angle out of it, going back and forth like getting out of a parallel parking spot, not knowing if the ceiling was going to collapse at any second. Boulders were rolling past the window.

"The guys who pilot these subs are pretty cool customers. This was the first time I could remember seeing a pilot get nervous, which made me nervous. Anyway, eventually we got out of the crack and surfaced. We fixed the thruster with spare parts on the ship, and went back the next day. Then I had better luck sampling." With deftly wielded chopsticks, Jim lifted a chunk of fish slathered in red pepper sauce to his mouth and swallowed.

"Because the pit was so deep and narrow, it acted as a kind of reservoir, keeping the temperature up and keeping out the amount of normal seawater you usually see around vents. I've never seen such rich life. We'd remove a huge mat from a rock, and the next day we'd come to the same spot and it would have grown back. I think we got a glimpse of what the biosphere must be like deep below the sea floor."

As our conversation progressed in the crowded little restaurant, I kept noticing other diners turning their heads at us in irritation, so I kept trying to quiet down. But I was grateful we had been so loud in our excitement and considered it a good omen for the coming expedition when our waitress, a young Hawaiian woman, admitted she had been listening and asked what I would be doing on the Big Island. I gave her a thumbnail version.

"What's your name?" she asked. I told her. "Oh, yeah, of course, you're the guy who wrote *Cave Passages*."

"You've read it?" I said, dumbfounded. "You're one of the twelve people not related to me who actually read my book?"

"Sure, a friend gave it to me who knew I like nature stuff. It was great." With that, she earned a tip entirely out of proportion to the quite reasonable price of the meal.

I recounted my conversation with Jim as I rode with Larry and Joel down the winding coast road toward the site of the only lava then flowing from Kilauea. For months, a river of magma had been sliding down the mountain just below the surface, emerging from an active lava tube at the water's edge to form a shield of new land. Larry didn't plan to collect samples near the hot flow itself, since microbes needed at least a few weeks to colonize fresh lava. We had decided to view the red stream simply as tourists, once we had finished with some caves not far from the road. At the entrance to one of these caves, a tight tunnel beneath precariously balanced boulders that shifted to the touch, we had been turned back by the strong stench of rotten eggs.

"That's hydrogen sulfide," Larry had warned, stopping short. "Deadly poison. In concentration, it can burn your lungs right up."

"How did you collect in here before?" I asked.

"It was never there when I was here before."

"What happens if the gas fills the cave while you're inside?"

"Hopefully you'd smell it in time and get out," Larry said. "But maybe not. Could be you'd just die." He added that, upon due consideration and reflection, he proposed to remove this particular cave from his sample list. Joel and I concurred, and the motion carried.

Thus we were following a winding road from a cool green forest of cycads down to rocky cliffs that overlooked the vast blue Pacific. Lava had crossed the road the year before, creating a new end of the line. We parked here, chatting for a while with a ranger who described the various eruptions she'd seen in two decades at the park. We then hiked a few hundred yards to where a crowd had gathered at the best lava-viewing area. A ranger shared her binoculars and answered questions. Several photographers had set up tripods on the rocks, supporting large telephoto lenses aimed at the flow. One of them let me take a look through his viewfinder.

At first, all I could see was a great cloud of steam at the water's edge, still some distance away. But the experienced lava watchers said we'd be able to see more after dark, so I found a comfortable rock and waited. As the sun gradually sank behind the mountain and a million stars emerged overhead, we began to see brilliant red tongues licking from the lava tubes, hissing new land into being, pushing the coastline a few feet in the general direction of Loihi and its pit of hidden life.

ELEVEN

APRIL 1997

And so these men of Indostan
Disputed loud and long,
Each in his own opinion
Exceeding stiff and strong,
Though each was partly in the right,
And all were in the wrong!
  —JOHN GODFREY SAXE
  from an Indian legend

EUROPA, EUROPA

"In light of the recent news that has brought us together," said Richard Morita, the world's preeminent expert on Antarctic microbes, "I think I should begin by pointing out that it was the noted microbiologist F. M. Harold who first recognized that each novel idea in science passes through three stages before gaining wide acceptance. The first stage is a response from the scientific community that the finding is simply not true. Second comes the admission that the finding may be true, but it is not important. The third and final stage is agreement that the idea is both true and important, but by then, of course, it is no longer new."

The comment drew appreciative laughter from the thirty or so invited scientists and one uninvited (but not unwelcome) reporter who had assembled in a basement conference room of the Pasadena Holiday Inn. We had gathered for a three-day event entitled "Exploring the Ice and Ocean Environments: International Workshop on Instrumentation for Earth and Europa." A few blocks away, at the Jet Propulsion Laboratory, the instrumentation team of the Galileo space probe was giving a televised press conference. They would list the reasons why all the data gathered by the probe thus far pointed to the existence of a liquid ocean beneath Europa's ice. Ron Greeley of the Arizona State University, a key scientist on the Galileo team, was at the JPL with them, but he had already given us the same talk before heading to the studio, showing us recently received slides of the Jovian moon.

Greeley had explained the evidence attesting to massive deformation of the ice: Some images suggested erosion from below by a fluid that had filled in impact craters before solidifying. Some scenes looked geologically old due to multiple craters superimposed upon one another, while others appeared relatively young—less than a million years, according to Greeley. Even I knew that in a geological sense, a million years was the same thing as a week ago Tuesday: whatever processes had smoothed over the older craters might still be occurring today. Put another way, the passages of Lechuguilla Cave have been in existence at least six million years longer than the present surface of Europa.

In Greeley's photos one could pick out individual blocks of ice that had rafted apart, broken up, and spun over a liquid surface that later refroze. He showed how they fit together like a jigsaw puzzle. Density studies by the Galileo probe indicated that the moon's water shell (whether frozen or liquid) was over 60 miles thick. Thus, if the frozen portion were only a few miles deep, then the liquid below it would represent more water than in all of Earth's oceans combined. Europa, not Earth, might be the wettest world of the solar system.

And now Rick Morita, who had been finding cold-loving microbes buried within the ice of Antarctica since the late 1950s, had the rapt attention of scientists who a few years earlier might have dismissed his work as nothing more than laboratory contamination and wishful thinking. Such was the reaction that much of the scientific establishment had heaped upon Dave McKay and members of his team with regard to their findings in the Martian meteorite. The scientific contentiousness had reached such a level that it had been noted by *Newsweek*, in an article which made some of McKay's opponents sound like prizefighters preparing to enter the ring. I had witnessed some of this arm-waving scientific disdain firsthand two weeks earlier, at the twenty-eighth annual Lunar and Planetary Science Conference (LPSC) at the Johnson Space Center.

In the classic children's story, six blind men of Indostan attempt to determine through scientific analysis the exact nature of the elephant. Their familiar (and wrong) answers are an elephant is very like a wall, a spear, a snake, a tree, a fan, and a rope. The moral: you can't assume the nature of a complex object merely by feeling one of its parts. It was a lesson worth remembering as I tried to make sense of the bewildering array of scientific evidence concerning ALH 84001 presented at the LPSC. In just eight months, the brownish doorstop had become one of the most studied objects in human history, subjected to far more scientific scrutiny than had been applied to the Shroud of Turin. The rock had been sliced like a salami, and dozens of fragments had been shipped to researchers all over the globe. Many of the researchers, including several teams funded by NASA, had reported evidence that appeared to negate the original paper's suggestions of life. They had found that carbonates had formed at extremely high temperatures, the PAHs were from the Antarctic ice, or that the magnetite crystals were nonbiological. Yet just as many studies supported the existence of fossilized Martian life, in some cases directly and convincingly refuting points raised by the doubters. If anything, the new studies had made McKay and Gibson more firmly convinced that the nanofossils were real than they had been when they first published the *Science* paper.

Each time a negative paper appeared, the host university of one of the authors would issue a press release and headlines around the world would flash: "Study Finds Mars Rock Lifeless." (I don't know why they used the same headline, but I saw this one several times, along with "Mars Life Declared Dead" and the slightly more hopeful "Mars Life on Life Support.") With each negative paper published to date, Gibson or McKay found and pointed out significant errors in the methods the scientists used, the conclusions they had reached from legitimate methods, or occasionally both their methods *and* their conclusions. These objections were mentioned at the bottom of each "Lifeless" article. This process repeated itself every few weeks. On the other hand, several new studies supported the team's findings, including two in the journal *Science* revealing apparently conclusive isotopic evidence that at least some of the carbonates in the rock had been deposited at relatively low temperatures conducive to life.

Nearly all of the researchers who showed up to debate the issue before an LPSC audience of over five hundred people agreed that the rock had been blasted from Mars by a meteoric impact some 15 million years ago and that it was chemically complex. All parties were also in agreement that a clean sample returned from Mars might be the only means of settling the question of life. Beyond that, all agreement ended. It was clear from the debates I saw in Houston that the "pro-lifers" and "anti-lifers" were becoming ever more entrenched in their beliefs, and that members of both camps had mustered reasonable scientific evidence to back them up. But, as with the elephant in Indostan, I realized that the rock's great age and amazing complexity made it easy to refute virtually every argument: Each piece is very different, and nearly every study had been based on evidence gleaned from a single tiny fragment.

Some of the key magnetite crystals could have been formed at low temperatures by ancient magnetotactic bacteria and others at high temperatures by natural—but lifeless—processes. Some of the meteorite's carbonates might well have been cooked into being at high temperatures as a result of impact shock, or even several major impacts during the billions of years that the rock lay in place on Mars. But the famous "Oreo cookie rim" carbonates and the fossils within them might just as easily have formed in relatively cool groundwater when the rock was young. A portion of the PAH molecules could have entered the meteorite via bacteria in Antarctic ice, while others had ridden from Mars undisturbed.

Despite more than a dozen major presentations at the LPSC, a dozen more at this conference in Pasadena, and over a hundred new studies of ALH 84001 then underway, many of those with whom I spoke were beginning to think that the rock would never produce a definitive answer regarding past life on Mars. But if the rock hadn't yet taught those in the space community about life on Mars, it had taught some of them a great deal about life on Earth. Dark-life topics were popping up in scientific conferences, space-related journals, and popular magazines such as *Scientific American* and *Discover* with increasing regularity.

Here in the conference room in Pasadena, I recognized some of the faces I had seen in Houston. But if the thousand scientists gathered for the LPSC had been largely argumentative, even belligerent, the handful here now appeared congenial and like-minded. Instead of debating the existence of nanofossils in an ancient rock, they spoke of their desire to bring back live bugs from beneath the earth and beyond it.

The workshop's five organizers included three mission planners from the JPL, an instrument designer from Abbott Laboratories, and a NASA scientist from the Ames Research Center whom many considered NASA's foremost exobiologist. The last was Chris McKay (no relation to Dave), who was also a noted expert on Mars, the outer planets, and their moons. He was a principal scientist of the forthcoming Cassini mission to Saturn. The workshop's purpose was to bring together the Russian experts who had discovered Lake Vostok; the Galileo instrument team and other experts in designing remote-sensing devices for interplanetary travel; and microbiologists who had successfully sampled extreme organisms from Antarctica, deep-sea vents, and Lechuguilla Cave. The idea was to have all these people, in the words of one JPL organizer, "think out loud with us." Specifically, after a series of formal talks representing each type of expertise in the group, the scientists would split into small teams to brainstorm robotic devices for sampling Lake Vostok in three to five years, to be followed by a mission to Europa a few years after that. In addition to Rick Morita, Chris McKay had invited Larry Mallory and his Biomes partner Miles

Hacker; Jim Cowen's shipmate and fellow University of Hawaii faculty member Gary McMurtry; and several other leading names in the hunt for dark life.

These scientists were to generate ideas for what to pack aboard a two-stage device tentatively dubbed the "cryobot." Shaped like a coffee urn and kept at about the same temperature, the cryobot would slowly melt its way through the ice of Vostok Station and later Europa, unwinding a thin communication cable and allowing the ice to refreeze behind it as a hermetic seal. Upon hitting water, the cryobot would release a small free-swimming probe called the "hydrobot," which would take off and look for life. At least that was the plan. How these machines might accomplish their missions had yet to be seen.

Chris McKay, a fit, tall, bearded man who looked like a caver (and was, with several Lech trips under his belt), was more direct in explaining the workshop mission at the meeting's start. He displayed the most recent version of the Tree of Life from Norm Pace's lab, saying, "We have only one data point for the study of life, and we're it. The fact that there is a single tree implies that there's a root for that tree, and this is a very important point for considering Europa. At some point on that tree is the ancestor from which the rest of the tree evolved, and that point, as is currently understood by the experts that map this kind of tree, is right here"—he pointed to a lower branch—"between the eucarya and the archaea. The interesting thing about that point is that it tends to be populated by thermophilic sulfur bacteria, so in theory, the common ancestor of life on Earth, the great-great-great-ancestor of all of us, was a thermophilic sulfur bacterium."

McKay discussed the possible implication: that thermophilic sulfur bacteria are at the origin of life. "But there's an important distinction here," he said. "What the tree gives us is what the common ancestor was like, but that organism could have just been the leftover, the sole survivor of some global catastrophe that wiped out all other life." Perhaps it survived merely by chance. Perhaps it was thermophilic and thus able to hide out in a deep vent, or perhaps life does originate in hot springs with sulfur-rich environments.

"What do we know about the origin of life?" he asked. "Precious little. Since we don't have good data, we do what the social scientists do, which is literature analysis instead."

After the laughter died down, McKay separated origin-of-life theories into three broad categories: extraterrestrial, terrestrial organic, and terrestrial inorganic. "Let me make a small philosophical point about life in the context of these theories. The fact that we only know about one type of life leads to the famous saying you can't compare apples and oranges." He took down the Tree of Life and put up another chart, listing genetic variations, and continued:

> In fact, this is a plot that compares apples and oranges, and the point is actually very important. If you want to understand fruit as a broad category, you have to compare apples and oranges, and you want to compare bananas and tomatoes as well. And this is the point we have in exobiology; we only have one example. We've got apples, if you will, or oranges. In order to understand life on a broad level, we need additional data points.
>
> There are three ways of looking into it: One, make life in the lab. People have been trying for fifty years but don't have much to show for it. Two, go find life on Mars, Europa, or extrasolar planets—go there and dig it up. Or three, wait for a phone call from other life, which is what the Search for Extraterrestrial Intelligence has been doing, with the same lack of success as those trying the first method. So with planetary programs, our approach is to go out and look.

McKay then listed the best criteria for identifying a place to "go look" for life: liquid water, carbon, and a few important trace elements. The solar system turns out to be rich in all of these ingredients except liquid water. Carbon, for example, is actually far richer in the outer solar system than it is here on Earth.

> So if you can find liquid water anywhere in the outer solar system, you have a good chance of finding the right ingredients for life. If you have an ocean on Europa, is it possible that life could have originated there? Well, at least one theory for the origin of

life would be consistent for having life originate in a deep subsurface vent on Europa, because this theory postulates that life
originated on Earth in a subsurface vent.

But is there any other way? One speculation is life can be
transferred from one planet to the other. It's becoming quite the
rage these days. Meteorites are scattering from one planet to
another. We now know that pieces of Mars have been knocked
off Mars and after orbiting the sun for a while crashed into Earth.
From what we've found in Antarctica, it's safe to say that at
least a couple hundred pounds of Mars falls on Earth every year.

It took little imagination, McKay suggested, to suppose that
by a similar mechanism pieces knocked off Earth might orbit
around and hit the outer solar system, on a trajectory that would
intersect Europa. The scientific paradigm has been that planets
are biologically isolated, but that may not necessarily be true.

We have life appearing on Earth almost instantaneously from a
geological perspective, right at the end of the early bombard-
ment, when there was still a lot of planet banging going around,
big impacts exchanging bits and pieces between the planets. As
a result of the intense study of the Allen Hills meteorite, we're
learning now that objects flung into interplanetary space by
impacts never heat up to a point that would sterilize life on
those objects. There's evidence now that the rock from Mars
spent ten million years in space, then crashed into Earth, but
never got hot enough to kill everything on it. In short, the planets are always swapping spit. Maybe life has made the trip back
and forth several times. Perhaps life on Earth originated on early
Mars, and we're all Martians.

After McKay's talk, a young woman from the Scripps
Oceanography Institute asked him, "In light of the tremendous
cost, what is the motivation to look for life on other planets?
Why do it?"

"I would answer in two ways," McKay said. "One is philosophical. To me, one of the most profound questions of the universe is, are we alone? Is Earth the one phenomenon of life? The

second is more mundane and scientific. We have life chemistry here in a particular way. Well, so what? Is that the only way to do it? Are there better ways to do it? We may learn a lot about life that could have practical advantages here by studying life from somewhere else." As he warmed to his answer, McKay began twirling his pointer like a baton and pacing across the room. "If we bring life back from Europa, it will teach us one of two things. Going back to the Tree of Life on Earth, all of the new things we're finding, even in exotic places like Antarctica or Lechuguilla Cave or deep-sea vents, are just adding new branches to this tree. That's great, and we learn a lot about life when we do that, but to find another tree"—at this he turned and tapped his pointer against his Tree of Life poster—"a second genesis"—tap! tap!—"a completely independent example of life"—tap! tap! tap!—"that would give us a whole different order of magnitude in our understanding of life."

McKay lowered his pointer and walked toward the woman who had asked the question. "That's one of the things we could get from life on Europa," he said. "But if we got there and found the other thing, life that was somehow related to one of the branches of the tree that we already have, well, that would be very interesting, too."

After McKay's talk, two Russians gave the history of the work at Vostok, speaking with almost impenetrable accents of their success in culturing live microbes from even the deepest portions of the borehole. They were followed by Larry Mallory, who showed numerous slides of Lechuguilla and discussed the hundreds of taxa he could pull from a single tiny pool. Miles Hacker then championed the idea that valuable natural products would inevitably flow from the discovery of new and exotic microbes, whether extraterrestrial or subglacial. After Ron Greeley and Steve Squyres discussed late-breaking Galileo results from Europa, Morita summed up for the crowd his four decades of experience in finding microbes where common wisdom had held that life could not exist.

"Although we have heard a great deal lately about thermophiles and hot environments," Morita said, "it is important to remember that the cold environment dominates. The polar regions make up fourteen percent of the planet's surface. The oceans make up seventy percent, and more than ninety percent of the oceans remain at a temperature below five degrees Celsius. Much of the remaining liquid water occurs not in streams and lakes, but in mountain glaciers, caves, and deep aquifers, all of which tend to maintain a cold temperature."

Morita used the term "psychrophile" for cold-loving organisms, which he defined as those capable of growth at freezing or near-freezing temperatures. He also added that he had collected "extreme psychrophiles" that were quite capable of growth below freezing, at -5° Celsius. These microbes, which created their own internal antifreeze, actually exhibited slower growth at temperatures a few degrees above freezing, and would quickly die off at temperatures even a few degrees above that. Morita also described "psychrotrophic" organisms in Antarctica and elsewhere that were seasonally cold. These tended to shut down all metabolism while frozen, growing only for short periods whenever sunlight on surrounding sediments melted the bit of ice that contained them.

From experience, Morita had learned that warm pipettes, petri dishes, or hands would quickly kill psychrophiles. For many years, tests of Antarctic ice had yielded no microbes, he explained, because the tests were conducted in heated laboratories, which killed all samples before they could be studied. But with properly cooled instrumentation and laboratories, it was actually quite easy to recover bugs from the Antarctic ice.

"For decades, the term 'viable but nonculturable' was applied to these bugs," he said. "This was a polite way of saying, 'Huh, I guess I killed them all.' " With care, Morita explained, he learned to keep his cultures alive, often for long periods of time. He possessed one Antarctic culture that had lived happily in cold storage since he had collected it in 1963. Another had spent the past three years at -5° Celsius, yet had doubled in size. He had cultured bugs from a subglacial clay that had been trapped beneath hundreds of feet of ice for 1.5 million years. This, he said, was relatively young. He accepted the validity of several studies published during the previous decade which had described live microbes cultured from amber up to 40 million years old and from dried specimens preserved in salt deposits in four different parts of the world at ages ranging from 225 to 275 million years.

Perhaps the most interesting thing about microbes preserved in stasis, whether by freezing or by drying in salt, was that they tended to shrink in size. "When starvation sets in," he said, "they will rapidly divide, forming what has been variously called nanobacteria or ultramicrobacteria. These very small forms, most of which will easily pass through a 0.2 micron filter, are in fact dominant in the cold environment." Beginning in 1988, when high-resolution scanning electron microscopes first made their detection possible, Morita had found nanobacteria in every type of ice he had examined. He now believed that they were common in all low-nutrient, oligotrophic environments, where the starvation strategy of at least some organisms was to shrink into the smallest possible packet that could start life over again when conditions improved.

The means by which they did this appeared to be the same method cavers used to preserve food for a long underground sojourn: dehydration. Frank Volke, a specialist in biological membranes at the University of Leipzig, had calculated that if small, spherical microbes could somehow squeeze excess water from within their cells, going from a typical 70 percent solution down to a water content of only 20 percent, they could perform all required cellular functions at a diameter of 75 nanometers. This was the exact size of many of Bob Folk's nanobacteria specimens, as well as some of the frozen cells Morita had extracted from Antarctic ice. Volke had shown that cells could theoretically survive at this size and water content by using the two-dimensional space of their cellular walls—made of a moist substance called phospholipid—as the medium for processes normally carried out within the wet interior of larger cells. Volke supported his 20 percent estimation for water content with experiments he performed on frozen protein solutions. In these solutions, the rapid speed with which certain enzymes reacted could only be explained by a 20 percent water content; within live cells, freezing seemed to encourage the production of similar enzymes.

After Morita's enthusiastic expansion of the extreme limits of "life as we know it," the group broke into four teams to consider the in situ study of Lake Vostok and Europa. Larry and Miles were assigned to the "geological issues" team, which included two of the workshop's initial organizers: Joan Hovarth, who manages JPL alliances with various businesses, and Tzyy-Wen Yeng, a spacecraft instrument designer from Abbott Laboratories. Also on the team were Lonne Lane, a senior member of the JPL Galileo instrumentation team, with experience on interplanetary probes going back to the Viking and Pioneer missions; Gary Wilson, a young Antarctic researcher originally from New Zealand; Bridget Landry, an equally young data specialist for the Mars Pathfinder mission; and Gindi Lynch, an undergraduate employee of JPL. Landry and Lynch had already begun testing prototype cryobot elements with a research group based at the University of Nebraska.

These eight grabbed soft drinks and coffee and found chairs around a folding table in "Justines 2," a windowless cubicle created by folding an accordion wall across a larger conference room. I sat at the table with them, promising those present (and myself) that I would listen and not participate in the brainstorming session.

"These are the key questions," Joan Hovarth began. "What are the important scientific questions? What must we determine to answer them? What must we measure, and how? With what relative prioritization? How will we take samples?"

"Well, we'd have to get into the liquid water to find life," Miles Hacker said, "But maybe we could find evidence of it within the ice itself."

"From my experience in Antarctica," Gary Wilson said, "you don't find life in ice or water, but in sediments. What I would want to do is look for trapped sediments, or, on Europa, look for sediments on the surface that have been splashed up by impacts."

Mallory agreed. In Lechuguilla, he seldom found organisms

on rock or free-floating in water, but nearly always found them at the interface between water and some other substance, whether rock, mud, air, or a glass collection slide. "You can't just poke randomly and expect to get anything," he said. "You need to get up next to it and choose the best interface. What we need to do is design a Mark I Hairy Eyeball that can do this."

The group began discussing various sediments and how one might spot them.

"Well," said Lonne Lane, "let's keep in mind that finding a viable life form would be enormously exciting to a lot of people. But I would deem the mission highly successful if we found an adequately organized organic molecule. So the question is, how dead can it be and still be a well-organized organic molecule?"

"So you're breaking down life into one well-organized organic molecule?" asked Hacker.

"That sort of leads to a whole different set of questions," said Larry.

"The question is strange," admitted Lane, "but a molecule is simple and therefore possible. I have been very fortunate to have been to seven of the nine planets, looking at, flying to, and trying to understand them." The pride in his voice couldn't have been more evident if he had made the journeys personally, as opposed to building a generation of space-faring machines. "I think that I have a well-honed feel for how difficult the problem is, even taking the simplest experiment out of the laboratory and putting it on a spacecraft."

"I agree," said Hacker. "I think if we find even a fingerprint of life, we're in good shape."

"Even if it's not a sustainable sample of life, is there a way of getting your sensor to know that it's there, or was there at some point?" asked Lane.

"Really that's two questions," said Larry. "One, is there fossil evidence of some sort of past life? Two, are biological compounds present?"

They began discussing the minimum size of an ice or sediment sample that could be reasonably examined in order to answer either of these questions. Lane clearly favored an approach for Europa that would avoid the hazards of a cryobot-type mission, finding life signatures instead on material thrown across the surface by impacts or ice volcanism—certainly, there would be no question of planning a mission through the ice until the exact depth was known. Although the early Galileo results had a number of experts speculating that the ice was no more than a mile or two thick, it could just as easily have been ten, twenty, or a hundred. But if life signatures could be detected by a surface examination, such a mission could be planned and launched on a far shorter time scale than what the cryobot-hydrobot would entail.

"What would be the disadvantage of having one payload go up and send out several different exploratory units?" Hacker asked. "Then we could have identified geography that we want to go after."

"The technology is certainly possible," Lane said, "but the reality of the budgeting process is such that separate landers would vastly multiply the cost of the mission."

"Absolutely," agreed Bridget Landry. "Having a separate probe on Galileo boosted its cost by a factor of . . . I think it was two point five. Even two identical probes adds a huge cost."

"But we also realize that if you go to any one location from orbital information only, there's a high risk that the location won't pan out as you expected," said Lane. "Therefore, our philosophy might be to make whatever we send simple and complete to try to replicate a life-sampling process that can be multicycled."

"Could you have real simple test points, then," asked Hacker, "that allow us to find the right elements? Then you'd have a complex machine that goes afterward to the best site."

"Oh, I'd love to do that," Landry said.

"Potentially a bad time-separation issue," Lane said. "How many vehicles do we have to insert into orbit and later separate? At what speeds do you have to maintain their orbits? I realize these are low-level, ugly questions, but they have to be answered right at the beginning."

"But that is an interesting idea," Landry maintained. "Have a network of very simple probes. If you get a ping off of one, then a more complex probe goes to see if it's actually life."

Lane agreed that with the proper wherewithal and well-timed launch windows, you could launch a sortie for initial assessment followed by a single complex lander. "But once you use two launch vehicles," he said, "you've tacked another seventy million dollars to your mission cost."

"Couldn't you send the complex probe on the first mission, but have it remain in orbit until the best site was found by the little ones?" asked Landry.

"It's feasible," said Lane. "But do you have it remain in a Jovian orbit or a Europan orbit? Either way, it's going to be far more difficult than what we've done with Galileo. Neither's easy, but the Jovian's probably less likely to give you problems than the Europan."

"First we need to know how we identify that one good site," said Wilson.

Mallory scribbled on the back of his workshop program. "Is this what we're looking for?" He turned the page around so we could see the words "HI, MOM."

Everyone laughed, but Larry went on to explain that he had a serious point to raise. He proposed a "magic button." This device, admittedly a long shot, would be very lightweight and easy to take along on any life-detecting probe. "What if you could get a dime-sized, low-cost, yes-or-no testing pad which would chemically recognize a segment of the 16-S subunit of ribosomal RNA common to all life on Earth? You probably won't get a hit, but if you do, boy what a payoff. You can still design traditional chemical tests and tests for fossilized remains, but you stick the magic button on whatever you launch merely as a lottery ticket."

And so the conversation went, all through the afternoon and into dinner at a wonderful Italian seafood restaurant in old Pasadena. The conversation was picked up and picked apart by the larger group the next day and by recombined breakout groups after that. Over lunch, Hovarth and JPL mission planner Jim Cutts explained to me that, at best, the first Vostok probe would be tried in 2002; the earliest launch for a probe to Europa would be 2008 or 2009. They reminded me that the conversations at this workshop were quite preliminary. Yet I felt that if I had not glimpsed the actual birth of the spacecraft that might one day find extraterrestrial life, I was at least witness to the ideas that would govern its ultimate creation. That life was there to be found had begun to seem a foregone conclusion.

.✦.

EARLY MARS

Throughout the spring of 1997, dark life seeped into public view. New Galileo images spawned newspaper and magazine speculations about extraterrestrial life; discoveries in Antarctica and the Columbia River basalts inspired revelations in the press of the inhabited depths of Earth. The journal *Science* devoted an entire issue to "The Revolution in Microbiology"; its cover story, written by Norm Pace, was nothing less than a new blueprint for the evolution of life. The issue also included an in-depth profile—rare for *Science*—of Carl Woese, which read almost like an official apology for the doubt and scorn the scientific establishment had heaped on him when he had first declared the archaea the third domain of life. Meanwhile, a Discovery Channel crew followed Larry Mallory on a collection trip in Mammoth Cave, featuring him in an hourlong special on mysteries of the microbial world. Finally, the lead story of the premier issue of *Natural-Science*, a much-hyped journal on the World Wide Web, was a personal account by Bob Folk of his discovery of nanobacteria in travertine, corroded metals, and a number of meteorites. This led to weeks of E-mail to the editor from doubters, believers, and those who argued for withholding judgment until other researchers could investigate Folk's claims.

I was thus not as surprised as I might have been by a story I stumbled upon in my mail after returning from the Vostok-Europa workshop in Pasadena. The newsletter of the Fulbright College of Arts and Sciences at the University of Arkansas contained a profile of Anne Taunton and her work with the Martian meteorite team. Illustrations included a photo of Anne at a microscope as well as a gift Kathie Thomas-Keprta had given Anne at the end of her internship: an image of Martian nanofossils looped into the letter "R," around which Kathie had typed the phrase: "Anne is a tried and true Razorback!"

I E-mailed Anne, asking whether I might interview her at some point. She promptly responded that she was presenting a poster on her senior project at an undergraduate research conference my university was sponsoring the following weekend. Moreover, a few days after that she planned to present additional research at a conference on early Mars sponsored by the Lunar and Planetary Society in Houston. I told her I had preregistered for the same conference several weeks earlier, and I looked forward to seeing her at both events.

The following Saturday morning, undergraduate science posters were arranged along the halls of the Garrison Student Center, the building in which my office was then located. Not twenty feet from my office door, I found Anne's presentation on electron microscopy. The poster focused on the differences between suspected nanofossils and nonbiological objects such as mineral filaments and gold-coating artifacts. She had shot a number of FESEM images of intentional false-positive biological signatures, then detailed the key differences between these images and those she had taken from evidently legitimate Columbia River samples. The poster explained how one could objectively study a series of FESEM photographs and eliminate the false positives, as well as techniques the FESEM operator could employ to avoid nonbiological "hits" when searching a mineral sample for suspected nanobacteria.

As I stood reading, Anne and her parents, who had driven to Arkadelphia from El Dorado, approached and introduced themselves. She and her father joked with each other, their eyes reflecting a similar humor and intelligence. When I asked what it was like to be a famous scientist, Anne's raucous laugh filled the long corridor, turning heads from the other posters and projects on display.

"Infamous is more like it," she said. "At least as far as my academic advisor is concerned."

"He doesn't buy into this stuff?" I asked, nodding toward her poster.

She smiled and rolled her eyes. "You could say that."

"And of course," added her father, "poor Anne here has never been one to question authority."

This set off another cackle from Anne, as it was clearly intended to do.

"They love to egg each other on," explained her mother. "Pay no attention; it only encourages them."

With Anne's noisy yet relaxed manner, her casually chic clothes, and her youthful good looks, she could have passed at first glance for a typical unfocused college student. But as she began describing the poster and the work at NASA, her face radiated a palpable depth of intelligence. After discussing her internship and the resultant publicity, Anne described her senior project: comparing images from ALH 84001 to nonbiological, nano-sized objects from lunar meteorites. At the end of an exhaustive search, she had at last found some mineralogical signatures on a single lunar sample that appeared somewhat similar to some of the Martian objects. She had just sent these out in a blind test to a group of microbiologists, she explained, and would display some of the images in a poster at the early Mars conference in Houston next week.

She promised to introduce me to Dave McKay and the other members of his team during the conference. To my obvious delight, Anne said she would see if she could get some time on the FESEM during the conference so that she could show me its operation. She mentioned that she had agreed to help Carl Allen, the senior research scientist for Lockheed-Martin at the Johnson Space Center. He had recently joined the ALH 84001 team with the purpose of searching for nanofossils and living nanobacteria in terrestrial carbonates.

"What sort of carbonates?" I asked.

"Travertines."

"Where are they from?"

"Only two places that I know of," she said. "We have some of Bob Folk's original Viterbo travertine and some samples from Yellowstone National Park that Carl collected."

"You wouldn't by any chance like a sample of hot spring travertine from a national park where there's been absolutely no previous microbial work, would you?" I asked. I described the tunnel beneath Hot Springs and the odd aragonite discs I had seen popping up from the underground flow in the Fordyce bathhouse display pool. "And what's neat is that these sites are all underground, so there's no photosynthesis taking place. I think I could get you some decent samples if you'd be interested."

"Would I be interested?" she asked. "I'd love some of that stuff! We definitely need more samples! Especially if you can get fresh deposits, without a lot of contamination. I should introduce you to Carl, and we can talk about it next week."

Anne and her parents soon left for a family gathering, but I couldn't stop grinning: I was going to get to look for my own nanobacteria.

As it turned out, I was nearly overwhelmed by the scientific Who's Who attending the Early Mars Conference in Houston. Among the 170 who had registered for the four-day event were Bob Folk, the nanobacteria guru; Todd Stevens, discoverer of the Columbia River basalt (CRB) microbes; T. C. Onstott, founder of Princeton's geomicrobiology program and co-author of a *Scientific American* article I had read on the CRB bugs and the subterranean biosphere; Rutgers microbiologist Anna-Louise Reysenbach, the former Norm Pace postdoc who had taught Diana Northup how to extract DNA sequences from the sulfur-reducing organisms from Parkers Cave in Kentucky; Ken Nealson, a microbiologist from the University of Wisconsin who was one of the leading experts on extremophiles; and Imre Friedman, a world-renowned microbiologist from Florida State University who had found rock-dwelling microbes in the Sinai Desert and the desertlike dry valleys of Antarctica. Friedman was the subject of a cover profile in that month's issue of *Discover*, an article entitled "Looking for Life in All the Wrong Places." Nealson had emerged as the leading microbiologist opposing the ALH 84001 objects as life forms on the basis of size; he insisted on calling nanobacteria "nanothingies" until someone could devise a test to prove they were alive and explain how they contain their chemistry in such small packages. Onstott had been the subject of several articles I had read describing his success in retrieving rock-eating thermophiles from the deepest, hottest chambers of a South African gold mine.

The planetary scientists attending the conference had even more impressive pedigrees than the microbiologists did. Michael Carr, Allen Tremaine, Chris McKay, Stephen Squyres, Fraser Fanale, Jack Farmer, Michael Drake, Chris Chyba, and many others whose names I had seen in major articles on Mars and Europa would present new work, as would the entire ALH 84001 team and many authors of the leading articles opposing the evidence of past life in the Martian meteorite. Harvard's Paul Hoffman and Heinrich Holland, two of the world's greatest authorities on the geological record of early life on Earth, would attempt to synthesize the latest findings in the field and apply them to the possible evolution of life on ancient Mars. Many of the spacecraft designers who had attended the Vostok-Europa workshop were present, as were other key scientists of the Pathfinder, Mars Global Surveyor, and Galileo missions.

Since so many separate disciplines were represented, each speaker would be addressing general topics in plain language that was often absent from specialized meetings such as the Lunar and Planetary Science Conference. "Keep it broad and simple," advised Michael Drake of the University of Arizona, who chaired the first session on Thursday, April 24, 1997. The meeting was to have been chaired by perhaps the most talented scientist of his generation in the art of speaking about extraterrestrial life in plain language: Carl Sagan. But Sagan had finally lost his long battle with disease four months earlier, so the conference was instead dedicated to his memory. Many of the speakers who had known the scientist would mention over the coming four days how much he would have enjoyed attending. It was clear that a great synthesis was taking place, an outpouring of knowledge from many distant quarters that pointed to the reality of what had been wild theory when Sagan had first propounded it two decades earlier: the conditions of early Mars, and the subsurface of Mars today, were ideal for the existence of microbial life.

I was one of only three journalists registered for the conference (the other two were from *Sky & Telescope* and *ABCnews.com*) and couldn't believe my good fortune. In the alphabetical listing of participants, I was placed between Anne Taunton and Kathie Thomas-Keprta; this is where I literally found myself on the first day of the conference. All of the presentations and discussions were scheduled for the same lecture hall, which seated only 150; on those rare occasions when all the registered participants attended the same session, it was standing room only. The physical closeness of the space contributed to the sense of excitement among the participants. As one dark-life researcher after another shared their findings with theorists who had postulated about early Mars without considering the deep biosphere of Earth, it became increasingly clear that the odds were tipping in favor of life on early Mars.

During a break on the first day, I wandered around the lobby of the Lunar and Planetary Institute, staring at three-dimensional views of Martian volcanoes and canyons displayed around the perimeter of the room. I noticed a knot of people gathered around a couch in the center of the room, where a small bearded man was pulling photocopied images from a battered leather briefcase and handing them to anyone who would take one. The briefcase, I saw, was covered in Italian travel stickers.

Dick Holland, the distinguished Harvard geologist who had just spoken, was staring down at one of the photocopied pages as though he had been handed a copy of *The Watchtower* by a Jehovah's Witness.

"I ain't saying they are, and I ain't saying they ain't," said the man on the couch. "But if those aren't cells, then what in the name of heaven are they? Those grapelike clusters are exactly like the *Staphylococcus* in a microbiology textbook. They're inside the Allende meteorite, which was collected before it even cooled down when it fell in 1969, so whatever they are, they ain't contamination. They arrived from space."

"Very interesting," said Holland, making a sideways move for the coffee urn.

I walked up and facilitated his escape. "Dr. Robert Folk?" I asked the man on the couch.

"That's me," he said. He was dressed in a pale blue oxford shirt, dark trousers, and a threadbare corduroy jacket.

I introduced myself and asked whether I could buy him lunch after the next speaker.

"Where?" he asked.

"Wherever you like."

He smiled broadly. "If this town has a Hooters, you're on."

Thus I found myself eating an enormous hamburger and drinking a draft beer brought by a barely clad waitress while the discoverer of nanobacteria lectured on his most recent work.

"The only thing that's going to convince the microbiologists these buggers are real is if we can culture them and get at their DNA," he said. "So I've found a partner in the biology department in Austin who's having a go at it. You know, as far as culturing goes, I can grow up all the nanobacteria you want on sterilized aluminum stubs placed in Austin tap water for forty-eight hours. Nothing to it. I mean the stubs will be positively coated with the buggers, and so they have to be in the city water supply. You can boil them for two hours, and it won't faze them a bit. Only thing that kills them is chlorine bleach. But trying to get a microbiologist to grow them up is a waste of breath. 'They don't exist, so why should I grow them?' is the attitude. Now, I ask you, what kind of science is that? It's like saying, 'The world's flat, so why bother sailing over the horizon,' and boy, would you check out that little redhead over there."

I couldn't believe that he wasn't a caver.

That evening, I attended a poster session during which I saw photographic evidence, gleaned from enlargements of old Viking orbiter data, of ancient Martian rivers, lakes, glaciers, and ocean shorelines, as well as possible sinkholes and dried cave springs. New, higher-resolution pictures of the planet were expected the following fall from the Mars Global Surveyor. Additional evidence of early water was expected from the Pathfinder lander, targeted toward what appeared to be the massive outflow channel of an ancient catastrophic flood. If these spacecraft confirmed the interpretations displayed at the conference, there would be no room left for doubt that Mars in its youth was a wet, warm planet very like Earth. As one poster boldly proclaimed: "It rained like hell on early Mars."

"If the early, wet Mars ever sustained life," Stephen Squyres of Cornell University had said that afternoon, "It's a safe bet that some of that life has survived. It's worth noting that if we took Earth, with all its subsurface bugs, and shoved it today out to the orbit of Pluto, they would keep plugging along for hundreds of millions of years or more. The rest of us would be icicles, but the deepest of these bugs wouldn't even register a change."

After the poster exhibit, I returned to my hotel room to finish a gripping book I had been reading on my flight to Houston. It was called *Deadly Feasts: Tracking the Secrets of a Terrifying New Plague*, by Richard Rhodes, and it outlined the growing threat from Mad Cow Disease (more properly called bovine spongiform encephalopathy, or BSE), scrapie, Creutzfeld-Jakob Disease, and the broad class of maladies known as "prion" diseases. Some researchers believed all of these diseases were caused by a prion, a deadly nanobacteria-sized protein that was capable of self-replication, like a life form. As the book explained, there were a number of holes in the prion theory, but what was certain was that BSE-type diseases destroyed the central nervous system by creating mineralized deposits called "plaques" in the brain. BSE was acquired by consuming or coming in contact with brain tissue from an animal that had died with the disease. The unknown disease agent resisted heat sterilization that would destroy traditional bacteria or viruses and could pass through a 0.2 micron filter. Confirmed cases had been transmitted via metal dental tools that had been "sterilized" in an autoclave, which surrounds objects with pressurized hot steam. There had been much in the news that month about the spread of Mad Cow Disease in humans in Britain, where people apparently contracted the disease by consuming cattle that had been fed the ground-up remains of diseased animals.

Although Stanley Prusiner was only six months away from being awarded a Nobel Prize in medicine for proposing that nanobacteria-sized prion proteins caused these incurable diseases, many researchers had publicly worried that acceptance of the prion theory was premature. While prions were unquestionably present in BSE-infected test animals, no one had ever transmitted BSE using prions alone. And yet the disease was easily transmitted between test animals via body fluids that had been run through a 0.2 micron filter. Moreover, there were many known strains of BSE disease, which suggested that the strain characteristics were stored via a nucleic acid—a bug. A prion protein alone would be incapable of handling such complex information. A series of articles published in the British journal *Nature* had suggested that prions merely accompany a very small hypothetical organism the authors dubbed a "virino."

This hypothetical organism had traits that I immediately recognized. As I reached the end of the book, I came upon a paragraph which, in light of my conversation at lunch, struck me as so suggestive that I dialed Folk's room number (he had mentioned at lunch that we were in the same hotel).

"Sorry for calling at ten-thirty," I said, "but I just have to read this to you. It's from page 240 of *Deadly Feasts*." I described the book, then read aloud:

In 1990, Paul Brown freeze-dried a sample of scrapie brain, sealed the sample into a glass ampule and baked it in an oven for one hour at 360 degrees Centigrade. Reconstituted, the sample still transmitted scrapie to a hamster. [Carleton] Gajdusek invokes minerals as nucleants to explain how an infection agent might survive being baked to ash at 360 degrees C. Mineral deposits containing aluminum and silicon have been found in nerve cells in high-incident clusters of ALS and Parkinsonism-with-dementia cases on Guam and other Western Pacific islands. Aluminum silicate deposits form the cores of Alzheimer's amyloid plaques. They may be crystals of a common form of clay, montmorillonite. Alzheimer's researchers have proposed, Gajdusek writes, "that they are the initiating elements of the amyloid deposition." It was this finding of aluminum silicate cores in Alzheimer's plaques that led to a panic a decade ago among users of aluminum cookware, although no connection between cooking in aluminum and Alzheimer's disease has ever been confirmed.

Folk was silent for a moment, then said, "I wasn't going to say anything about this, because we just applied for a National Science Foundation grant to do the work, but we plan to look for nanobacteria in arterial plaques as the cause of arteriosclerosis. I've found them in dental plaque from my own teeth. It's disgusting, but I've found them in my own excrement, for that matter. If Alzheimer's and Mad Cow Disease involve the formation of mineral plaques, they're sure worth looking at too." He mentioned that the Finnish team that had already found nanobacteria in blood and commercial blood products was now studying them as the possible causative agent of kidney stones.

"What about gallstones?" I asked.

"Could be," he said. "This is all so new and so controversial that the medical establishment just isn't aware of it. No one in your average research hospital would know how to look for nanobacteria, let alone how to find them." What's more, Folk explained, Kajander had suggested that the calcite shell in which nanobacteria appeared to encase themselves would shield them from traditional tests designed to detect pathogenic microbes. Nature had equipped them with a kind of stealth technology. Until now, they had easily flown under the radar of modern medical science. Folk asked me to give him the name of the book, which I did, promising to E-mail him some additional virino and Alzheimer's citations after the conference.

Two nights later, I attended the poster session in which Anne displayed six new images of ALH 84001 as well as six little squiggles and balls in lunar meteorites, without identifying which was which. "Care to take a shot at it?" she asked me.

"Sure," I said. "Martian, Martian, Lunar, Martian," and so on until I had gone through the list.

"On what did you base that?" she asked.

"On whether it looked like bacteria or something mineralogical," I said. She smiled and said, "Well, you got all but one set right, which seems about average so far."

As we stood talking, several of the noted scientists at the convention tried her test. Heinrich Holland got them all right, as did Marilyn Lindstrom, curator of the Antarctic meteorite collection at the Johnson Space Center. Lindstrom had with her a clear box containing a large piece of EETA 79001, the SNC-class object that had confirmed the identity of all Martian meteorites via its trapped gas bubbles. She let me hold the piece of Mars while she identified Anne's lunar and Martian images, then she called over Todd Stevens to try the same thing. The rock would have made a nice paperweight on my desk; for a few seconds I contemplated a larcenous dash for the parking lot, wondering how far I would get. But after Stevens also correctly identified the suspected biological images in Anne's selection, I was surprised to see that he seemed as eager to hold the bit of Mars as I had been, and I passed the object reverently to him.

I had hoped to visit Building 13 that night after the poster session, but Anne told me that she'd been unable to sign up for time on the FESEM, as it was being used by other projects. She was still interested in acquiring some of my Hot Springs National Park samples, she said, suggesting that maybe later in the summer I could drive them down and help her shoot them on the machine.

"Well, I got to hold a chunk of Mars," I said. "I guess that's good enough for one trip."

The highlight of the last day of the conference was a formal debate about life in ALH 84001. Dave McKay had just recovered from heart bypass surgery and was visibly weak as he stood to speak; Kathie Thomas-Keprta had just given birth to a son and was strong but exhausted from the sleepless nights of a new parent. Yet they and the other members of the team gave a strong, cogent defense of their findings, citing additional new information that seemed to back them up. As with every debate on the rock, however, nothing firm was decided, because the rock's complexity left so much open to individual interpretation. As the crowd debated the issues after the principal speakers had finished, the talk kept coming back to nanobacteria.

"The key issue is size," said Ken Nealson, who had earlier drawn laughs by stating he was neither "pro-life" nor "anti-life," but "pro-choice." "We simply need more data. If life can really exist in such a small package, then perhaps these objects can be called fossils. But if life really can be so small, fossils on Mars are nothing compared to the other implications such a finding would have. Remember, it hasn't been that long since exobiology was lumped with pyramid power and other pseudoscience. More work needs to be done; it is premature to conclude anything."

"What someone needs to do," suggested Imre Friedman, "is to extract DNA from nanobacteria. I believe this would convince everyone."

A tall, clean-cut man with dark hair, who had been sitting in the back row throughout the conference without saying much, raised his hand and was recognized. "We're hoping to do exactly that here at JSC," he said, "with nanobacteria from terrestrial travertines. We're trying to find a way to remove isolate nanobacterial cells, identify cell walls, and remove DNA, but it's too early to know if we'll be able to do it or not. Stay tuned."

The conference ended a few moments later. I struggled through the crush of people rushing for their rental cars and a mass exodus to the airport. I saw the man in the parking lot, getting into a car. But before he vanished, he turned and I was able to read his nametag, which identified him as Carl Allen of Lockheed-Martin Engineering. After returning to Arkansas, I E-mailed him to introduce myself and ask about his comment at the end of the conference. Our correspondence grew.

As Anne had predicted, he was very interested in obtaining some samples of travertine from Hot Springs National Park.

TWELVE

August 9, 1997

Big bugs have little bugs,
Upon their backs to bite 'em,
And little bugs still smaller ones
And so on ad infinitum.

—After Jonathan Swift

Building 13

On a table to our right the vacuum pump clicked off, having removed nearly all air from the sealed chamber of the FESEM in Building 13. It was nearly midnight at the Johnson Space Center.

By pointing a computer mouse, Anne Taunton rotated the disc inside the chamber like a high-end CD changer. A video camera recorded the position of particular sample stubs as they passed beneath the XL40 field emission gun. The bulk of the gun hid in a gray cylinder rising above the sample compartment. The portion we could see on the monitors resembled the tip of a gigantic ballpoint pen. Anne stopped at the sample labeled "Iron Nub, Tunnel Spring #1, Hot Springs National Park," and raised the disc until the rock almost touched the active end of the gun.

She clicked a bar on her monitor, flooding the sample with waves of electrons far smaller than the wavelength of visible light. Reflected electrons bounced through banks of lenses into the eye of a highly specialized video camera. The image on the two monitors before us suddenly shifted to what this camera saw. Under high magnification, the pebble—any pebble, regardless of its planet of origin—became a mountainous plateau broken by canyons and boulder fields. We hovered above a desolate landscape.

All day we had been traversing these miniature deserts looking for signs of life. We were ostensibly examining only the Hot Springs travertine—our time at JSC was running out—but we couldn't resist peeking once or twice into Mars. After all, it was already on the plate, placed there the day before by Dave McKay. Just before breaking for dinner at 9 P.M., Anne had called up a file of some of McKay's most recent images. The most striking depicted four or five jellylike blobs, apparently of biofilm—a substance, I had learned, that many mineral-dwelling bacteria release into their environment. The microbial mats of deep-sea vents and certain sulfur caves are woven together with biofilms, as are the acidic "snottite" formations of Cueva de la Villa Luz in Mexico.

To my eye, the biofilm images looked far more "biological" than any of the segmented worms that had been published a year earlier. After showing me McKay's photos, Anne took me directly to one of the biofilm sites in the Martian carbonate. Starbursts of fossilized jelly hung over projecting rock faces like clothing casually tossed over bedroom furniture. The sample had an undeniably "lived-in" look.

"Why hasn't he published these in *Science?*" I asked. "Why hasn't he released them to the press? What's he waiting for?"

"You'll have to ask Dave," Anne said. She guessed that with all the flak McKay and the team had received, he probably wanted to have plenty of supporting material before he released these images to the world.

This made a great deal of sense. At the opening of the Martian meteorite discussion during the Early Mars Conference, McKay had said, "I'm not a fan of formal debate, as I don't believe it's conducive to good science. It promotes adversarial relationships between teams and encourages both sides to overstate their case." He had looked as though he felt physical pain each time an opponent made a categorically negative—or, just as often, clearly mean-spirited—comment during the course of the public deliberation. McKay never allowed himself to issue a more categorical statement than the one in his conclusion: "The data are strong enough now that we can say there is very strong evidence that life [in ALH 84001] is a reasonable hypothesis."

I knew that Bob Folk, like McKay, had been subjected to increasingly personal attacks by some scientists. In 1996, Folk had co-authored a study, published in *Science*, of the role of nanobacteria in creating a vast copper sulfide deposit in Chile. This had prompted a few microbiologists to write vitriolic letters attacking the whole notion of nanobacteria. Yet I also knew that many of these same microbiologists made one exception to the 0.2 micron minimum-size rule: *mycoplasma*, a gluey, stringlike bacterium allowed special size dispensation because it lacks the rigid cell wall common to most bacterial species. According to some of the papers I had read, mycoplasmas could grow to only 0.1 micron, or 100 nanometers, in length. Different strains had been shown to speed the development of AIDS in HIV-infected cells and to cause such diseases as "walking pneumonia" and urethritis. But biologists opposing the existence of nanobacteria often, and quite conveniently, forgot about mycoplasma, sticking to the 0.2 micron definition drummed into them as undergraduates.

Curious as to how small these wall-less organisms could actually get, I had tracked down two mycoplasma specialists, Maureen Davidson at the University of Florida and Ken Bott at the University of North Carolina at Chapel Hill. I E-mailed both, asking, "What's the minimum size for mycoplasma?" Their answers were the same: they didn't have a clue.

Davidson confessed to having heard the term "nanobacteria," but she didn't know to what the term actually referred, and she had not followed any of the controversy surrounding it. She wrote:

> I'm afraid I can't be of much help here. The published dogma on mycoplasma species (the common use term for all members of Class *Mollicutes*) as per *Bergey's Manual of Determinative Bacteriology* is that the physical size of mycoplasmas ranges from 300 to 800 nanometers. Thus, mycoplasmas should be outside of the

range for the organisms (?) termed nanobacteria. The *Thermo-plasmas* (100 to 300 nanometers; originally isolated from self-heating coal refuse piles and, I think subsequently, from hot springs after much looking) were first classified as belonging to Class *Mollicutes* because they lack a cell wall. They have since been moved to the archaea (I think—I lost track of them after they were moved out of the mycoplasma domain). Those organisms would seem to fit in the physical size area of the "nanobacteria." I have no idea how the size was determined, but I assume it was by the "standard techniques" for such things, whatever they are.

Davidson then hit upon the crucial problem with all mini-mum-size arguments concerning microbial life, including all the size arguments I had heard thus far against Folk and the McKay team:

[Size measurement of bacteria] is not something most scientists would ever do since usually it has already been done by someone else. My guess would be electron micrograph measurement [would work best for mycoplasmas], since this would seem to be the most "direct evidence" technique available. However, there are myriad "artifacts" that can be introduced by EM processing techniques (including changing the size of mycoplasmas and probably other bacteria as well, but to a lesser extent since they have cell walls) . . . Since excellent EM work is almost an "old fogy" methodology today, my guess is that there aren't many people remaining in the work force who actually know how to do it well. This is a shame, since one does actually need the technology occasionally, even in this day of molecular biology and "sexy" techniques [that don't require direct observation]. My guess is that organisms as small as "nanobacteria" could exist. Obviously organisms at the high end of their range do exist in the *Thermo-plasmas*, so probably there are other bacteria of that size as well. But we haven't looked for them before so we COULDN'T find them.

The scientists who "believe in them" will simply have to prove their point scientifically in a rigorous manner. Nonbelief in nature's weirdness is as common in scientists as in the general population. Remember that it hasn't been all that long since the electron microscope was invented, the atom was split into smaller parts, the genetic code was discovered, and we actually discovered that there was a use for the "other strand" of DNA. I can remember asking a professor in college, "What's the other strand do?" He replied, "Nothing." I didn't believe him—I just didn't think nature was that wasteful. Obviously, others besides me also asked the same question and decided to pursue a legitimate answer.

Davidson added as an aside that mycoplasmas are generally believed to have the smallest genome sufficient for free-living life. However, she and other researchers had proved that they can "throw off" parts of their "necessary" DNA and still survive, at least under lab conditions (which, as she pointed out, might not mimic life in the "real world").

Scientists used to think that there was just one genetic code, but we have found that is not true as well. Mycoplasmas have several weird codons that do different things in mycoplasmas than they do in other bacteria. They use their small genome quite efficiently. My guess is that we haven't even begun to find all the unusual forms of life on earth. We should keep an open mind and never say "never."

Ken Bott was more circumspect in his reply. Still, like Davidson, his expert opinion was that the experts didn't know exactly how small a living organism could be. He wrote:

Although I work regularly with *Mycoplasma genitalium*, I cannot profess to be an expert about its size. We *do* often quote that this is the smallest organism. Certainly the genome is the smallest yet identified. . . . The main snag is that since mycoplasmas are wall-less they are very pleomorphic [meaning they flow like a jelly]. Within a single species they range from extremely small things that will pass through filters retaining most bacterial species to larger filamentous and amorphous sizes. All of these forms would contain at least one genome's worth of DNA, but they would not be of consistent size as would organisms bounded by a typical cell wall.

Bott attached to his E-mail an SEM photo of M. *genitalium* with a 0.1 micron scale bar. A fingerlike appendage protruded from a rounded organism perhaps 600 nanometers in diameter. "The photo was taken to depict the protein 'adhesion' molecules on the tip structure," Bott explained. "Since this species typically parasitizes mammalian cells, they can differentiate into the form seen here. But if you observe photos in [standard mycoplasma reference books], you will also see the fragmented and tiny versions [of the same form] that are common in populations cultivated in cell-free growth medium."

I understood this comment to mean that ample SEM images of nanobacteria-sized mycoplasmas do indeed exist, but that no mycoplasma researcher to date has cared to shake the foundations of biological wisdom by pointing out that such photographs depict organisms plainly smaller than the "minimum" size for life.

Anne stood for a moment to twist two knurled focusing knobs, roughly fixing the beam by hand. Then she aimed the mouse at a pull-down menu, adjusting a half dozen numeric values affecting the power and shape of the electron field. Most of the microfossils we had seen throughout the day fell within the familiar dimensions of known bacteria. This alone was interesting; it proved that Hot Springs National Park is a source of unrecognized thermophiles. Moreover, because the water at the park is heated by the geothermal gradient, as opposed to the volcanic processes heating the springs of Yellowstone and Viterbo, it contains much less sulfur than typical hot springs. The species that inhabit its depths are likely to be quite different from those studied at other springs.

So far, Anne and I had spotted the broken remnants of only a few smaller cells, exploded somehow from within, perhaps during the fossilization process, perhaps during preparation of the sample for electron microscopy. But these just barely fit accepted descriptions of some of the smallest known thermophiles; they were still giants compared to the Martian analogs we were hunting. In the travertine we had seen occasional examples of what *might* have been structures like those in ALH 84001. In one of the floating discs from the Fordyce display pool, we found hundreds of pencil-shaped aragonite crystals, bound together at their interstices by a substance resembling biofilm. A number of spheres with diameters of about 75 nanometers rested in the gluey film deposits. Anne photographed these with a Polaroid unit built into the FESEM.

Still, we hadn't seen anything that a doubter—of which there were many—couldn't have shrugged off as appendages broken from larger cells, or mineral filaments, or artifacts of the gold-coating process used to make samples "visible" to the electron beam. What we'd seen had been just tempting enough to bring us back after dinner for a few more tries.

I had gathered these samples over numerous trips during the course of the summer with help from Steve Rudd, the natural resources specialist for the national park, as well as with the assistance of several colleagues from my school's biology department. The morning before I headed to Houston, I had met Rudd at his office. We had ventured into the basements of several of the closed bathhouses, where I sampled water and bits of travertine from seeps and display pools. In one of the unused structures, called the Hale, a dead tarantula was curled up just outside a low window into a native hot spring no more than two feet in diameter. The pool's perimeter bristled with formations that resembled miniature aragonite Christmas trees poking into the water. I collected one of these, marveling at how different these formations were from those in the Fordyce pool a short walk away—a difference I couldn't help but attribute to separate species regulating mineral growth in each pool.

When I had arrived at JSC late that night, I learned that Carl Allen, who had authorized my presence there, had traveled out of town to a conference. Anne and I had spent a few hours that night and most of the next day prepping my samples across the complex in Building 31. We fixed the travertine with glutaraldehyde, etched it with acid, dried it, mounted it on metal stubs, and coated it inside a sealed jar that glowed with a purple haze of gold and palladium atoms. By the time everything was ready for Building 13, we had been left with only a single day for actual examination with the microscope.

Anne's second NASA internship was nearing its end. Both of us were scheduled to leave JSC the next afternoon. This night and very early the next morning offered our last shots at uncovering new, definitive images of nanobacteria. During the course of Anne's summer, she had fallen in love with Steve Symes, a postdoctoral researcher from the University of Arkansas working on lunar soils in Building 31. That she was spending the last night of her internship locked up in Building 13—as opposed to out with Steve—was a testament to the promise of these Hot Springs samples.

Using the mouse to fly us over the mineral wasteland, Anne slowed and descended toward one of a dozen canyons. Because of different contrast settings, the single image shared by the two monitors where we sat varied slightly. The scanning electron beam and the complex magnification optics caused the pictures to wobble a bit, intensifying the illusion of a landscape viewed from a great height. I pointed out a roughly textured area to the lower right.

"Can we check that?"

"Sure," Anne said. "No problem." With a click of the mouse button, we appeared to fall between steep canyon walls toward a protected valley. The magnification jumped to 20,000, then 50,000. The valley and its inhabitants zoomed into sharp focus.

"Oh my God," said the young scientist.

Chains and clusters and loops of cells were everywhere. Some were clearly frozen in the act of cell division. Tiny filaments linked some of the spherical objects to larger cells, like a line of ducklings trailing their mother. The largest of the cells before us was the approximate diameter of a large virus, such as HIV. Viruses, however, are not technically "alive." They borrow the reproductive machinery of host cells in order to make copies of themselves, which is the only thing viruses can do (often with disastrous consequences for the host cells). They cannot eat, digest, excrete, grow, attack invaders, or carry on any of the regular functions of living beings. But these cells looked nothing like viruses. They looked exactly like textbook illustrations of living bacteria, except that quite a few of them were much, much smaller than anything science had definitively classified as life.

I had seen Folk's images; what lay before us now was sharper, clearer than the best he had ever produced. The image left little room for ambivalence, for calling these objects coating artifacts or mineral filaments or figments of wishful thinking. We were looking at something important. Any surviving remnants of my journalistic objectivity took flight and vanished. I sat staring at images that were in themselves news, at a new reality, and I felt a hunger to learn, study, and explore this dark life. I no longer was content merely to report on the birth of a new science—I wanted to join its front ranks. I wanted to show the things before us to the world and prove that they lived.

"Have you ever seen anything that looked like this?" I asked at last.

"My God, no!" Anne said. "Nobody has ever seen anything like this."

She followed a looping filament with her finger. It wound around clusters of spheres, as well as loose nanobacterial rods aligned end to end in twos—a position called "diplobacilli" in my microbiology text. Anne used the mouse to pull ruler lines from the sides of the computer screen to measure the cells. The rods were approximately 90 nanometers wide by 200 long. The larger spheres ran about 280 nanometers in diameter, while the smaller spheres associated with them remained a consistent 75 to 80 nanometers. A few chains of spheres dropped just below 50 nanometers.

"How do these sizes compare with what's in ALH 84001?" I asked.

"We're right there in the same size range, at least with some of these." She turned to me, smiling, and said, "Mike, I have to tell you, this is some good stuff. Let's get out a couple of boxes of film. We've got a lot of pictures to take."

⋆

Il Poeta e Il Postino

Anne and I shot fifty-four Polaroids of suspected nanobacteria from the "Iron Nub" and two other samples. It was a two-person operation. I loaded a film cartridge and timed each exposure before pulling the paper backing off the print, while Anne selected images to photograph from the FESEM terminal. For each significant scene, she would take a series of three or four "locator shots," marking images in decreasing magnification that would allow her to return to a specific spot during a later FESEM session with the same sample. In addition to controlling the film exposure, the computer printed a caption line at the bottom of each Polaroid listing the sample name, its unique image number, the exact magnification power, the strength of the electron beam, and a scale bar to identify the precise size of any objects in the scene. After taking a Polaroid, Anne would create a computer file for the image, saving it to her personal folder in the microscope computer's hard drive.

I noticed that the largest four files in the hard drive were labeled "Dave," "Kathie," "Annie," and "Carl." The knowledge that samples I had personally gathered were joining this inter-planetary database heightened my sense of involvement, of complicity. I felt like Walter Mitty, NASA Scientist. I wanted to pick up the phone and call somebody, anybody, just to brag. These Hot Springs samples—unlike any stored elsewhere in the FESEM database—had never been exposed to sunlight. (Although, I had to admit, photosynthesis was a possibility in the Fordyce samples, due to the fluorescent bulbs the park used to light the display pool; the display pool in the basement of the unused Hale bathhouse, however, had not been illuminated for decades.) My dark life had been collected at its point of emergence, without the possible contaminating influences of surface algae or other organisms. Anne was right—it *was* good stuff.

I began thinking of ways in which I could prove that it was actually alive. I could grow fresh cells on sterilized glass slides; I could run spring water through a 0.2 micron filter, place it in a sterilized container inside the spring to maintain constant temperature, and see what grew; I could place filtered water on a thermophile growth medium and try to produce visible colonies. The possibilities kept running through my brain, and I kept jotting messy notes while timing Polaroid exposures. Anne and I had been at the task for so long we were both beginning to feel punchy, making bad puns and inane comments.

"You know what all this means, don't you?" I asked at one point.

"No. What?"

"It means that two or three years from now, you're going to see Julia Roberts or Jodie Foster staring at a computer screen full of nanobacteria and saying, 'Oh my God!' "

"Hah!" Anne released a guffaw worthy of Jo Anne Worley. "They can find someone better-looking than that, can't they? I mean, I could live with Jodie Foster, if I had to, but Julia Roberts? Forget it. She's a stick with a big mouth."

We finally knocked off at 2 A.M., after double-exposing one shot and ripping the paper from two other prints only to see that we had failed to expose them—dumb mistakes obviously caused by fatigue. We agreed to meet back at seven the next morning to prospect on the FESEM for another couple of hours before stopping to sort and organize the images. Anne wanted to leave behind a well-ordered portfolio of the Hot Springs images for Carl and the rest of the team before she headed out for Arkansas later in the day.

Yawning and full of coffee, we started the morning with the "Aragonite Xmas Tree" I had retrieved from the Hale bathhouse. Each sample that Anne had prepared had been etched briefly with a solution of hydrochloric acid; slightly altering the duration of the etching could sometimes lead to dramatic differences in the number of visible cells. In this sample, the acid had sharpened the edges of cells but had not remained in place so long as to destroy the delicate biofilm membranes between them. We saw strings and fabrics of gossamer film so fragile that the beam of electrons that made them visible caused them to break apart and curl as we looked on.

The films connected a mass of ball-shaped cells in two distinct sizes: the larger ones were 150 nanometers in diameter, the smaller 80. These balls and adjoining films had clearly formed in sheets, and by skimming across the sample we could move through different layers and see the same composition permeating the structure. In its home spring, this Christmas tree had been indistinguishable from an aragonite bush in Lechuguilla Cave. Its entire mineral content was inextricably bound up in life, and once again I wondered how much of the cave geology I had picked up in two decades of caving could have been more properly termed biology.

As we looked through the sheets of uniform cells and films, two interesting solitary objects stood out. One was a classic rod-shaped bacterium, complete with flagella, that was a respectable single micron long (1,000 nanometers) by a slim 130 nanometers in diameter. The other was a tiny sphere, a mere 56 nanometers in diameter, that appeared to be surrounded by the stiff, hairlike projections known as *fimbriae* on larger bacteria. These are the grappling hooks by which disease-causing organisms attach themselves to host cells or structures. Two longer, wavy projections resembled *pili*, the sexual organs of some bugs. Through pili, separate strains and even different species of bacteria freely transfer genetic material. The increased antibiotic resistance of dangerous bacteria; the new, deadly strains of *E. coli*; and a great deal of additional microbial mischief plaguing the world in the 1990s began in recent history with one bug poking pili at another before anchoring its fimbriae in a host. And here was a ball well within the size range of the ALH 84001 fossils, making what appeared to be a microbial mating call. It was a picture that could launch a thousand sci-fi screenwriters.

Our time at the microscope soon passed. We began cleaning up the mess of nearly twenty-four hours of frenzied work. Anne copied several of the most arresting pictures we had taken that morning and the night before to a computer diskette and gave it to me. She also allowed me to keep one of the several Polaroid originals of what I had begun to think of as the "Oh My God Valley." After profusely thanking Anne for allowing me to participate in the scientific adventure of a lifetime, I checked out of my Clear Lake hotel and headed for Austin.

Before I had made the trip down, Bob Folk had agreed to meet me in his office at the University of Texas that Sunday afternoon in order to look at some of my Hot Springs samples. I had set several of them aside for him while at JSC. He had also offered to show me some of the more interesting work he had done recently with samples of his own. Halfway there, I realized that the drive would take an hour longer than I had expected it to, so I phoned his home from a gas station. Bob's wife told me he'd already gone to the office. I called him there, apologizing for my tardiness. He said not to worry, he planned on spending the whole afternoon working anyway, and by the way how did my trip to Houston go?

"I'd have to say it went pretty well," I admitted. "In fact, I've got a picture that I'd really like you to see."

"Bring it on," he said, giving me directions to his building.

I spotted the place with little difficulty, as it was an ugly, institutional high-rise visible from several blocks off. Because it was a Sunday, I quickly found free parking on a nearby street. I walked behind a fountain to a basement entrance Bob had told me would be open, then took the stairs to his floor. I knew I'd found the right place when I saw a corridor plastered with nanobacteria posters and images under a big, laser-printed banner asking, "What are they?!!"

The office door was open. I can be fairly absentminded and disorganized myself, and I've certainly seen a number of messy faculty offices throughout my years as student and teacher, but the view through the open door was of the most cluttered academic space I had ever beheld. Scientific journals and manuscripts were stacked like stalagmites between sample cabinets that were nearly buried under boxes of rock and loose paper. Yellowing photos of Italy and former students covered every available inch of wall space. Huge decks of index cards, containing the notes for various class lectures and scientific articles, were bound together with rubber bands and balanced in teetering columns. The office sink in which Folk had grown nanobacteria on aluminum strips in tap water was black with old stains and contained a number of unwashed beakers and instruments.

I couldn't see a person through the opening, however, so I pushed the door further and stepped inside. "Hello?" I called.

Bob Folk rose from his desk against a far window and began threading his way through the complex path to the door. The office was quite large, which was, I realized, what allowed it to become so spectacularly messy. Like a goldfish, the physical corpus of four decades' work had grown to fit the available space.

We shook hands, and before saying anything else, I pulled the "Oh my God" photo from my briefcase and handed it to him. "What do you think of that?" I asked.

He stared at it for several seconds, then grabbed my hand again. "Congratulations!" he said, not letting go. "This is absolutely the best photo of nanobacteria I've ever seen. This is what I've been waiting for. This is it. This is the stuff. They can't call me crazy anymore."

He grinned. I grinned. He finally let go of my hand and then suggested that I get Anne to send it to *Science* right away. I promised to ask about her team's publication plans. I mentioned that I had brought some of the same samples with me.

"Let's go take a look at them," he said. "And while we're at it, I've been wanting to look inside this." He pulled a gray triangular stone, just over an inch long, from his desk. "This is hardened volcanic ash I just brought back from Italy. Have you seen the movie *Il Postino?*"

Confused by the non sequitur, it took me several seconds to realize what he was asking. "As matter of fact," I said at last, "my wife and I watched the video with some friends no more than two weeks ago."

"Remember the bar where the postman meets the beautiful girl?" he asked.

"Sure."

"They used a real bar on the actual island in the movie. It sits smack up against a volcanic outcrop, so while we were drinking there, I went out back and chipped off this piece of stone. I've been looking at basalts and other volcanic rocks lately, and it appears that nanobacteria can colonize them just as readily as they do carbonates."

Before taking me to the room where the geology department's SEM was kept, Bob showed me a small metal cabinet sitting on a table near his office door. He pulled out a drawer stuffed with hundreds of envelopes, each the approximate size for holding a greeting card.

"Pick out any envelope and open it," he instructed.

I grabbed one and saw that it was numbered and listed a name and location. Inside was an SEM Polaroid of nanobacterial spheres resembling the specimens in sheets that I had seen in the aragonite Christmas tree.

"That's pyrite in precious opal," Bob said. "Look what's building it. It's layer upon layer of nanobacteria." He asked me to pull out another envelope. This image was a now familiar assortment of spheres in a white mineral that I took to be calcite.

"That's concrete from the Biosphere," he said. "I heard that the place was condemned because the concrete had become 'corroded.' People are supposed to be working in a simulation of deep space, totally isolated from the rest of the planet, but the concrete walls fall apart and everything gets contaminated. So I got a sample of one of the concrete blocks, and you can see what's doing the corroding."

He pulled out other envelopes. I saw tiny rods in Virgin Island beach sand, more spheres in a piece of chert Bob had collected at the age of ten, and vast clusters of nanobacteria clinging to rust from a Texas water well. Bob mentioned that it was easy to find nanobacteria in rust; in his opinion it was impossible for metallic corrosion to occur *without* the presence of nanobacteria. Like the decay of flesh or the souring of cream, rust was a biological process carried out by invisible organisms.

"That's why Mars is red," he added. "It's covered with billions of years' worth of iron rust caused by nanobacteria. The little buggers are everywhere."

After returning the envelopes to their proper places, Bob took me to a lab on another floor of the building. There he ran through a shorter version of the sample preparation Anne and I had performed two days earlier in Houston. He then led me into a small dark room, little more than a closet, which housed the machine on which he had discovered nanobacteria and taken many thousands of subsequent images of them. I quickly realized why Anne's picture was so much better than any that Bob Folk or anyone else had ever taken. In comparison with the FESEM in Building 13, the machine before us—considered state-of-the-art in 1988—now looked like a prop from a Buck Rogers serial.

The well-worn instruction sheet for powering up the microscope ran three pages. Despite his familiarity with the routine, Bob traced each step with his finger, reading aloud as he performed the called-for action. Each function that Anne had controlled via mouse and pull-down menu, Bob controlled by turning a large black dial. There were many dials, and his hands flew as he caressed them into optimal settings. A bank of round gauges sat above the dials, their black needles jumping as if on an aircraft's instrument panel. Where Anne and I had watched separate large, high-resolution computer screens, Bob had only a tiny green window that resembled the porthole of a bathysphere.

The electron beam washed rapidly through the image on this screen. Staring at it was like watching a 1952 Zenith. The vertical hold seemed to roll and jump; fuzzy afterimages lingered each time Bob changed the view. I found it nearly impossible to focus on the green-and-black representation of the sample before us, a chip of the rock from behind the *Il Postino* bar. I began to marvel at how truly sharp some of Bob's images were, considering the device with which they had been taken.

Not all of the sites that Steve Rudd had led me to in Hot Springs were underground—I had brought with me samples gathered from a few surface springs and seeps on the hillside behind Bathhouse Row. Anne had understandably wished to concentrate on subterranean carbonates during our limited time in Building 13, but now Bob was placing one of the more interesting surface samples I had collected into the tiny vacuum chamber of his SEM. The sample was twig with a bit of an attached green leaf, which had evidently fallen into the steaming pool where many of the park's unique thermophilic algae had been previously studied. The twig, no more than one-eighth of an inch in diameter, was coated with a quarter-inch blob of white mineral that appeared to be aragonite. I had retrieved it because it was good evidence for the speed with which new deposits could be laid down in the hot flow.

"You can see it's just a solid mass of aragonite crystals here next to the wood," said Bob.

I studied the flashing green screen and saw the edge of the twig blown up into a surprisingly smooth section of black wall, surrounded by a brilliant field of rippled crystal.

"But watch what happens when we move to the outer edge of the deposit." As Bob deftly maneuvered the sample and refocused the wavering beam, the aragonite mass began to separate into spaghetti-like strands of individual crystals. "Look at the tip of each crystal," he instructed, increasing the magnification as he spoke.

I saw what he meant. The growing crystals were not pointed, as one might expect. Each and every one was tipped by a single round sphere approximately 75 nanometers in diameter.

Bob pulled out a box of Polaroid film to record photos of the sample; the machine lacked any sort of computer for storing images electronically. The type of film his department stocked was more complicated than what Anne and I had used and had to be washed with a small chemical sponge in order to develop. "It's about fifty cents cheaper per photo," he explained. "That may not mean much to NASA. But in a university, that's reason enough to do it this way."

After coating the prints and rinsing them in a sink just outside the darkened microscopy cubicle, he hung them by clothespins on a wire stretched across the room. Slowly, the image I had seen on the irritating green screen appeared in black and white, the round heads atop each crystal plainly visible.

"That's how you get aragonite in spring water," Bob said, pointing to the spheres. "Each cell builds itself a platform that somehow grows beneath it as it metabolizes food. When the cell divides you get two platforms and so on until you have a visible mass of aragonite. They get so thick that most of them are trapped and fossilized, but there's always enough growing at the edges to keep the colony alive." He smiled wickedly and added, "Of course, it's absolute heresy to say such a thing. If you try to publish these pictures with such an explanation, expect to be burned at the stake."

THIRTEEN

DECEMBER 1997

Life abounds with little round things.
—LEWIS THOMAS

MAIL FILE 1

Date: Mon., 18 Aug. 1997 8:18:31
To: Carlton C. Allen
From: Michael Ray Taylor
Subject: Hot Springs travertine

Hello Carl,

I expect that by now you have had a chance to see the images Anne Taunton obtained from the Hot Springs samples I drove down last week. To my wholly untrained eye, they were nothing short of amazing. To Bob Folk's undeniably biased eye, they were the proof he's been waiting for since '92. But I'm very curious to know what you and other senior scientists at JSC think about them.

I'm sorry that I wasn't able to deliver the samples at a time when you were there, but in the very brief messages I've gotten from Anne this week, it sounds like there's interest among your group in doing more serious work with this travertine. If there is any way I could volunteer to help, whether through collecting further rock or water samples, guiding you or others to collection sites, etc., please let me know. As I indicated in my last E-mail to Anne, I don't have strong confidence in the electronic pH meter I used at the sample sites, so I intend to return and double-check my readings in the next couple of weeks. Also, in that at least three of the springs seem to deposit minerals at a fairly rapid rate, I think it would be possible to obtain current depositions on collection slides placed in the spring flow over specific time periods. I'd be happy to set up such an experiment, should you have any interest in it.

Anyway, I just wanted to say that I feel wonderfully privileged to have collected samples from a site that may be useful to your team, especially should they eventually help prove the existence of nanos. This is a tremendous opportunity for a science journalist. I guess I was lucky enough to be in the right place at the right time.

Thanks again, and keep in touch.

Mike

Date: Mon., 18 Aug. 97 08:46:05 CST
Subject: Re: Hot Springs travertine

Hi, Mike—

Yes, I did see Anne's pictures and I'm thrilled. We definitely will be continuing this work, with the intent of submitting a paper in the next couple of months.

I have been leading the carbonate springs project, and with Anne heading back to school I'll pretty much have it to myself. My first effort will be to pick up on Anne's work and try to get chemical compositions on the bacteria, etc. We really need to know if these are cells (living or dead), fossils, or in some cases inorganic precipitates. Along these lines, I would very much appreciate any data you have on water chemistry, as well as details on your collecting locations and technique. Also, what bacteria have been identified up to now at Hot Springs?

My overall direction is to compare bacteria in carbonate

samples from Hot Springs, Yellowstone (which I've been studying this summer), and Folk's "discovery" location in Italy. This work has the potential to stretch our definition of life by pushing its lower size boundary. It is also extremely applicable to the possible Martian microfossils (also found in carbonates) as well as to questions of where on Mars future missions might search for signs of ancient life.

I look forward to continuing to work with you on this exciting project.

Carl Allen

.✴.

PROGRESS REPORT

Eight of us crowded around the small conference table at the center of Dave McKay's office at the Johnson Space Center. After three and a half months of successful growth and filtration experiments in the tunnel and the basement display pools of the Fordyce and the Hale, Roger Giddings, superintendent of Hot Springs National Park, and Steve Rudd, the park's natural resources manager, had requested this December meeting. Carl Allen, Dave McKay, and Kathie Thomas-Keprta shook hands with Rudd and Giddings while we waited for Everett Gibson, who stood at McKay's desk talking on the phone with a reporter from the Associated Press.

Hap McSween of the University of Tennessee, one of the more vocal critics of life in ALH 84001, had just published in the prestigious British journal *Nature* his findings that the carbonates in the meteorite had been created under hot, dry conditions incompatible with life. McSween had been propounding the same theory since the month before the life-on-Mars announcement, when he and Ralph Harvey of Case-Western Reserve University had published a paper theorizing a high-temperature formation of carbonates in ALH 84001. The JSC team had criticized the earlier study and had published a critical response to the new *Nature* paper in the same issue. McSween's university had issued a press release about the *Nature* publication while the JSC team had not, so reporters kept calling to ask JSC team members whether they now conceded that the Martian meteorite had in fact been proved lifeless. As Gibson reiterated, they most assuredly did not concede, for the several reasons listed in their *Nature* response. He then referred the reporter to the article he had co-authored with McKay in the current issue of *Scientific American*. In it, they restated the case for life in ALH 84001 and detailed several lines of evidence further supporting the original paper.

At last Gibson's phone call ended, and McKay began the meeting by apologizing for the interruption. "At least it's better than yesterday," he said. "Alan Alda and a crew from his Smithsonian show on public TV were here all day, interviewing all of us. Nobody got any work done. I asked him for his autograph, and he asked me for *my* autograph, so at least it was fun." For the benefit of the park service visitors, McKay—with occasional interruptions from Gibson and Thomas-Keprta—once more explained the history of ALH 84001, from its creation on Mars to its collection and ultimate recognition on Earth. He listed the four lines of evidence that had led the team to the conclusions announced in August 1996, and explained the additional supporting work that had been done since then.

Carl Allen then described his work, which included studying organisms preserved in travertine not only to understand ALH 84001 but also to prepare to look for possible fossilized life in future robotic missions to the suspected sites of ancient Martian hot springs. The Mars Global Surveyor was then in the process of aerobraking, using the planet's thin atmosphere to drag it into a circular, pole-to-pole orbit. Once that orbit had been established, the satellite would map the whole surface of Mars. Carl and others at NASA had high hopes that it might pinpoint deposits from ancient thermal springs, one of which could be targeted as a future landing site.

"I'm currently trying to do two things," he said. "One is to tie together common microbes that live in basically similar hot spring environments around the world. Wherever you look in terrestrial hot springs, these guys are there in some form. But going to Hot Springs, Arkansas, has opened up possibilities I was not seeing at Yellowstone or in Italy." Carl explained that the water chemistry at HSNP was significantly different from the sulfur-rich thermal springs he'd studied elsewhere. This, coupled with an absence of sunlight and concurrent algae growth, made the site particularly rich. He detailed the processes by which the spring samples were analyzed—not only visually but also chemically through X-ray diffraction. Other attributes of a sample could be studied through transmission electron microscopy (TEM) and with a device called the ion microprobe. He also mentioned that members of the team planned to attempt DNA replication and analysis of both "normal"-sized thermophiles and suspected nanobacteria from the HSNP site.

"The other thing I'm interested in is how well these things are preserved," he concluded. "In the next go-around, I'd really like to find old carbonate deposits from extinct hot springs of a known age and compare them with fresh samples."

It was my turn. I spoke briefly about my role in the collection and experimentation that had led to this meeting. I described the circuitous means by which I had evolved from journalist to field investigator, and I detailed the methodology I had used in working with the samples. After the initial session with Anne in August, the most interesting images had come from numbered slides placed for varying lengths of time in one particular tunnel spring and also in the Hale display pool.

To ensure that any life on the slides was not contaminated by surface organisms, I sprayed them with a new two-step commercial substance called "DNAZap." It was guaranteed to degrade any and all DNA from treated surfaces. (Carl had shipped the two small bottles from NASA in a large, well-padded box. The instructions had contained the disconcerting warning: "Wear gloves at all times. . . . Since the full toxic effects of the aerosol mixture are not known, we recommend that the two solutions NOT be sprayed simultaneously.") After zapping away unwanted DNA, I rinsed all the slides with distilled water, then ran them through a traditional autoclave. Using sterilized clamps and wires to hang them directly in the hot flow, I placed them in springs for periods ranging from twenty-four hours to three weeks. They were always placed in pairs.

I would treat one slide immediately upon removal from the spring with microscope-grade glutaraldehyde, another expensive and highly caustic solution. It had come shipped in dry ice, and I kept it in my freezer along with the bags containing my original tunnel samples (and ice cream, beans from last year's garden, etc.—which was why I used a permanent marker to label the boxes "Daddy's Bug Stuff—POISON!"). The glutaraldehyde would instantly fix—or kill and preserve in its exact shape—every microorganism on the slide. I would preserve the unmolested twin slide in a sealed container of spring water for later comparison with the fixed sample.

I explained that all of the slides I had treated and placed in the springs had produced colonies of organisms as well as masses of biofilm thick enough to be visible to the naked eye. More recently, I had placed treated slides inside jars of water that had been run through 0.45 micron filters (Carl preferred to try these before dropping down to the 0.2 threshold). I left these sealed jars in the spring to maintain constant temperature. I placed alongside them, as a control mechanism, slides in jars of unfiltered water in addition to one slide hung in the open flow. Although the slides in the filtrate lacked the thick coatings of travertine that accumulated on slides placed directly into the spring, they were also coated with a light, filmy substance visible to the naked eye. The day before, Carl had prepped some of this material for the FESEM. It was now in the process of "critical point drying." Rudd and Giddings would join us in examining it in Building 13 after lunch.

After the two administrators had been brought up to date, they explained several of the reasons why they had come to Houston. Steve Rudd's immediate background was in law enforcement; he had had long stints policing Yellowstone and the Grand Canyon. But decades earlier, in a previous professional incarnation, he had been a JSC technician assigned to the military precursor of the LANDSAT program. Steve had assisted me in a number of bathhouse collections and growth experiments. He had caught my excitement in the swirls of color and fresh mineral growth we had found on sterilized glass slides placed in the Hale or the Fordyce for forty-eight hours. Both he and Roger wanted to understand what was living in their park, to discuss the ways in which NASA and the National Park Service might cooperate in exploring what was quickly revealing itself to be a significant scientific resource. Another reason for visiting NASA was merely financial: special federal grants were available for cooperative studies between agencies, and this work seemed a likely candidate for such a grant.

However, while the park administrators were clearly as delighted as the JSC team and I were by the things we had found, they also had a number of legitimate causes for concern. Whenever science revealed strange new microorganisms, bioprospectors tended to follow in increasing numbers. A month earlier, Steve's counterpart at Yellowstone National Park had brokered a first-of-its-kind deal with Diversa Corporation, a West Coast biotech firm. The deal guaranteed the cash-strapped park a large up-front payment for the nonexclusive right to sample thermophilic algae, archaea, and bacteria from Yellowstone's many hot springs, plus a small, undisclosed percentage of any profits ultimately arising from useful bugs.

Several environmental groups saw this arrangement as "selling off America's heritage," akin to allowing mining or timber operations in a national park—despite the fact that all of the extracted "resources" could fit into a thimble. At the same time, other critics, including members of Congress, had attacked the deal because they felt the park was getting too small a share in what could become a bonanza for Diversa—despite the fact that nearly a dozen other biotech firms then held far less controversial permits to sample microbes in Yellowstone for potential commercial applications. None of the others had offered to share a dime of future profits with the park. In any event, the Diversa deal had exploded into a public relations nightmare.

Giddings and Rudd hoped to avoid such an occurrence at HSNP by developing a policy for research in the park well in advance of granting any permits to individual companies. They felt some urgency because bioprospectors had already begun to sniff around. When the Diversa deal had hit the news, a retired patent attorney living in Hot Springs had contacted HSNP to ask whether any thermophile research was underway there. Steve had referred him to me. Boyd Surran told me he had worked with biological weapons researchers at the Army's Pine Bluff Arsenal in Arkansas for over a decade. More recently, he had helped the University of Arkansas Medical School acquire drug development support from Pfizer, the pharmaceutical giant. He took me to lunch, and I tried not to say too much.

Steve and Roger were concerned about bioprospectors, but they were genuinely worried about the reality of microbes in spring water long believed to be sterile. Thermal water was the park's primary resource, its reason for existence. People swallowed and bathed in millions of gallons of it annually. "No other park in the system is charged with giving away as much as possible of its primary resource," Steve explained.

"The hot springs of the Wachita" had been considered one of the prime parcels of the Louisiana Purchase in 1803. It became the first federally protected natural resource, set aside explicitly for public use in 1832, long before the birth of the National Park Service. Generations of bathers had attested to the "restorative" powers of the springs. Until the advent of penicillin in World War II, a month at Hot Springs had been the U.S. Army's standard prescription for venereal and many other diseases soldiers managed to acquire in foreign lands.

During every visit I had made to Hot Springs since moving to Arkansas in 1991, I had seen pickup trucks and dusty station wagons, many bearing Texas and Louisiana plates, lined up at the public spigots bordering Bathhouse Row. People filled one- and five-gallon jugs by hand, one at a time, until their trunks and truck beds could hold no more. A few times, I had wandered up to ask why. Older, clearly rural folks had claimed unlikely and even miraculous medicinal effects: gout and digestive problems diminished; ulcers, colon polyps, and stomach tumors destroyed. Others told me they just liked the taste.

In any event, the spigots were a public water supply. The Environmental Protection Agency had empowered state health departments to regulate public water quality at federal facilities. So far, the state of Arkansas had demanded that the park meet quality standards only in the water drawn from its cold-water springs, which originated closer to the surface than the thermal springs. At great expense, the park had recently installed two ozone purifying systems for the two largest cold springs. This was the only state-approved treatment method proven to kill bacteria without affecting the water's natural taste or chemistry. (At least, the process was proven to kill the familiar and harmful coliforms that contaminate surface lakes and streams—no water treatment system in the world is able to kill *all* bacteria.)

"I can see a point in time," Steve said to the assembled group, "when this same regulatory crew comes to us and says, 'You're gonna have to treat the hot water.' That could create a real dilemma if we end up with a situation in which you folks identify a genetically unique beast in our water, something that by mandate we would not be able to hurt."

"That's a very distinct possibility," Carl agreed. "The people in the extremophile business say ninety-nine percent of the stuff out there is unknown. Almost every organism that you find in hot springs, especially in a place with the unique chemistry that you have in Hot Springs National Park, will be a 'genetically unique beast.' You folks should be funding your own program for looking at what's in there preemptively, which is something I'm setting up with the Yellowstone folks right now. But they're in a different business. They don't sell their water."

"We don't sell it either," Roger reminded him. "We give it away."

"We give it away wholesale!" echoed Steve. "Tens of thousands of people drive from all over—New Orleans, Dallas, you name it—to get this stuff. During the federal budget shutdown, we had to close the springs for a week. We almost had riots, people were so ticked off."

"They drink it?" asked Dave.

"Absolutely," Steve, Roger, and I said in unison.

"And they've been told for decades that it's sterile," Carl added.

It occurred to me there had never been any legitimate chemical explanation for the health benefits that generations of drinkers claimed to derive from the water. Having seen the active warfare going on in Larry Mallory's petri dishes, I found it easy to speculate that perhaps unusual thermophiles in the water could indeed ward off disease. If so, then Pfizer had good reason to be interested in the park, and killing off the water's dark life was tantamount to killing unknown cures.

It would be no easy task, however, to explain to the taxpayers lined up at the spigots that bizarre bacteria had been found in their drinking water. *Yes, it was being studied by NASA as a possible analog to Martian life, but not to worry, the wee beasties couldn't hurt you. Drinking them might even be good for you.* I didn't envy the poor sap charged with writing *that* NPS press release and the accompanying visitor brochure. For the moment, no more than a few people beyond the room in which we sat knew that the park's springs emerged in a state far from "naturally sterile." When and how to release this knowledge to the public was a concern not only for the current administration but, Steve later assured me, also for those higher up in the NPS chain of command. He hinted that certain people in Washington, whose names were evidently not to be uttered, were personally interested in the outcome of the discoveries in the park. If the nanobacteria were really there, the scientific significance of a public announcement could prove an asset to the park, rather than a P.R. liability.

"The classic paradox," said Steve, "would be that the EPA tells us to treat the water. Our mandate tells us we can't hurt unique life forms. The only solution would be to stop giving out the water, but then the public would be outraged."

"I don't think they need to worry about this," said Kathie. "It's highly unlikely that whatever's there has developed any pathogenic traits while living in deep rock strata at near-boiling temperatures. Standard water tests would never even detect them."

"Nanobacteria are probably in every public water supply already," I said, remembering Folk's aluminum strips in Austin tap water. "The ones in the park water might actually be good for you." But I added that perhaps other species, more familiar with the human body through long association and co-evolution, were not. I said that Folk had received the National Science Foundation grant for which he had been invited to apply, to further study nanobacteria in travertine, but he was also undertaking a yearlong search for nanobacteria in the human body. The week before, he had E-mailed me that he had looked at several arterial plaques under the SEM, "and the answer is YES!!!" His next plan was to examine calcium deposits associated with arthritis. I mentioned my own speculations concerning Mad Cow Disease and Alzheimer's, and other diseases associated with mineral plaques such as MS, Crohn's disease, and Type II diabetes.

"Not that I think all of these are actually caused by nanobacteria," I hastened to add. "But their causes remain unknown, so looking for nanos couldn't hurt." While it had been shown that some people were genetically predisposed toward Alzheimer's and other diseases, such findings did not mean that a gene literally *caused* the disease. It was just as likely that certain people *lacked* a gene that produced some natural defense against a virulent nanobacterium.

Dave mentioned Folk and his dental plaques. I added that the Finnish team had found nanobacteria in commercially available blood plasmas and serums, and I repeated what Folk had told me, that the Finns were now looking into kidney stones. I guessed that they might soon examine gallstones as well.

"I think the fact that people are drinking this water is reason enough to figure out what's in it," Dave said.

"We do perform a standard mineral analysis every three years," said Roger.

"What do you analyze for?" asked Dave.

"Minerals and trace elements. It's mostly silica, calcium, a few salts."

"What you really need is to categorize the biota. That can be done."

It can be done, I thought, but it will probably take decades. In one spot in the tunnel I had found three small, very hot trickles flowing down the wall, no more than two feet apart from each other. Each produced different-colored travertine: orange, red, and a blue so deep it was almost black. The last was the same color as some cyanobacteria deposits in Yellowstone. I suspected this might be the case in the darkness of the tunnel as well, for although cyanobacteria *can* photosynthesize sunlight, many are capable of drawing on chemical energy sources when sunlight is absent. The waters from these three different-colored springs mixed in a pool perhaps a foot wide, four feet long, and six inches deep.

The pool held fuzzy, pea-sized balls of suspended mineral lace that dissolved with the slightest touch. Spiky aragonite clubs poked from the bottom, draped in curtains of white slime. Wafer-thin calcium rafts rode lightly on the surface, clinging to the travertine edges. Tiny pink and brown dots of who-knows-what floated here and there, along with many other biological-looking blobs. Each visible object in the pool was more likely to represent an intricately ordered community than billions of members of a single species. If this small pond were a rain forest, these objects were its trees; each great canopy was a village populated by large and small creatures.

A good geomicrobiology dissertation project could be built around cataloging the fauna of this one pool, I realized. The park contained approximately 140 separate springs. Each outflow channel doubtlessly hid similar levels of complexity. I could almost understand the frustration Anton van Leeuwenhoek must have felt upon realizing the vastness of the microbial world that surrounded him, with the full knowledge of how few educated people of his day believed it even existed, let alone made any serious attempt to study it.

After the meeting, Carl, Roger, Steve, and I went to Building 13. Before we looked at the new samples, Carl called up some of the stored images from Anne's file on the hard drive, pointing out the lassos and dividing spheres. The previous August, Anne and I had looked at only mineral samples removed from the site.

Today, all of the samples Carl had prepared were of fresh growth on slides I had placed in emerging spring water for forty-eight hours. These had been allowed virtually no chance of contamination by anything other than native spring organisms.

I had removed them from the tunnel two days before, assisted by Jamie Engman, a biologist at my university, who, by chance, had once been the office mate of Serban Sarbu, the principal explorer of Movile Cave. A thunderstorm had broken as we were hiking back from the spring area, and runoff had begun to pour in sheets from street drains along Central Avenue. Although I had assured Jamie that it took a full day of rain to flood the tunnel to dangerous levels, he was understandably nervous at the sight of so much inrushing water. We beat a hasty retreat through rapids and small standing waves.

Most of the sample thus rescued remained still undisturbed in its original fixative container. Carl had removed only a tiny flake of mineral from the slide for our examination. Within minutes of starting up the FESEM, we were flying over bacteria shapes of all sizes, as well as strands and sheets of biofilm. Here and there, crystals poked from the smooth surface; these were always surrounded by greater numbers of bugs. Carl zoomed in on a pair of dividing rods, each perhaps 500 nanometers long by 80 nanometers wide. They appeared plump as fresh sausages, but under the concentrated beam of the electron gun, they began to shrivel and cook before our eyes.

"Amazing," said the superintendent of the park in which they had grown. "I had no idea we had anything like this. No idea at all."

✦

BLOWUP

Anne Taunton was absent from our meeting at JSC. I was certain she would rather have been with us—or anywhere else on Earth—than where she was, which was sitting in Derek Sears's office at the

University of Arkansas, delivering her completed honors thesis. Ever since the Early Mars Conference, her relationship with her advisor had deteriorated. According to Anne, he had been angry that she had allowed researchers at the conference to see her lunar and Martian FESEM images, and angrier still that so many of them seemed to have little or no trouble distinguishing nonbiological artifacts from objects that appeared to be of biological origin. He blamed it on the atmosphere of the conference and the influence of like-minded observers upon each other.

The month after the conference, Paul Benoit, an assistant research professor working in Sears's office, approached Anne and asked whether he might include some of her lunar and Martian images in a paper he was preparing for an engineering conference in August. Anne resisted, saying she "didn't think it was a good idea." When Benoit promised that he would include only images she had already presented in public in her Early Mars Conference poster, she relented. She agreed to write a section of Benoit's paper describing how the FESEM images were prepared and taken. She also included her interpretations of the several differences between lunar and Martian microstructures. She mentioned in the section that she wrote for his paper that the results of a survey of microbiologists had not yet come in, so her interpretations might not hold up.

"I saw it as putting my ass on the line because I didn't known what the surveys said at that point," Anne recalled later. "If the surveys said I was wrong in my interpretations, I was fully prepared to admit it at that point. Heck, I'm only an undergraduate." She assumed, incorrectly, that Paul Benoit would mention the paper to Sears before submitting it to his conference.

Later in the summer, Anne had gone to Fayetteville for a weekend meeting with Sears to go over her thesis outline, in which she had also included her interpretations of the differences between lunar and Martian microstructures.

"You have no right to put in your opinion!" she later recalled him shouting. "You're making premature conclusions! You shouldn't even be working on your outline in Houston where *those people* can influence you." He then criticized her for abandoning an earlier study on crystalline lunar spherules that she had begun under Sears before taking the first NASA internship. He ordered her not to work on the thesis outline further until she completed her internship and would no longer be exposed to the McKay team. "This outline is bad science," he said. Anne left his office in tears.

She returned to Houston, where she spent part of her time helping her new boyfriend, Steve Symes, polish a lunar study he was publishing. Symes had earned his Ph.D. under Sears, who considered him one of his star pupils. The study Symes was conducting listed Sears as co-author; he told Anne he'd also like to list her as co-author, in light of work she had done on the lunar project during the year before her NASA internship.

"It's not necessary to put my name on it," Anne said. "All I did was sort stuff for size."

No problem, he assured her. "You did some good work. Of course your name is on it."

After her second NASA internship ended with our investigation of the Hot Springs samples in early August, she returned to Fayetteville and met early in the semester with Sears, hoping that by now he had cooled off. Although the first meeting was strained, they agreed to meet every Monday to discuss her thesis project. He informed her that the survey results had begun to come in, declining to say anything more about them. Instead, he gave her an unrelated assignment that he guessed would take her two weeks to finish. "But if you could finish it in one," Sears concluded, "that would be great."

She finished most of the assignment the following week, as well as work on a paper for another class, before she and Steve got into a telephone argument that distracted her for several days. Steve had taken her name off his lunar paper, but he had failed to say anything to her about it. She wasn't so much angry at having her name taken off the paper, she later recalled, as she was upset that Steve had never talked to her about it. She assumed that Sears had something to do with it. The discovery was what she would later call "the beginning of the end" of their relationship.

Sears's wife, Hazel, worked in his office as the administrative assistant to the cosmochemistry group. One day Anne confided to her that she and Steve were having problems and it was affecting her work. The following Monday, she handed Sears the portion of the assignment she had completed, asking if she could have a few more days to complete the rest of it.

"You're falling behind," he snapped. "How many more fights are you going to get in with your boyfriend?" He then accused her of undermining the thesis study by putting her opinions into the Benoit paper, which he had just read.

She left his office in a rage. A week later, she returned with the completed assignment and tried to ask him about her outline and the survey results. The results had been sent in care of his office, although they were addressed to Anne. "I can't talk to you about it," he said, according to Anne. "You're making me take too much time from my graduate students. They're more important than you and your study."

"I can't believe you'd say that!" she said. "You designed this whole study. It was your idea, not mine, and I feel like I've done some pretty good work with it. I've spent hundreds of hours with these data, and no one knows them like I do. I should be allowed to make my *educated* interpretations, then see whether or not the survey results support them. I thought that was what science was—you form a hypothesis and then you test it."

"I have no respect for you or your science," she heard him say.

Again she left his office in a rage.

During this time she also learned that Diann Schneider, a graduate assistant in the cosmochemistry group, had removed Anne's name as co-author from a paper she had written and which Anne had helped to prepare. Again, she suspected Sears. Anne had asked him that she be assigned to another advisor for her honors project, but Sears had insisted that by appointing him, she was contractually obligated to remain with him. However, he told her in a memo, he would no longer be available for assistance. She would have to rely on other faculty for that. He would take over the survey and respond to her finished thesis at her defense. In a later discussion with him, she repeated his comment about "having no respect for you or your science" and asked how he could continue to be her advisor. Sears responded that he had only intended to goad her into doing better work. He believed in the project and wanted to stay with it, he told her.

Anne concluded that his reason was to make sure she didn't provide any additional ammunition for those idiots, as she felt he regarded them, in Houston. The last thing in the world he wanted was for the data from a study he created actually to support life in ALH 84001 by suggesting that lunar FESEM squiggles appeared mineralogical and Martian ones appeared biological. Sears had rewritten virtually every question on Anne's survey to ensure there would be no hint of a "pro-life" bias, and he had made sure all the survey results were sent to his office.

"At least let me see the surveys," Anne recalled asking the following Monday. Sears refused. She demanded to know why.

"I'm going to evaluate them and make sure they're done right."

"This is my project," Anne said. "Even though the surveys are more your design, I put them together, gathered the addresses, sent all the stuff out, AND they came back with my name on them. Me. Thus mine."

Sears stormed across the office, retrieved twenty-two survey envelopes from a locked cabinet, and shoved them forcefully at her. "Here!" he shouted. Several fell across the floor. Anne gathered them and hurried out without another word.

At home, she discovered why Sears had been so reluctant to part with them: they showed a clear statistical distinction between the Martian and lunar images. Most of the microbiologists who had responded had also sent comments and even pictures of similar objects they had found. Their comments were what Anne described as "a mixed bag." Several of the experts surveyed congratulated Anne on the quality of her work, while a few said it was poorly done; some got very excited by what she had sent them, while others didn't really seem to care. But after applying every statistical analysis she could think of to the survey data, it was clear that a random group of experienced microbiologists thought that lunar objects looked dead and that the worms in ALH 84001 *looked*, at least, very much like the remnants of microbial life.

The next week, Anne recalled that she went to Sears and again asked that he step down as her advisor. He refused.

"Under university policy, we have a contract," he told her. "You'll do this to my satisfaction, or you won't do it at all."

She left his office determined to find another advisor anyway. A few weeks later, she did find a faculty member who agreed to step up if Sears would step down, but the chemistry department chair advised her that forcing Sears to do so would be more trouble than it was worth. She would have to go before a committee, in Anne's words "with Derek and God and everyone else, and listen to him rant about how bad a researcher I am." It was something that she agreed she didn't want to do. Several faculty members consoled her, telling her that she wasn't the first student Sears had given such a hard time. She recalled that other students had privately confided that Sears had a reputation for being harsh with several graduate students.

She had had no contact with Sears after that until December 3, when she came to his office for the last time, to deliver her finished thesis. The defense was scheduled for December 9. She informed him when and where it would take place. Anne had feared that Sears might call members of the committee in an effort to sandbag her project. Luckily, Sears had added a biologist, Tim Kral, to Anne's committee, promising that he wouldn't oppose the thesis if Kral approved it. Faculty members assured her that her project was not in any danger. This was, after all, only an undergraduate honors thesis—not a doctoral dissertation. But she also knew she would have to make her presentation in Sears's glowering presence.

What's more, he later told her, regardless of the content of her thesis, he intended to publish the lunar images, in order to show how easily researchers could be misled into thinking tiny mineral objects in meteorites are evidence of past life. "I've already written it up," he said. "If you want to be a part of it, you can read the abstract and talk to me."

She declined. "I don't care what your thesis says," he added.

"The surveys aren't valid. Little squiggles in lunar samples look like little squiggles in ALH 84001, and therefore the whole idea of calling them fossils is patently absurd."

.✦.

Mail File 2

Date: Sun., 14 Dec. 1997 15:20:29 -0400
To: Michael Ray Taylor
From: Emily Davis Mobley
Subject: "Hot" cave trip

Dear Mike,

Did you know about the trip to Mexico on Jan. 3–10 that will be visiting Villa Luz, the H_2S cave? Diana Northup as well as Louise Hose will be going. Art and Peggy Palmer, too.

Bob Addis really wants to go and was over and it really seemed like your thing.

He hopes to drive through Ark. on his way. Want to join him?

Emily

P.S. He hopes to do Cholleodero (the water cave pull-down through trip) and some Mayan ruins as well.

Date: Mon., 15 Dec. 1997 16:00:28 -0500
From: Robert Addis
To: Michael Ray Taylor

Mike,

Confirming yesterday's E-mail thru OLDBAT, the trip to Mexico is for real and I thought that you might enjoy it. I will drive thru Ark. 1/1 or 2, meet a private plane in Tx., and fly to Villahermosa by 1/3. The first 3–4 days is cutting-edge science in Cueva de Villa Luz, studying the microbiology of hot

H$_2$S-laden cave water—the Palmers, Diana, Hose, and a cast of thousands! Guaranteed journal article, the first with color photos. Louise Hose's Westminister College is sending two cameramen to promote their school. Later in the week the trip gets more serious/fun with a wild wet cave called Cholleodero. Thru trip that pulls down the ropes and you jump a few waterfalls! Fly out of Mexico on 1/9, drive back 1/10 & 11.

You must start malaria medicine before Xmas. It wouldn't hurt to get a tetanus shot too. Word is that the political unrest in Chiapas has not caused any problems in Tabasco, although we will be right on the border. You will want (are you ready for this?) an acid gas mask for Villa Luz since H$_2$S levels can be high, especially a concern on repeat trips.

Probably a shorty wet suit or an 1/8 inch would do. How do you do in chill water? Rappels only of <150', seat harness, device, and maybe a cow's tail ascender, but basically it's down only! Water chutes to ride and the biggest jump to a plunge pool is 31'!

What say you? I think it would be great if 2 Big Guys got dehydrated caving together again!

Bob

Date: Fri., 19 Dec. 1997 09:00:43 -0600
From: Carlton C. Allen
To: Michael Ray Taylor
Subject: Caves and Hot Springs

Mike—

Did you catch the report on National Public Radio's Morning Edition about the formations known as snottites in the Mexican cave? Norm Pace and Louise Hose described acid slime, poison gas, etc. Is that the expedition you are thinking of joining? I suspect that a chapter on snottites would cut sales of your next book by 10%!

Otherwise, I've been thinking about what to do with all of the data we're amassing from Hot Springs. My current plan is to submit the highlights for the poster session at the Lunar and Planetary Science Conference. I'm putting together a parallel poster on the stuff we're finding from Yellowstone, so the side-by-side comparison should be interesting. To tie it all together I plan to present a talk at the conference on the implications of our hot springs studies for Mars sample return.

Anne Taunton has agreed to co-author and present the Hot Springs poster. (By the way, she successfully defended her honors thesis last week—a real load off her mind.) Would you be interested in also being a co-author and coming to the conference to help her present? I intend to have an abstract for both of you to mark up the first week of January.

Carl

Date: Mon., 22 Dec. 1997 23:08:09 +0000
To: Michael Ray Taylor
From: Martin Belderson
Subject: *Nova* episode

Dear Mike,

The film will be made. We are officially in production. Thanks, in part, to all the advice and information that you gave to me.

Right now, the pressure is off. The film does not have to be finished until the autumn, which is plenty of time to organize everything. I cannot see us filming in Lechuguilla before April–May at earliest.

The next stage is for me to write a treatment that makes *Nova* happy. Right now they want me to shift away from the specific story on microbes—i.e., your "Dark Life" angle—and make it a more general story on cave genesis (two-thirds will inevitably be still on microbes).

By the way, have you heard of Louise Hose's and Jim Pisarowicz's "snottites"—soda-straw-like microbial growths above volcanic vents in a cave in SE Mexico? They drip H_2SO_4 (pH 0.5–3.0). The latest *Journal of Cave and Karst*

Studies apparently has two abstracts on it. To my untutored ear, it sounds very promising. Perhaps they would be willing to put a new expedition together for Easter, so that we could film the native festival at the cave? Maybe Diana Northup would come as well?

Happy Christmas,

Martin Belderson
Four Winds Productions
Leeds LS6 2LN
United Kingdom

FOURTEEN

MARCH 19, 1998

Jack Benny used to say that when he stood on the stage in white tie and tails for his violin concerts and raised his bow to begin his routine—scraping through "Love in Bloom"—he *felt* like a great violinist. He reasoned that, if he wasn't a great violinist, what was he doing dressed in tails, and about to play before a large audience?

—GEORGE PLIMPTON
in *Paper Lion*

GOING PUBLIC

Space Center Houston, a nonprofit tourist attraction that serves as the official visitor center for the Johnson Space Center, sits on the John Glenn Parkway just outside the southwest entrance to the complex. Inside the airy, hangarlike museum one can find actual and mock-up spacecraft, hands-on activities for kids, and a large cafeteria and gift shop. On a Thursday evening during the twenty-ninth Lunar and Planetary Science Conference, Space Center Houston was closed to the public and opened to over a thousand scientists who filed past posters that filled the vast lobby and halls. Most of those attending the poster session had already sat through four long days of scientific presentations on planets, moons, and meteorites. Absorbing so much information was thirsty work. Nearly everyone who arrived at Space Center Houston made a beeline for the coolers of iced beer and long tables of free food that had been set up in the cafeteria. They turned left at the giant Lego astronaut and scooted past the vintage Soviet space suits without a glance.

Hundreds of scientific posters were on display that night, each relating the results of work by as many as twelve authors. More than forty posters were devoted to Mars, including ALH 84001 and other Martian meteorites. Nine of these were grouped under the topic "Life on Mars and Earth." Four of the nine were arrayed as a single unit just outside the food and beer line, where they were guaranteed a crowd of observers throughout the evening. These related posters had been authored by various members of the original JSC Mars meteorite team working in conjunction with other researchers.

One of the central posters in this group was by Carl Allen and David McKay. Entitled "Biomarkers in Thermal Spring Carbonates: Implications for Mars," it discussed the ability of hot springs mineral deposits to preserve fossil microbes on Earth. The text argued that seeking out ancient carbonates on Mars was the best way to find possible evidence of past microbial life, no matter how long ago that life may have existed. The poster displayed FESEM images from my Hot Springs National Park samples, as well as micrographs of samples from Yellowstone, Viterbo, and the famous carbonates of ALH 84001. I stood beside the other central poster, just to the left of the McKay and Allen, cold beer in hand and dopey grin on my face, as the doors opened and the scientists began streaming by.

"Microbes in Carbonate Thermal Springs: Hot Springs National Park," the title read, right beside the round blue-and-white NASA logo crossed by a red streak—an emblem that somehow always made me think of "The Jetsons." The authors were listed, in order, as Carlton Allen, Anne Taunton, Michael Taylor, and David McKay. Below the authors' names their sponsoring institutions were listed: Lockheed-Martin, JSC, and Henderson State University. The poster displayed four FESEM images of bugs and biofilms I had grown on sterile slides. There were nanobacteria-sized spheres frozen in the apparent act of cell division—the first for public display. Other photographs (or micrographs, as electron microscope images are more properly called) depicted bizarre spiral filaments over 5 microns long but only 100 nanometers in diameter—living telephone cords that closely resembled known species of bacterial spirochetes.

There was a ball 150 nanometers in diameter attached to a tail 3 microns long and 120 nanometers in diameter. The tail ended in a circular loop about a micron in diameter. Whatever this was, it was a common feature of all the tunnel samples. Anne, Carl, and I referred to them collectively as "lassos." Mixed among the apparent nanobacteria were small but acceptable-sized rods ranging from 500 nanometers to just over 1 micron long.

The poster also included a photo of me retrieving the "iron nub" sample amid a shower of hot water and steam. One shot showed glistening red and white travertine accumulations below a spring outlet; another showed me collecting a slide from the Hale bathhouse display spring. Noticeably absent was the "Oh My God Valley," where Anne and I had found groups of apparently related spheres ranging in size from 200 nanometers down to less than 50—the image which had so pleased Bob Folk.

Carl had explained that this was the first-ever presentation of microbial cells and fossils from this location. He wanted to establish the validity of hunting for microbes in carbonates before jumping aggressively into the controversy surrounding nanobacteria. He thought the dividing spheres would provide more than enough controversy for this first outing. There would certainly be other publications later. It would be better to find plenty of supporting evidence, such as DNA, RNA, or live cultures, before going public with the smallest objects we had seen.

As we waited for the first scientists to make it through the beer line, Carl asked me about Villa Luz. I explained that I had backed out of the New Year's expedition due to family commitments but that I was now scheduled to fly down to the cave in April with Louise Hose, Diana Northup, Penny Boston, and a crew from the PBS series *Nova*. "I was worried about how I could afford the New Year's trip anyway," I said. "Now *Nova's* sending me for free. And we'll be there for La Pesca, the Indian ceremony where they harvest the cave fish. All I have to do is help carry film gear through poisonous gas and dripping acid slime. What a great deal!" Carl looked dubious.

To the left of the Hot Springs poster was another for which Carl was the lead author. It focused on microbes in Yellowstone National Park carbonates and included FESEM images Carl had taken of clusters of possible nanobacteria. Thin filaments connected the individual spheres in the manner of *Staphylococcus aureus*. The micrograph was almost an exact duplicate of an illustration I recalled from my microbiology textbook, except the balls and filaments from the Yellowstone spring were about one-tenth the size of those from human skin. On the other side of the Allen and McKay poster was one prepared by a team led by Frances Westall of the University of Bologna in Italy, who was currently taking an extended sabbatical at JSC. It contained FESEM imaging of some of the world's oldest known fossils: hydrothermal vent microbes preserved in carbonates approximately three and half *billion* years old, collected from a site in South Africa.

Taken together, these four posters provided a solid argument that bacterial fossils were likely to be present in all hot spring carbonates on Earth, and, if life ever existed there, on Mars. Although each poster depicted nanobacteria-sized objects, Westall had suggested to me at lunch that she believed most of the objects Folk and others had termed nanobacteria were in fact something else. She thought they were polysaccharides released by larger microbes in a process similar to the one that creates biofilm. These complex sugars could assume a cell-like shape, Westall explained. Weak electrical charges could make them line up in chains, and they could be entombed in carbonates along with regular fossil cells. They were not free-living organisms, she argued, but could still be taken as evidence of life in any rock in which they were found (including, presumably, ALH 84001).

I was willing to accept her explanation for some of the tiny chains of balls in the "Oh My God Valley" that did indeed resemble a line of magnets stuck together. But some of the slightly larger spirals, lassos, and filament-lined clusters in the

Hot Springs and Yellowstone samples were absolutely identical to photos of common bacteria in all respects but size. When properly prepared and imaged on a high-quality machine such as the one in Building 13, it took a stretch of the imagination to call them anything but microbial life.

Rick Morita, Olavi Kajander, Frank Volke, and other talented microbiologists with direct, relevant experience had all put forth plausible theories of how such dwarves might contain necessary life chemistry at a size smaller than 0.2 micron. They could perform some chemical functions within the material of their cell walls or even outside their cells in the surrounding medium. Perhaps they shrank and divided under stress. Perhaps, as some viruses had been shown to do, they could snip their DNA or RNA into two sections, with one cell holding one half and the other the second half. When conditions were favorable, they might reassemble their genetic code, much like the separate partners reassembling the map to the "Treasure of the Sierra Madre." The more I studied what was known about small organisms such as mycoplasma and Morita's psychrophiles, the more a 0.2-micron size limit looked like a human-imposed rule that nature had chosen to ignore.

Ralph Harvey, a longtime proponent of high-temperature formation of the carbonates in ALH 84001 and therefore a vocal opponent of Martian nanofossils, had begun at conferences to show a slide comparing a large, normal-sized bacterium with a nanobacterium from Folk's original paper. Next to these was a still smaller wormlike segment from ALH 84001. In the slide, Folk's object is about the same proportion to the bacterium as a rat is to an elephant; McKay's object is no larger than the smallest shrew. Harvey's intent with the slide was to show that because of the vast differences of scale, the Folk and McKay objects were simply too small to be termed bacteria. This had struck me as a very poor sort of proof. After all, elephants, rats, and shrews are all mammals, despite corresponding differences in scale. They eat similar foods and reproduce by sexual union. They give live birth to live babies and nurse their young. They share a common ancestry, one far closer in a genetic sense than that of any three microbes from a typical thermal spring. Natural selection has made the shrew and the elephant the optimal sizes for the evolutionary niches they occupy, just as it did for the guppy and the blue whale, the flea and the ultrasaurus.

I shared these thoughts with the first scientist to examine the Hot Springs poster. Considering the audience, I wasn't exactly going out on a limb in making this argument. He wore a red T-shirt depicting wormlike squiggles similar to those in ALH 84001. A photo cutout of a bearded face that matched the shirt's wearer topped each squiggle. The shirt read, "Vagaries of Nannobacteria Fan Club." Bob Folk nodded in agreement to my elephant-and-shrew analogy, making a face at the mere mention of Harvey's name. Then he turned to the poster, staring intently at each image before carefully reading the text that Carl had drafted and that Anne, Dave, and I had helped to revise.

Others began to file past and crowd around. Both Roger Giddings and Steve Rudd had traveled down from Hot Springs National Park. So far, word of the microbes in the thermal water—the park's primary resource—had not reached the public, but they realized that it probably would after this presentation. The two administrators shook hands with Carl and Dave, who stood before their central poster, which tied the other three together. I saw several scientists whom I recognized from earlier talks. Others I didn't know bore nametags identifying them as faculty from Stanford, Harvard, MIT, and other universities considerably larger than Henderson State. Several asked me technical questions, which I answered as best as I could. All the while, Folk continued to stare at the Hot Springs poster, his thick glasses inches from the text.

"You don't go far enough," he pronounced at last. "I see you misspelled 'nannobacteria.' Well, I've gotten used to that from NASA. But spelling aside, you had better nanobacteria pictures than these in the group you showed me in August. Where are they? And you say here that the films on your slides precipitated abiotically, because light films grew in water run through a 0.45-micron filter. I know you've got all sorts of organisms that can fit through that size filter. They might have precipitated the films.

When are you gonna show them all you've got? That one picture you showed me"—we both knew the one he meant—
"should have run in *Science* months ago."

I looked for Carl. He was deep in conversation with another
scientist, so I began explaining Carl's reasoning, as I understood
it. Yes, between the Hot Springs and Yellowstone samples we
had what were undoubtedly the best visual images ever
recorded of nanobacteria. But no matter how compelling they
were, they were just that: visual images. We couldn't convince
the Ralph Harveys and the Ken Nealsons of the world that they
were alive unless we could amass other, stronger lines of evidence to support the visual. With both Andy Steele and Frances
Westall now working on the team, I felt that such evidence
would be found in due course. I also planned several additional
growth experiments, including one involving grades of various
sizes of filter, which might help establish whether the little balls
and rods were free-living organisms, or were, as Frances Westall
believed, some sort of released metabolite.

"This poster is just a start," I concluded. "But I think it's a
nice start."

Folk asked whether Anne had come to the conference; he
wanted to question her on her sample-preparation technique. I
explained that the job she had been promised at NASA after
graduation had fallen through due to a grant problem. She had
broken up with her boyfriend at NASA, and she had faced a
miserable time in her honors thesis defense. She had decided to
skip the conference, I explained, and stay home with her parents
in El Dorado. But she had been accepted into a top geomicrobiology graduate program at the University of Wisconsin. She was
going to start in May, and I told Bob that I was certain we'd hear
more from her.

As we were talking, I saw Kathie Thomas-Keprta walk up to
Dave McKay with a look of barely contained anger on her face.
She spoke to him for a moment. He literally turned red and
stormed down the hall. Curious, I excused myself from Bob and
followed him. I found him just a few yards away, in the ALH
84001 poster section, speaking loudly with a smiling Derek Sears.

"How could you even use this image?" It was the closest to shouting I had ever heard from the mild-mannered scientist. "It is absolutely nontypical for a lunar meteorite. Anne spent months, hundreds of hours on the microscope, finding this one image. And it's the only one she could find. This is just, just unconscionable." McKay's hand trembled as he pointed to Anne's most "lifelike" lunar meteorite image. It accompanied her least biological-looking ALH 84001 micrograph on a poster entitled "SEM Imaging of Martian and Lunar Meteorites and Implications for Microfossils in Martian Meteorites" by Derek W. G. Sears and Timothy A. Kral of the University of Arkansas.

Sears merely smiled and shrugged at McKay's accusations. "The pictures speak for themselves," he said. "If you were impartial, you'd see that." Sears was clearly savoring the moment.

Dave walked back to Kathie, Carl, and Sue Wentworth. I heard him mention filing some sort of formal protest against Sears. The others were clearly against the idea, arguing that it could come back to haunt Anne later in her career. I returned to Sears's poster and read the text, which compared the structures in five lunar meteorites with those in Allen Hills. "Although in smaller numbers, we have found similar atructures on lunar meteorites," it read.

After reviewing the controversy over nanobacteria and the problems of identifying very small objects seen through SEM only, the poster made its case:

> Our argument is that the moon, with its lack of water, lack of an atmosphere, extreme temperature range and hostile radiation environment, is currently a sterile environment. There is no evidence that it was ever suitable for life. If the lunar meteorites contain objects similar to those in ALH 84001, then it is highly unlikely that the objects seen in the Martian meteorite were biological in origin. On the other hand, the lunar and Martian meteorites have experienced virtually identical terrestrial histories.

The text described the samples studied (without mentioning who actually performed the study), then revealed,

Submicrometer-sized objects were found on many surfaces. Some objects were clearly lying on the surface of the meteorite, some apparently grew out of the surface, while some were located on highly textured surfaces and their relationship to the surface was unclear. We sorted the images into the following morphological classes: areas containing elongated objects, areas containing spheres or approximately spherical objects, areas containing both of these objects and two areas containing long thin strings of material, i.e. "snake-like" features. The Martian meteorite contained many ~100 nm-long elongated forms, while most of the objects on the lunar samples were ~20 nm approximately spherical (or ovoid) forms, but both forms were found on both types of meteorite.

The poster concluded:

We have not attempted to identify the true nature of all the objects we found, although some are clearly the result of processes occurring at the edges of crystals, some are coating artifacts, and some are probably surface contaminants. Rather our objective is to point out that original and fracture faces of lunar meteorites, when examined in the same manner as the ALH 84001, contain objects with the same dimensions and structures as those reported by McKay et al., albeit in smaller numbers. Since the lunar meteorites came from the most sterile environment known but have shared the same Antarctic and laboratory history as ALH 84001, we argue that the objects described by McKay et al. may not be due to ancient biological activity on Mars.

The poster made no reference to Anne's survey of microbiologists or the results of that survey; in fact, it contained no mention whatsoever of Anne Taunton. Kral had become a co-author long after Anne had taken the original images, agreeing with Sears that he saw similarities in those objects. Kral was unconcerned about dropping the opinions of other microbiologists as expressed in the survey, because, as he later explained to me, "Even if you have the opinions of hundreds of microbiologists, it is still just opinion." Carl later explained to me that Sears had first listed Anne as a co-author along with Kral and had showed her the abstract without allowing her to change it. With effort, she had managed to talk him into at least removing her name. No wonder she had stayed in El Dorado.

When I returned to the Hot Springs poster, I found a bearded man with a yellow press nametag reading it. I greeted him, and he introduced himself as David Chandler of the *Boston Globe*. A total of forty-one talks and posters presenting new evidence on ALH 84001 were scheduled for the conference; Chandler explained that he was attempting to work his way through all of them. We agreed that some of the most interesting Martian meteorite results would likely come out the next morning in the conference's closing session: Kathie Thomas-Keprta and others were scheduled to present the results of significant new studies on the rock's magnetite crystals and PAH molecules.

I was distracted from Chandler by a professor from the University of Chicago who wanted to know if I would be willing to share some of my Hot Springs samples. I said sure, then pointed him toward Steve Rudd, who would have to grant permission for me to pass the samples along. I turned to find Chandler dutifully reading another poster. He continued past new images from the Mars Global Observer to Chris McKay's poster suggesting methods for finding caves on the surface of Mars. Poster by poster, Chandler receded slowly toward the Space Shuttle in the distance.

The next Saturday, the front page of the *Boston Globe* carried his article with the headline "Mars Life Theory Gains Momentum." The story focused primarily on evidence presented during the closing session of the conference that while some magnetite crystals in ALH 84001 do in fact appear to have been produced through mineral processes, others are of a type that on Earth can be produced only by bacteria. All efforts to produce this other type of crystal in the laboratory have failed; only biology seemed capable of explaining its presence in the rock. (Although it remained at least possible that magnetite-producing bacteria had somehow penetrated the rock as it lay in Antarctica, rather than on Mars.) After outlining the evidence presented at the Friday sessions, Chandler wrote:

> Several other presentations added ammunition to support the claim that tiny cell-like shapes found in the Mars rock may be fossils of ancient microbial life. While many biologists have questioned whether it is possible for a living organism to be as tiny as the fossils, numerous researchers have now found living microbes on Earth that are comparable in size.
>
> Several of these tiny organisms, sometimes called nanofossils, have been found in water from thermal springs at Yellowstone National Park and at Hot Springs, Ark., among other places.

For a journalist, I felt that I was in pretty good company. Chandler's indirect mention of my work excited me in a way that reading my byline in *Sports Illustrated* or *Audubon* had never managed to do. Scientific discovery offered a seduction akin to that of caving. I began to understand how some scientists, like some media-savvy cavers I had met over the years, might resort to unconscionable acts in order to enhance their professional reputations. But my caving mentors had taught me that the beauty and delicacy of the cave always take precedence over the person who finds it. Likewise, I realized, a new scientific truth is more important than the person lucky enough to stumble upon it.

Back home in Arkadelphia, I resisted the urge to tape Chandler's article to my office door. I drove up to Hot Springs to place some more filter slides in the Hale, and I began packing gear for Mexico.

FIFTEEN

APRIL 18, 1998

Yet half I seemed to recognize some trick
Of mischief happened to me, God knows when—
In a bad dream perhaps. Here ended, then,
Progress this way. When, in the very nick
Of giving up, one time more, came a click
As when a trap shuts—you're inside the den!
            —ROBERT BROWNING
                "Childe Roland to the Dark Tower Came"

INTO THE LIGHTED HOUSE

At the junction of the Oxolotán (pronounced "Oh-show-low-ton") and Amatán rivers in the highlands that rise south of Villahermosa in the state of Tabasco sits the hillside village of Tapijulapa ("toppee-who-loppa"). It is one of those increasingly rare Mexican towns not yet overrun by Wal-Mart, Kentucky Fried Chicken, and other northern invaders. True, a couple of satellite dishes poke above the canted tile roofs that reach toward the ancient stone cathedral overlooking the town. While the restaurant on the square does contain a large-screen TV— usually tuned to soccer, Mexican soap opera, or bullfights—in Tapijulapa one will find no phones, hotels, or gas stations. Children play barefoot in the shaded Zocaló. At midday, dogs and chickens wander unmolested down cobbled streets.

As the afternoon heat gives way to hazy sunset, most of Tapijulapa's population wanders down the steep hill to the rivers to bathe, just as their Chol and Soque ancestors have done for centuries. Unlike most places I have traveled in Mexico, here the strong influence of Catholicism has not changed traditional bathing habits: while most of the teenagers sport modern swimsuits, many of the children and their parents and grandparents allow the strong, spring-fed current to wash over their nude bodies. Groups of women wearing brightly colored skirts and nothing else chat casually as they launder clothing in the wide, shallow Oxolotán. Bending to pound cloth against stone, they form tableaux that Gauguin might have painted.

Teenage boys occasionally walk through the strong current to the deepest part of the Oxolotán, which is no more than three or four feet deep during the dry season. By hand, they lift rounded limestone cobbles from a narrow boat channel and pile them on a nearby bar that has been rising for decades. This keeps the river open to the town's water taxis, which offer passenger service to smaller villages upstream and to the region's only tourist attraction, La Cueva de Villa Luz, sometimes called La Cueva de las Sardinas. The cave is part of an extensive park that includes waterfalls, swimming holes, picnic areas, and the vacation villa of a former governor of Tabasco, now opened as a museum.

Each morning for a week in April, I joined the scientists Louise Hose, Diana Northup, and Penny Boston in journeys upriver to the Villa Luz dock. There, along with film crews from *Nova* and CNN, we hiked two kilometers through pasture, cane fields, and thick jungle alive with tropical birds. We turned right at the governor's villa, taking the path that followed the milk-colored cave river to its source. Long strands and mats of sulfur bacteria swayed in the white current like skeletal weeds. We could smell an overpowering sulfurous odor ten minutes before we saw the cave entrance.

During La Pesca de la Sardina, the populations of several towns gather at a nearby waterfall to watch a group of Soque women pound *barbasco* roots to a pulp. Released into the cave stream, the pounded roots rob oxygen from the water and drive the fish to the stream edges, where they are easy to catch. A group of men and boys pack the *barbasco* and fresh flowers into baskets, which they carry to the cave. After performing a dance in which they offer the flowers and their thanks to the gods of the cave, they walk to the music of drum and flute down a short staircase to the underground river. They wash the roots in the stream, wait a few minutes, then leave with their baskets full of fish.

The date of La Pesca is not fixed, falling sometime around Easter and traditionally signaling the start of the rainy season. A village leader had assured Martin Belderson, the director of the *Nova* documentary, that we would be able to film the Pesca. In fact, however, the village decided to hold the festival several days before the *Nova* crew arrived. Not to worry, we were told— they'd simply hold another one. The cave contained plenty of fish for a second harvest.

In most caves, troglodytic fish live solitary lives, with one or two individuals often taxing the available food of a typical underground pool. To remove even a half dozen native fish from a cave in the Ozarks or Kentucky could destabilize and perhaps destroy an entire population. But in Villa Luz, one could scoop up a half dozen fish in one hand as hundreds more danced around one's ankles. It was easy to see why the cave had so excited biologists. Unlike Movile, the famous H_2S cave in Romania, Villa Luz was not sealed off from the surface. Far from it: the many skylights that gave the cave its name of "lighted house" rained leaves and other organic debris into the main passage, while tiny springs and vents of sulfurous gas continually fed chemical food sources from below. The resulting mixing zone offered the best of both worlds—oxygen and rich organic humus from above, bacteria-laden water from below.

The cave could be thought of as a terrestrial analog to the black smokers of the deep ocean. There the microbes could also live solely from chemicals rising from inside the earth, but the larger organisms—crabs, shrimp, giant tubeworms—all remained indirectly dependent upon photosynthesis, for their gills extracted dissolved oxygen from seawater. Undoubtedly the vent ecosystem made use of the constant rainfall of organic material from the ocean above, while the erupting dark life provided an unending source of free hot food. Place a forest of Pacific tube-worms beside a black smoker on Europa, however, and despite the ample food it provided, they would soon suffocate. Like the heat-loving worms, the larger creatures of Villa Luz seemed uniquely adapted to exploiting the dark life from below and a rain of jungle nutrients from above.

It was a wonderland of life, far richer in organisms than any cave I had ever explored. In addition to the ubiquitous fish (a cave-adapted molly, or miniature carp, called *Poecilia mexicana*), the cave contained amazing numbers of flying insects, spiders, amblypygids, centipedes, millipedes, crabs, and bats. Standing in any part of the cave, I could see at least a dozen types of spider, ranging in size from tiny specks to sleek black monsters as big as my hand. One chamber housed an enormous colony of bats that, unlike all other known cave bats, appeared never to feed on the surface. Instead, they wheeled constantly about the room in which they lived, consuming midges and other flying insects that were always present. Two low, watery crawlways near upwelling springs and sulfur vents—where the microbes tended to be the thickest—were so full of swarming midges that you could hear their amplified wings before you reached them. Jim Pisarowicz had named these tunnels "the Buzzing Passage" and "the Other Buzzing Passage." The only creatures in the cave that lacked an on-site food supply were the vampire bats that roosted in small colonies in side passages. They left at night to feed on horses and cattle on nearby farms.

Somehow, the bats had adapted to the poisonous hydrogen sulfide that surrounded them. At least, they had learned to avoid those parts of the cave where the gas was most concentrated. On an earlier expedition Pisarowicz had led, he had tested H_2S levels only occasionally, using a limited supply of disposable testing rods. But for this expedition, Martin Belderson had purchased an expensive electronic gas monitor. Designed for rescue operations in mines and collapsed buildings, this small, handheld unit gave us a constant readout on gas levels every time we entered the cave. We soon discovered that the rooms favored by the bats were fairly low in H_2S, while other rooms near upwelling springs often fluctuated between deadly levels and levels where one could safely breathe without a mask. In some transition zones, I noticed the desiccated remains of bats, still clinging to the ceiling. Evidently, they had attempted to roost at a time when levels were low, only to be killed in their sleep by rising H_2S.

To keep gas "spikes," as we called them, from similarly surprising us, we carried masks bearing two disposable filters designed to remove hydrogen sulfide. When gas levels were low, we could work for up to two days with one set of filters. When levels were high, the filters would clog after just a few hours in the cave. Breathing would become harder, and the air would taste stale; if you didn't change filters at that point, you might begin to feel light-headed or to develop a sudden, throbbing headache. Each time I unscrewed a clogged filter to replace it with a new one, I was amazed at how heavy it had become. Trapped sulfur gave the disc the heft of a hockey puck. I shuddered to think what such a concentration of the chemical might have done to my lungs.

Ostensibly, my role on the crew was to assist in the lighting of cave scenes and haul gear. Each day, I carried from the dock and deep into the cave several lighting batteries the size of big-city phone books, as well as an unwieldy blue metal trunk containing a heavy 300-millimeter lens, which I balanced on my shoulder. I spent so much time with the blue box that I gave it a name, Bertha, and began to converse with her whenever we stopped to rest.

The lighting of the cave scenes was supervised by Sid Perou, a strong, easygoing British caver who turned sixty-one during the expedition. An influential filmmaker in his own right, Sid had created dozens of cave documentaries for the BBC and had won an Emmy for his photography of Lechuguilla in a National Geographic special. His specialty was lighting cave scenes in such a way that the light moved along with the cavers, creating the illusion that the chambers they passed through had been illuminated only by their helmet lamps. Assisting this effect sometimes required me to hold hot lamps in awkward positions. I would stand or recline for an hour or more in acidic mud beneath dripping snottites while buzzing hordes of midges committed suicide in the hot movie lamp and fell in black piles at my feet.

Despite the rigors of such work, however, I had ample opportunity to sneak away for science and did so almost every day. I collected snottites for Carl Allen and another microbial researcher. I assisted Diana in her collection of snottites and various life-encrusted minerals. And now, on Saturday, the final day of the expedition, I looked forward to assisting Louise Hose in mapping one of the last unexplored passages of Villa Luz, "Jim's Itchy Crawl."

Jim Pisarowicz had discovered the crawl while exploring an extensive side passage during the big expedition the previous January. Pisarowicz had scooted only a few feet into the low tunnel before feeling a powerful burning and itching sensation. He had hurried out of the cave to find his body covered with red welts, as though he had acquired an instant case of poison ivy. While Louise suspected this had been a skin reaction to acid in the mud of the crawl, it remained possible that he had suffered a histamine reaction to some unusual microbe in that part of the cave. For this expedition, Louise had purchased Tyvek environmental suits that, along with our masks, would keep the itchy stuff out. We hoped.

But before Louise and I could go mapping, we had one more scene to film with Diana, in a back room of the cave, where the hydrogen sulfide levels were the highest. Louise was needed by CNN at the entrance. While *Nova* had sponsored Louise, a geologist, and Diana, a microbiologist, for this trip, the Sunday magazine program *CNN-Time Newsstand* had sponsored Penny Boston, an exobiologist. The CNN program was to focus primarily on Villa Luz as an analog to possible environments for life on Mars. Penny liked to say it was "as close as she could get to Mars on Earth." She compared snottites to the "horta," an acid-secreting, cave-making creature in an episode of the original *Star Trek* series. The *Nova* program, in contrast, would concentrate on the microbial and chemical processes that created unusual caves like Lechuguilla. Because the two crews were covering different subjects, they had decided to film at the same time so that they could swap scientists. Thus Louise hung back near the entrance with CNN guys, while I once more found myself slogging toward the back of the cave with Diana, Martin, Sid, and the other members of the *Nova* crew.

We were going to the part of the cave where gas levels were the highest, so Louise had given me the monitor. I had made several trips back and forth to the entrance to ferry gear for the film crew throughout the week, so I had learned the shortest route to the back room and was leading the team. Every fifteen seconds the monitor let out a reassuring beep to let me know it was working. Should any of several poisonous gases reach dangerous levels, the beeping would become sudden and insistent. Ten minutes into the passage, we dropped to our hands and knees for a crawlway about thirty feet long. As I expected, the monitor beeped an H_2S warning and we donned our masks. The flat bottom of the crawlway was pocked with finger-sized holes, some of which spouted a small amount of water and burped continual bubbles of H_2S.

The smooth floor was slick with scum, a microbial zoo that Diana had termed "green slime" in her sample collection. The water was no more than two or three inches deep, so I could rest Bertha on low rocks that poked above the surface at the side of the passage. I slid along with one hand on the lens box and the other palm-out on the floor, gliding along as if on grease. I wore the monitor like a necklace and could read it at a glance. As I crawled I watched the H_2S levels climb up to 38 parts per million—high, but no problem with our masks. The levels dropped briefly on the other side of the crawl, where a skylight at the top of a fissure brought in fresh air. But fifty yards further down the passage we ducked into a large, water-filled room where several springs came together and the levels again set the monitor to beeping.

I turned off the audible warning, as I knew that the H_2S levels would stay in the danger zone the whole time we were here. A hill of mud rising from the water led up to "Snot Heaven," an area thick with snottite curtains. Many of the rubbery, living formations hung where I could see them. The mud hill was actually limestone, if you dug far enough into it, but microbial action had transformed the outer few feet of it into a highly acidic, crumbling paste of gypsum and microbes. The active H_2S system was excavating new cave passages from rock at a rapid rate, just as geologists argued it had done at Lechuguilla long ago. To look up this slope toward Snot Heaven was to see the process that had carved Glacier Bay and the Western Borehole.

The pH of the mud on the slope averaged about 3.0. The faster-dripping snottites had a pH around 1.5 (similar to the average car battery), but the slow-dripping snottites, which evidently collected more microbial waste before dropping to the floor, had pH levels that had been repeatedly measured at a remarkably acidic 0.0. When a drop from a slow-dripper hit you, you felt it immediately and jumped in the water. The next day you would find a tiny dissolved circle at the point where the drop had hit your clothing. The atmosphere quickly corroded batteries, so periodically we had to clean the electrical contacts of our caving lamps. At the base of the gypsum slope, right at the water's edge, was a tree-trunk-sized hole encrusted with bright yellow sulfur. This appeared to be one of the primary H_2S sources in the cave. Whenever we were filming or sampling near this hole, gas levels would sometimes spike to 140 parts per million.

There was some debate among Louise, the Palmers, and other geologists as to the actual source of the gas. The most popular theory was that it rose from the edge of a subsurface petroleum deposit. Tabasco was, after all, an oil-rich state. Or, as with black smokers, the H_2S might just as easily come from deep volcanic activity. There is an active volcano to the west in Chiapas, where in 1982, explosive eruptions of El Chichón destroyed dozens of villages and killed more than 2,000 people. But volcanoes tended to release a variety of gases in addition to H_2S, some of them even more poisonous, and none of these had ever been detected at Villa Luz, or even tested for.

We worked our way past the gypsum bank to a small, snottite-laden room around a corner from it. A few days earlier, Martin and his crew had filmed Diana sampling a snottite here as she discussed the strangeness of multiple life forms adapting to such an extremely acidic microenvironment. The snottites held perhaps hundreds of strange microbial species wrapped in gypsum crystals, and also small spiders and gnats that ranged freely up and down them, appearing wholly unperturbed by the acid. One of the things Diana and Penny had noticed was that the snottites grew primarily in areas where tiny spiders had connected protruding gypsum crystals with a tiny network of webs. They had theorized that the webs were a prerequisite to snottite formation, perhaps providing a platform for fungal growths that in turn supported mineral-precipitating and H_2S-oxidizing microbes. Although the interview had been fascinating by itself, Martin had wanted to get a few close-ups of snottite sampling to go with it.

So, applying the process I had learned in Lechuguilla two years earlier, I was once again dipping Diana's Leatherman tool in denatured alcohol and flaming it with a lighter. While the sound and camera ran and a crew of four looked on, I opened a specimen bottle containing fixative. Diana clipped a snottite from the wall with the sterilized tool. The formation dropped into the bottle and curled up like a white worm. Once during the process I nearly dropped a sample bottle when a six-inch amblypygid scampered up the wall beside me, evidently agitated by the bright lights. It looked like a combination of spider, scorpion, and cave cricket. Its two front legs had evolved into feelers that allowed it to move in the dark with astonishing speed.

Diana labeled a sample jar with a permanent marker and prepared to fill another. In Jim's and Louise's previous trips, they had observed that the location and number of snottites seemed to vary widely with the seasons, so we believed that the microbial population would soon recover from our intrusion, just as the fish recovered from the annual harvest by the Soque. Diana and Penny had begun doing electron microscopy work on the snottites at the University of New Mexico and had found them to be home to a wide variety of microbial life. Although they had not specifically searched for nanobacteria, they were finding that many of the cells most closely associated with snottite mineral crystals were extraordinarily small for bacteria, often less than one micron in diameter.

We had sampled and filmed the collection of three snottites from different angles when Penny approached, asking whether Diana might be free to show her the way to the "Red Goo" passage, where a wall was corroding into a blood-red paste (Diana preferred to call it the "Ragú" passage after the spaghetti sauce it resembled). Martin said he was done with Diana and excused her but asked me and the rest of the crew to remain for a few more detail shots of the area where we had sampled the snottites.

Diana and Penny retreated toward the faint blue glow of a distant skylight, and the crew set up for the close-ups. While they worked, I wandered about the shallow nearby stream, finding two crabs and the decaying remains of an ancient native torch. Martin had just said "Action!" when the monitor around my neck began to scream.

"Sorry," I said to the crew. "I thought I turned the H_2S warning off."

I looked at the display as I began pushing buttons and quickly realized that I had turned it off. Although the H_2S levels had reached a dangerous 152 parts per million, the warning indicator that had started the beeping was flashing "CO," for carbon monoxide, at 38 parts per million and climbing.

"Guys, this doesn't look too good," I said. As I spoke, yet another warning on the monitor went off, indicating dropping oxygen levels. The surrounding air contained 11 percent oxygen, then 10, then 9.6. The H_2S spike was remaining the highest I had seen. "I think we'd better get out of here."

"This is the last shot," Martin said. "We just need a couple of details. Honest. Then we can pack it in."

I looked at the monitor. Hydrogen sulfide levels were moving back toward the safe zone, but oxygen was still low and carbon monoxide was still present in dangerous concentration. "Our masks don't faze carbon monoxide. This stuff does in people who shut the garage door and start the car. They say you get a headache and then drift off to sleep, and that's it."

"I've got a headache," said John Murphy, the sound recordist. "And I'm a little dizzy."

"I feel okay," said Martin. "Just a few minutes more. Today's our last chance."

Nervously, I kept watch on the gas levels. The H_2S spike was down to 38, barely in the danger zone. The CO and O_2 levels, while still in the warning range, were moving toward normal. I figured we could wait ten minutes before I forced the issue. After five minutes, the carbon monoxide warning shot up briefly, and I repeated that we should start heading out, but the CO just as quickly began to dissipate. No wonder so many dead bats were glued to the wall in this particular room. Even if they had somehow adapted to hydrogen sulfide, the occasional burps of carbon monoxide would have done them in. The CO episode suggested that volcanic action was indeed taking place somewhere far below the limestone in which the cave had formed. I wondered how many of the species living in the snottites had arrived from the hot zone below, erupting like the microbial blooms of Jim Cowen's undersea volcanoes.

True to his word, Martin finished filming in ten minutes. We rapidly broke down the gear and boogied out of the cave. John said he felt faint—he did indeed look very pale—but I carried his pack and he was able to exit the cave unassisted. After a few minutes on the surface his color returned.

Louise had finished her interview with the CNN crew, and I told her about the carbon monoxide and low oxygen readings. She agreed that they were not to be taken lightly. The previous year a fit of wooziness similar to what John had experienced had come upon Louise and several others working the same room. She wondered whether that might also have been caused by carbon monoxide.

"It's a good thing we have the monitor on this trip," she concluded. "But at least we won't need to worry this afternoon, because Jim's Itchy Crawl is in a part of the cave where the gas levels have always been fine."

I had almost forgotten that I had a mapping trip yet to come.

•   •   •

After lunch on the surface, Louise and I donned white coveralls made of Tyvek, the durable, impermeable material used to make FedEx envelopes. We walked down the stairs into the cave, then downstream past the Red Goo/Ragú passage to the entrance to a long labyrinth of stoops and crawlways that ran parallel to the river. Jim's Itchy Crawl lay less than an hour down this passage. The irregular fissure would occasionally open to short sections where we could stand, but soon we would climb through a hole and be on our bellies again. Louise took pH readings at several points and was surprised to find the soil nearly neutral in this part of the cave, with no indication of acid. She was an expert caver, editor of the journal *Cave and Karst Studies*, and she had done hard-core caving trips in the Rockies with Norm Pace in the 1970s. I was thus somewhat surprised when, ten minutes into the passage, a bat fluttered past and she screamed bloody murder.

"Sorry," Louise said. "I'm deathly afraid of bats. Always have been. I just scream. Don't let it bother you."

My heart pounded in my chest. "No problem."

"There are lots of vampires back here. A few of them wherever there's a high spot in the ceiling."

"How can you tell?"

"Look." She pointed to a two-foot puddle on the floor beside us. It was dark red and sticky-looking; it resembled a festering scab. Directly above the wet circle a dark hole opened in the ceiling.

"Their diet is entirely liquid," Louise explained, "so they have to urinate frequently. The urine is tinged the color of blood." As she said this, one of the vampires dropped from above and fluttered past us, and Louise let loose another blood-curdling scream. I succeeded, barely, in not joining her. We slithered forward.

After twenty minutes and another five screams we were there. Our Tyvek suits were mud brown instead of white and ripped in several places. But with just the two of us working our way through the crawls, we had reached our destination much quicker than a larger survey team could have managed. Louise had promised Diana and Penny samples of the mud that had caused Jim's reaction, so I lay in the main crawlway while Louise pulled out sampling tubes and an electronic pH meter before we entered the virgin passage we were to map. We lay in an inch or two of water and thick, slimy mud—conditions much more akin to what I thought of as normal caving than I had encountered elsewhere in Villa Luz.

There were actually two entrances to Jim's Itchy Crawl, separated by a pillar of stone, both of them opening to the right of the "main" crawlway in which we lay. I scooted forward to the second entrance, through which I could look back at Louise as she sampled the mud. Like the mud in the passages leading to the crawlway, it wasn't at all acidic. As in a "normal" cave, the mud was actually slightly alkaline—although we found a small snottite with an acidic pH of 3.3 growing on the ceiling only a few feet from the entrance to the crawl.

From this angle, with Louise's light shining through it from behind, I saw something I was sure Jim Pisarowicz had missed: an ethereal curtain of dozens of strands of a gauzelike substance, perhaps fungal hyphae. They hung across the first entrance to the crawl, swaying in the scant cave breeze like gossamer snakes.

"There's the source of Jim's itching." I flashed my light on the strands so Louise could see them.

"Could be," agreed Louise, "although some of this mud just got on my wrist, and I have to say it's itching pretty good."

I admitted that I had ripped a hole in the leg of my Tyvek suit, and I too felt an itching from the mud against my thigh. It was uncomfortable, but nothing unbearable, akin to the sensation of brushing against a nettle bush in the Arkansas woods. We collected several strands of the waving curtain, then pulled out mapping equipment and bypassed the living threads via the second entrance.

Behind this curtain lay unknown cave and unknown life. I moved forward, measuring the darkness and feeling very much alive.

AUGUST 5, 1998

We shall not cease from exploration
And the end of all our exploring
Will be to arrive where we started
And know the place for the first time.
—T. S. ELIOT
in "Four Quartets"

SEWANEE

The crenellated stone castles of the University of the South perch Oxford-like amid green lanes at the edge of a cave-riddled plateau near Monteagle, Tennessee. More than 1,400 cavers have invaded this lush yet dignified place for the 1998 National Speleological Society convention. On a Wednesday afternoon halfway through the convention, I pause to take stock. Two years have passed since the Wednesday of the Colorado convention when I first heard of ALH 84001. Then, like today, the Terminal Siphons were scheduled to play at the convention's midweek dance party in the campground.

The science and exploration sessions of this convention have met in well-appointed lecture halls and august chapels—but most of the attendees are camped in a vast horse pasture on the edge of campus. A rambling tent city surrounds a row of caving vendors, the convention office, and a large temporary pavilion. In just a while, I'll climb on the stage, unpack my cherry-red

Fender Precision bass guitar, and help set up the sound system for tonight's show.

This morning, Diana Northup and Penny Boston gave a wonderfully comic presentation on microbial diversity in caves, entitled "Penny and Diana's Excellent Adventure." They've been a dynamic duo all week, following their Sunday night appearance on CNN. The Villa Luz segment aired complete with *Star Trek* clips and commentary by Bernard Shaw. At one point Penny flexed a bare biceps and said, "We are macho caving she-women!" At another point the CNN field correspondent asked Diana, "There are still a few things you don't know about this cave?" She and Penny dissolved in laughter. Diana finally managed to say, "There's *lots* we don't know about this cave!" By chance, ninety convention-goers returning from a geology field trip caught the show on a big-screen TV at a local restaurant. It was a hit.

Since Monday afternoon, an updated version of the NASA–Hot Springs National Park poster has hung on display in a stone gallery near the cave map salon. The display has already led to a future collaboration with a cave-diving scientist who has been growing bacteria on slides deep in a sulfur spring in Florida. And it has pulled in a microbiology doctoral candidate who may come to Hot Springs to begin the thorough cataloging of species that so urgently needs to be done. Despite the *Boston Globe* story, there's been very little public attention to microbes in the thermal springs. Steve Rudd is now drafting a press release to describe the NASA work to local media and others within the park service. I've joked with my wife that it's a good thing my university has no graduate microbiology program, or I'd be tempted to start several years of study and do the work myself. I am still growing new bugs in the Hale bathhouse, refining the filtrate experiment to determine just how small the smallest actual life in the spring might be.

Science progresses slowly. But like a great ship, once it achieves momentum in a particular direction, it becomes nearly impossible to stop. I was drawn into the story of dark life two and a half years ago. I've learned enough of it now to no longer expect a conclusion, at least not a definitive one, anytime soon.

The best I can hope for is to record fragments of the journey, to glimpse moments in time.

What follows are a few such fragments, glimpsed from the vantage of August 1998 and arranged in alphabetical order.

ALH 84001—Yesterday the Associated Press released a story summarizing the scientific scrutiny of the life-on-Mars claim. The story, picked up by ABC and NBC as well as papers across the country, concluded that after two years of examination scientists are no closer today to a definitive answer than they were at the time the announcement was made. "So far, no one has found absolute, incontrovertible evidence that the potato-sized chunk ever contained life," the story reads. "Then again, nobody has proven that the team led by Gibson and McKay was wrong." Hundreds of studies continue. Hap McSween, one of the original proponents of high-temperature formation of the rock's carbonates, now concedes that a low-temperature formation is more likely—so life in the stone cannot be ruled out on the basis of temperature. But just because life cannot be ruled out, McSween cautions, does not mean that Gibson and McKay have come any closer to proving it was there. Meanwhile, plans are well underway for the return of a pristine sample from Mars by 2008.

Carl Allen—Like all scientists at JSC, Carl remains involved in several projects at once. He's working with experts from the Centers for Disease Control in Atlanta to design fail-safe systems to keep future Mars samples from being contaminated by microbes from Earth and to keep any microbes brought back from Mars from ever being released into our environment. He continues to work on carbonate springs, in addition to projects on producing fuel and water from lunar soil. Along with Dave McKay and Everett Gibson and other members of the JSC team, Carl was recently awarded a major grant to participate in NASA's Astrobiology Institute, a broad-based program to investigate extraterrestrial life. He's waiting for some new HSNP samples that I promised him several weeks ago. Eventually, I hope, he'll be lead author of a major paper on hot springs nanobacteria, drawing in part on the Hot Springs results.

Jim Cowen—In January 1998, the Axial Seamount, a feature of the Juan de Fuca Ridge in the northern Pacific, erupted with nearly twice the force of the Gorda Ridge eruption two years earlier. Once again, Cowen led the early response team and a number of subsequent measurements of the rivers of dark life thrown up during 8,000 separate earthquakes over a period of twelve days. In the past month, he has made a series of dives to the Axial site in the research submarine *Alvin*. He continues to investigate; many of his latest results are posted on the Internet at www.soest.hawaii.edu.

Bob Folk—Bob has just returned from "a great summer in Italy, mainly spent sampling the hot springs." He E-mailed me, "Yes, we have nannos galore, even with 'pros' doing the microbial sampling." The "pros," he explained, were a group of microbiologists—not mere geologists—whom he had cajoled into accompanying him and applying standard microbial sampling techniques. Now that he's back in Austin, Bob and Professor Brenda Kirkland-George will continue their National Science Foundation–funded study of nanobacteria in minerals. He has published a new paper, with F. Leo Lynch, on nanobacteria-like objects in the Allende meteorite and in other carbonaceous meteorites from Mars. He intends to collaborate with a medical microbiologist on a paper about nanobacteria in the human body to be submitted within the next year. At my request, he is trying to locate plaque-containing tissue samples from patients with Alzheimer's and Crohn's diseases. He promises to let me know what he finds.

Louise Hose—Yesterday, Louise held the stage during an international exploration session of this convention, when she spoke about the exploration and study of Villa Luz. Her slide show included a shot of the two of us in Tyvek and gas masks, coated with brown smears of Jim's Itchy Crawl, giving the camera macho "thumbs-up" in a friendly poke at the *National Geographic* poses favored by a friend of hers, the prominent cave diver Bill Stone. The crawl beyond the fungal curtain had meandered around two corners before becoming too tight to continue. Until someone finds a new passage or the snottites create one, Villa Luz is now considered fully mapped with the exception of the water-filled end of "the Other Buzzing Passage," which will require scuba gear to penetrate. Louise plans to continue studying the relationships between the cave's unusual chemistry and its fauna.

E. Olavi Kajander—The Finnish nanobacteria expert was lead author of a study published in the July 7 issue of the *Proceedings of the National Academy of Sciences.* The study concludes that kidney stones are caused by nanobacteria, which make the deposits by precipitating the calcium phosphate mineral apatite. The Finnish team used FESEM to examine a collection of human kidney stones, and they also extracted and cultured nanobacteria from the stones. The nanobacteria cultures continued to precipitate apatite in the lab. Kajander tried to kill them with a number of standard antibiotics; only one could penetrate their stone fortresses successfully. Although the team's examination of thirty or so human kidney stones was an insufficient sample size for publication in a major medical journal, the news has been reported in *Science, Nature,* and throughout the popular press. It is now a virtual certainty that other kidney researchers will attempt to investigate Kajander's claims. If they also find nanobacteria, the next decade will see serious medical investigations into nanobacteria as the possible agents of dozens of other diseases involving mineral precipitation in the body.

Lonne Lane—The JPL engineer is testing a prototype life-detection probe in the "giant kelp forest exhibit" of the Monterey Bay Aquarium. If it works as designed, later this year Lane will board a submersible in order to pilot the robotic probe into the hottest vent of the Loihi eruption area off the coast of Hawaii. Among other mission goals, he hopes the probe may collect the highest-temperature thermophiles ever gathered. The Loihi mission, a joint project of JPL, the University of Hawaii, and the Monterey Bay Aquarium, will provide field performance data that Lane plans to use in designing second-generation probes for Lake Vostok and Europa.

Lechuguilla—As of a mapping expedition just last week, the known length of the cave is now 98.8 miles; it will probably pass the century mark by year's end. The National Park Service has instituted several new protocols for cavers working in Lechuguilla; all are designed to minimize contamination of microbial habitats. In 1995, explorers found Lake Okeechobee, a deep blue pool almost as broad as Castrovalva. The cavers who discovered it could see a formation-lined virgin chamber on the opposite shore. They elected not to enter the water and explore until Larry, Diana, or another approved microbiologist has had adequate time to sample and analyze the pool's life.

Larry Mallory—Larry and his Biomes partners are concluding negotiations with "a large firm" for licensing agreements on the various chemicals that Jim Bigelow has managed to isolate from the company's inventory of cave organisms. Because of a confidentiality clause, Larry can't tell me anything about the deal except "I'm happy about it. It's a good thing." Initial drug testing should begin within the next year. Meanwhile, Larry has taken a day job to make ends meet, performing computer analyses for the Gallup organization. "I help bring the nation its daily Lewinsky poll." Having sold their house in Amherst, Larry, Carolyn, and the kids have moved into a house in Olney, Maryland, not far from his parents. Larry and his work in Lechuguilla are to be featured in an IMAX documentary on the cave, which may be filmed there next year.

Emily Davis Mobley—On Tuesday, Emily and Diana Northup signed the first copies of *A Guide to Speleological Literature*, a massive scholarly undertaking that took a decade for them and two other editors to assemble and edit. In one volume it lists 4,000 nonfiction books and monographs in English that deal with caves, including introductions to specific sections by leading scientists in various cave specialties. The biology section alone is a rich resource for anyone seeking to study subterranean microbes. I owe Emily, big time.

Kenneth Nealson—The lead story of the August 1, 1998, issue of the electronic magazine *Science News Online* relates Kajander's findings. The article quotes Nealson as a leading nanobacteria skeptic:

> While bacteria generally have diameters of a micrometer (1,000 nm) or more, biologists have for many years recognized the existence of tinier bacteria, whose diameters range from 50 to 200 nm. Below such sizes, Nealson and others claim, there's simply not enough room to contain the machinery of life as we know it.
>
> Even a bacterium 50 nm in diameter—the smallest that Kajander describes—would be jam-packed, assuming its cell walls were about 10 nm thick and the microbe contained DNA and even one protein-making ribosome, which is 25 nm in diameter. "At 50 nm, one could imagine that things could stay alive. When you get much smaller than that, it's really hard to imagine," says Nealson. . . .
>
> By calling their microorganisms nanobacteria and citing Folk's work in their paper in the July 7 *Proceedings of the National Academy of Sciences*, the Finnish researchers give the geologist an undeserved legitimacy, contends Nealson. That association may also cause microbiologists to treat the research connecting nanobacteria to kidney stones with more than the usual skepticism, he suggests.
>
> "One could have left out the word 'nanobacteria' and had the paper be ten times better," says Nealson.

For me, Nealson's comments contain a hidden revelation: Just a year and a half ago at the Early Mars Conference, I heard him insist that the smallest theoretically viable life form would occur somewhere in the 100–150 nanometer range. Now he's come down in his thinking to 50 nanometers. That's within 30 nanometers of the smallest objects Folk claims to have found and *smaller* than most of the forms in ALH 84001.

Diana Northup—Diana is the principal investigator for a major grant awarded by the National Science Foundation's Life in Extreme Environments. Working with Penny Boston and Larry Mallory, Diana has genetically identified six novel low-temperature archaea from Lechuguilla cave. She and Penny plan to culture these, using methods developed by Larry. If they succeed, it will be the first time low-temperature archaea from any source have been cultured. "If we can grow these bugs, we'll be on the front page of *The New York Times*," Diana predicted at her presentation this morning.

In addition to showing excellent micrographs of Villa Luz bugs, she and Penny presented an image of a six-pointed star from Lechuguilla. It measured about 800 nanometers from tip to tip, resembling a microscopic starfish. At first, they assumed the object was an unusual crystal, but Diana has since determined it is a type of previously recognized iron-oxidizing bacterium. Although its size falls within accepted bacterial limits, the star shape makes its volume scarcely larger than one of Folk's objects. I hope to assist Diana in some Lechuguilla collections later in the year, when Martin Belderson plans to film her there for his forthcoming *Nova* documentary.

Steve Rudd—The natural resources manager has caught my fever. He continues to help me place sample collections in Hot Springs National Park, and he's come up with new sites for us to check along Bathhouse Row. Steve has several good ideas for experiments that we can try at the main collection springs up on the hillside. He's applied for an internal NPS grant to fund a thorough classification of microorganisms in the hot springs. If the grant is awarded, he hopes to personally assist any microbiologist who does the actual classification. With help from Roger Giddings, Steve has also rewritten the official visitor's brochure, eliminating the paragraph that declared the water "naturally sterile."

Derek Sears—I E-mailed Sears, asking whether he would discuss his differences with Anne. His response was to send me the following press release which has gone out to science publications and news organizations. "I cannot discuss Anne with you," he wrote. "That would be inappropirate and non-productive."

EMBARGOED FOR RELEASE UNTIL FRIDAY, AUGUST 14, 1998

THE DEATH OF LIFE ON MARS?
New scientific evidence from three independent sources disputes 1996 claim of early life on Mars. Meanwhile research on Mars is booming.

CONTACT: Derek Sears, Editor, *Meteoritics and Planetary Science*, University of Arkansas . . .

FAYETTEVILLE, ARK.—Some 15 million years ago, an asteroid knocked a rock off the surface of Mars and hurtled it into space. The potato-sized rock fell onto an Antarctic ice field (Allen Hills) 13,000 years ago, where it stayed until scientists discovered it in 1984 . . .

Today (August 14), three papers in the new issue of *Meteoritics and Planetary Science* conclude for entirely different reasons that McKay's group was mistaken.

In the first paper, University of Arkansas researchers Derek Sears and Tim Kral compare worm-like shapes in lunar meteorites found in Antarctica with the features in the Martian meteorite described by McKay and co-workers. They found these features to be identical on both the lunar and the Martian meteorites.

"Since the moon has no water, no atmosphere and extreme temperatures, it cannot support life," Sears said, "meaning that these features cannot be evidence of life on Mars."

The University of Arkansas research suggests that these features may be due to contamination on Earth, either in the Antarctic or in the laboratory; or, they may be due to processes that commonly occur on the surfaces of minerals, seen now for the first time because of the high microscope powers used. . . .

The other two papers mentioned in the press release repeat arguments for high-temperature formation of the meteorite's carbonates—arguments raised and largely refuted at the March meeting of the LPSC. An AP story that will result from the press release will quote Sears as saying, "Within an hour of looking at the lunar meteorites, we knew. We found objects on the lunar meteorites that we cannot distinguish from the Martian meteorites." Sears will tell a reporter from ABC News that when comparing lunar and Martian FESEM objects, he found: "They're both the same size. They have the same little quirks. Everything is there."

Anne Taunton—Regarding Sears's study, Anne E-mails me: "I was hoping the paper wouldn't go to publication, but oh well. I'm pretty pissed off at the fact he's making a big deal out of it. And the '30 minute' thing—I WANTED TO SCREAM!!!! It took me hundreds of hours to find anything even remotely similar to ALH 84001 in a lunar meteorite. I'm trying to decide whether or not to deal with it. I can't wait to see the actual paper."

Meanwhile, Anne began her geomicrobiology graduate training at the University of Wisconsin with a field trip to Australia in May 1998. She's assisting the program's director, Jill Banfield, in a study of the role bacteria play in weathering terrestrial rocks. Although Banfield, Anne's new advisor and a longtime colleague of Ken Nealson, remains highly skeptical regarding nanobacteria on Earth or Mars, she has encouraged Anne to keep in contact with the McKay team.

Anne's ultimate career goal is to collect direct, firsthand evidence of Martian microbial life. "I want to keep involved in the search for Mars life," she says, "so when they bring the rocks back or choose a crew for a manned mission, they have to let me go because I'm the best they've got."

Mike Taylor—We're on. The mountain air is cool and clear. Iced kegs of red ale fill the beer tent. Keith's hot tonight on lead. He recently landed a geology job in New Orleans, but he still manages to work regularly with two different blues bands. He's been playing so much and so well that he pulls the rest of us to a new level. Cass cooks on drums. Cave photographer Kevin

Downey adds a third guitar to the band this year. When he solos, he runs through jazz riffs he picked up from Gypsies in Romania. Albert is a wild man, full of energy and reeling them in as always. The two or three hundred people in and around the pavilion circus tent can't seem to get enough of him.

I stand next to Cass and we're tight, putting down a beat they can dance to. Familiar faces whirl through the crowd. There's Louise Hose dancing with my old friend Ron Kerbo, the senior cave specialist for the National Park Service. Here's Don Coons, perhaps the greatest vertical caver who ever lived, certainly the most graceful on rope, in motion across the floor with Patty Kambesis, a legendary cartographer and one of the discoverers of the Chandelier Ballroom. Behind the dark tree line that borders this field atop the limestone of Tennessee, the stars rise and the planets wheel.

Mars and Jupiter dance in the sky, and I play to them.

SUGGESTED READING

BOOKS

Amy, Penny S., and Dana L. Haldeman, eds. *The Microbiology of the Terrestrial Deep Subsurface.* New York: Lewis, 1995.

Broad, William J. *The Universe Below: Discovering the Secrets of the Deep Sea.* New York: Simon & Schuster, 1997.

Brock, Thomas D. *Biology of Microorganisms.* Englewood Cliffs, N.J.: Prentice-Hall, 1970.

———. *Milestones in Microbiology.* Englewood Cliffs, N.J.: Prentice-Hall, 1961.

Brown, Dee Alexander. *The American Spa: Hot Springs, Arkansas.* Little Rock: Rose, 1982.

Clifford, S. M., A. H. Treiman, H. E. Newsom, and J. D. Farmer, eds. *Conference on Early Mars: Geologic and Hydrologic Evolution, Physical and Chemical Environments, and the Implications for Life.* Houston: Lunar and Planetary Institute, 1997.

Crane, Stephen. "The Merry Throng at Hot Springs." *Stephen Crane: Uncollected Writings.* Ed. Olov W. Fryckstedt. Uppsala: Uppsala UP, 1963.

De Kruif, Paul. *Microbe Hunters.* New York: Harcourt, 1926.

Dixon, Bernard. *Power Unseen: How Microbes Rule the World.* New York: Freeman, 1994.

Dobell, Clifford. *Antony van Leeuwenhoek and His "Little Animals"; Being Some Account of the Father of Protozoology and Bacteriology and His Multifarious Discoveries in These Disciplines.* New York: Dover, 1960.

Fortey, Richard. *Life: A Natural History of the First Four Billion Years of Life on Earth.* New York: Knopf, 1998.

Gold, Thomas, *The Deep, Hot Biosphere.* New York: Springer Verlag, 1998.

Goldsmith, Donald, and Daniel Goldsmith. *The Hunt for Life on Mars.* New York: Dutton, 1997.

Gould, Stephen Jay. *Full House: The Spread of Excellence from Plato to Darwin.* Reprint ed. New York: Random House, 1997.

Kushner, D. J., ed. *Microbial Life in Extreme Environments.* New York: Academic, 1978.

Lunar and Planetary Institute. *Lunar and Planetary Science XXVIII.* Houston: LPI, 1997.

———. *Lunar and Planetary Science XXIX.* Houston: LPI, 1998.

Moore, George W., and Nicholas Sullivan. *Speleology: Caves and the Cave Environment.* Rev. 3rd ed. St. Louis: Cave Books, 1997.

Postgate, John. *The Outer Reaches of Life.* Cambridge: Cambridge UP, 1994.

Rhodes, Richard. *Deadly Feasts: Tracking the Secrets of a Terrifying New Plague.* New York: Simon & Schuster, 1997.

Sasowsky, Ira D., and Margaret P. Palmer, eds. *Breakthroughs in Karst Geomicrobiology and Redox Geochemistry.* Bristol: Taylor & Francis, 1994.

Scully, Francis J. *Hot Springs, Arkansas, and Hot Springs National Park: The Story of a City and the Nation's Health Resort.* Little Rock: Hanson, 1966.

Taylor, Michael Ray. *Cave Passages: Roaming the Underground Wilderness.* New York: Scribner, 1996.

Tortora, Gerard J., Berdell R. Funke, and Christine L. Case. *Microbiology: An Introduction.* 5th ed. Redwood City: Benjamin/Cummings, 1995.

Wells, Oliver C. *Scanning Electron Microscopy.* New York: McGraw-Hill, 1974.

Widmer, Urs, ed. *Lechuguilla: Jewel of the Underground,* 2nd ed. Schoharie: Speleo Projects, 1998.

ARTICLES

Achenbach, Joel. "The Genesis Problem." *Washington Post,* 2 Nov. 1997:1.

Ackerman, Diane. "Worlds Within Worlds: Symbion Pandora, a Creature That Breaks All the Rules." *New York Times,* 17 Dec. 1995: 13–14.

Chafetz, Henry S. "Travertines: Depositional Morphology and the Bacterially Constructed Constituents." *Journal of Sedimentary Petrology* 54 (1984): 289–315.

Chyba, Christopher F. "Life Beyond Mars." *Nature,* 15 Aug. 1996: 576–577.

Ellis-Evans, J. Cynan, and David Wynn-Williams. "A Great Lake Under the Ice." *Nature,* 20 June 1996: 644–650.

Folk, Robert L. "SEM Imaging of Bacteria and Nannobacteria in Carbonate Sediments and Rocks." *Journal of Sedimentary Petrology* 63 (1993): 990–999.

———., and F. Leo Lynch. "The Possible Role of Nannobacteria (Dwarf Bacteria) in Clay-Mineral Diagenesis and the Importance of Careful Sample Preparation in High-Magnified SEM Study." *Journal of Sedimentary Research* 67 (1997): 583–589.

Frederickson, James K., and Tullis C. Onstott. "Microbes Deep Inside the Earth." *Scientific American*, Oct. 1996: 68.

Ghiorse, William C. "Subterranean Life." *Science* 275 (1997): 789.

Gold, Thomas. "The Deep, Hot Biosphere." *Proceedings of the National Academy of Sciences of the United States of America* 89 (1992): 6045–6050.

Gould, Stephen Jay. "War of the Worldviews." *Natural History*, Dec. 1996: 22–28.

Grady, Monica, Ian Wright, and Colin Pillinger. "Opening a Martian Can of Worms?" *Nature* 382 (1996): 575.

Hillis, David M. "Biology Recapitulates Phylogeny." *Science* 276 (1997): 218–219.

Hulsenbeck, John P., and Bruce Rannala. "Phylogenetic Methods Come of Age: Testing Hypotheses in an Evolutionary Context." *Science* 276 (1997): 227–232.

Kajander, E. Olavi, and Neva Ciftioglu. "Nanobacteria: An Alternative Mechanism for Pathogenic Intra- and Extracellular Calcification and Stone Formation." *Proceedings of the National Academy of Sciences of the United States of America* 95 (1998): 8274–8279.

Kerr, Richard A. "Martian 'Microbes' Cover Their Tracks." *Science* 276 (1997): 30–31.

————. "An Ocean Emerges on Europa." *Science* 276 (1997): 355.

Linden, Eugene. "Warnings from the Ice." *Time* (1997): 55–59.

Liu, Shi V., Jizhong Zhou, Chuanlun Zhang, David R. Cole, M. Gajdarziska-Josifovska, and Tommy J. Phelps. "Thermophilic Fe (III) Reducing Bacteria from the Deep Subsurface: The Evolutionary Implications." *Science* 277 (1997): 1106.

McDonald, Kim A. "Discovery of Life Deep Beneath the Earth's Surface Produces a Revolution in Biology." *Chronicle of Higher Education* 43 (1997): A13, A14.

McKay, David S., Everett K. Gibson, Jr., Kathie L. Thomas-Keprta, Hojatollah Vali, Christopher S. Romanek, Simon J. Clemett, Xavie D. F. Chiller, Claude R. Maechling, and Richard N. Zare. "Search for Past Life on Mars: Possible Relic Biogenic Activity in Martian Meteorite ALH 84001." *Science* 273 (1996): 924, 930.

Morell, Virginia. "Microbiology's Scarred Revolutionary." *Science* 276 (1997): 699, 701.

Pace, Norman R. "A Molecular View of Microbial Diversity and the Biosphere." *Science* 276 (1997): 734.

Palmer, Jeffrey D. "The Mitochondrion That Time Forgot." *Nature* 387 (1997): 454.

Petit, Charles. "The Walls Are Alive." *U.S. News & World Report* 124 (1998): 59–60.

Pope, Victoria. "Is There Life on Other Planets?" *U.S. News & World Report* 123 (1997): 38–39.

Sillitoe, Richard H., Robert L. Folk, and Nicolas Saric. "Bacteria as Mediators of Copper Sulfide Enrichment During Weathering." *Science* 272 (1996): 1153.

Travis, John. "Nanobacteria by Any Other Name." *Science News* 154 (1998): 76.

Valley, John W., John M. Eiler, Colin M. Graham, Everett K. Gibson, Christopher S. Romanek, and Edward M. Stolper. "Low-Temperature Carbonate Concretions in the Martian Meteorite ALH 84001: Evidence from Stable Isotopes and Mineralogy." *Science* 275 (1997): 1633.

Wade, Nicholas. "Mars Meteorite Fuels Debate on Life on Earth." *New York Times*, 29 Jul. 1997: C2–C3.

Webb, Robert. "Cave Men Find Miracle Drugs in Mud & Muck." *Boca Raton Sun*, 25 Mar. 1997.

Wright, Ian P., and Colin T. Pillinger. *Science Spectra*, Issue 9 (1997): 26–31.

Zimmerman, Robert. "Moon Rivers." *The Sciences* 37 (1997): 11

USEFUL WEBSITES

The Astrobiology Web, at *http://www2.astrobiology.com/astro/index.html*

The Astrobiology Workshop, at *http://astrobiology.arc.nasa.gov/workshop/*

Biomes, Inc., at *http://www.biomes.com/*

Cueva de Villa Luz, Biological Investigations, at *http://www.i-pi.com/~diana/villaluz/*

Evidence for Past Life on Mars?, at *http://www.sji.org/ed/marslife/marslife.html*

Life at High Temperatures, at *http://www.bact.wisc.edu/Bact303/b1*

The Lunar and Planetary Institute, at *http://cass.jsc.nasa.gov/*

NASA Jet Propulsion Lab, at *http://www.jpl.nasa.gov/*

NASA Johnson Space Center, at *http://www.jsc.nasa.gov/*

NaturalScience Magazine, at *http://naturalscience.com/ns/nshome.html*

Panspermia: Life from Space, at *http://www.panspermia.org/*

Princeton Geomicrobiology, at *http://geo.princeton.edu/geomicrobio/intro.html*

Recent Scientific Papers on ALH 84001Explained, with Insightful and Totally Objective Commentaries, at*http://cass.jsc.nasa.gov/lpi/meteorites/alhnpap.html*

The Space Policy Institute, at *http://www.gwu.edu/~spi/index.htm*

The Vents Program, at *http://www.pmel.noaa.gov/vents/home.html*

The Why Files, at *http://whyfiles.news.wisc.edu/*

ACKNOWLEDGMENTS

So many people deserve my thanks that it's hard to know where to start, but I suppose the logical place would be with the person who first brought me the story: Emily, I still owe you.

A great many contemporary scientists—many more than I could hope to list in a single volume—have made important contributions to the understanding of microbial life underground. To those few who provide the examples that make up this book, I shall always remain grateful. For graciously allowing me into their research and their lives, I thank Larry Mallory, Diana Northup, Bob Folk, Anne Taunton, Carl Allen, David McKay, Sue Wentworth, Kathie Thomas-Keprta, Louise Hose, Joan Hovarth, Jim Cutts, Jim Cowen, Todd Stevens, Hank Chafetz, Sean Guidry, and Penny Taylor.

For assistance in travel, I'm grateful to the Henderson State University faculty development and research committees; to Ben Metcalf of *Harper's*; to Greg Henderson and Lori Cuthbert of *The Discovery Channel Online*; to Jeff Black of *ABCnews.com*; and to Martin Belderson of Northern Light Productions. And thanks to the following dedicated public servants in the U.S. National Park Service for help in a variety of ways: at Carlsbad Caverns National Park, Jason Richards, Dale Pate, and Bobby Crisman; at Hawaii Volcanoes National Park, Bobby Camara; at Hot Springs National Park, Steve Rudd and Roger Giddings; and at the southwest regional office of the NPS, my dear friend, and a friend to caves and cavers everywhere, Ron Kerbo.

For field assistance in and under Hot Springs National Park, often in less than pleasant conditions, I thank David Stoddard, Jamie Engman, Randy Duncan, Doug Gilpin, Mica Treece, and Dan Marsh. I'm grateful to Jimmy Bragg for meaningful instruction and the loan of useful equipment.

In writing *Dark Life*, I experienced what many authors would consider a corporate publishing horror story: assignment to five different editors as one after another left Scribner for other houses. But in my case, each of the five embraced my project enthusiastically and each provided useful guidance along the way. So thanks all around to Hamilton Cain, David Roth-Ey, Scott Moyers, Blythe Grossberg, and Jake Morrissey—although Blythe deserves the lion's share of credit, for pulling the finished draft out of me, chapter by slow chapter, throughout the summer of 1998. I am grateful also to Nan Graham and Susan Moldow at Scribner for their kind words of support during the long editing process.

Thanks to my principal reader, Lea Ann Alexander, and also to readers Kathy Taylor, Joyce Taylor, Dan Marsh, Anne Taunton, Carl Allen, Everett Gibson, Bob Folk, Larry Mallory, Diana Northup, Emily Davis Mobley, Thom Engel, Louise Hose, Steve Rudd, Lara Crane, Carl Miller, Angella Baker, and Donald Davis for offering useful comments and suggestions along the way, and thanks to Josh Barnett and Brad Parker for clerical assistance. For computer help of various sorts, always on short notice, I thank Jennifer Ford, Griff Ferrell, Joan and Charley Johnson, and my parents, Dan and Joyce Taylor.

Finally, although many a better writer has said it before me, I have to thank Esther Newberg for being the greatest literary agent of all time.

Index